CHANGING VALUE PATTERNS
AND THEIR IMPACT ON ECONOMIC STRUCTURE

A REPORT TO THE OECD

CHANGING VALUE PATTERNS
AND THEIR IMPACT
ON ECONOMIC STRUCTURE

Edited by
YOSHIHIRO KOGANE

UNIVERSITY OF TOKYO PRESS

Publication of this volume was supported by a grant from The Toyota Foundation.

The Organisation for Economic Co-operation and Development (OECD) was set up under a Convention signed in Paris on 14th December 1960, which provides that the OECD shall promote policies designed:
—to achieve the highest sustainable economic growth and employment and a rising standard of living in Member countries, while maintaining financial stability, and thus to contribute to the development of the world economy:
—to contribute to sound economic expansion in Member as well as non-member countries in the process of economic development:
—to contribute to the expansion of world trade on a multilateral, non-discriminatory basis in accordance with international obligations.
The Members of OECD are Australia, Austria, Belgium, Canada, Denmark, Finland, France, the Federal Republic of Germany, Greece, Iceland, Ireland, Italy, Japan, Luxembourg, the Netherlands, New Zealand, Norway, Portugal, Spain, Sweden, Switzerland, Turkey, the United Kingdom and the United States.

CONTENTS

v

PREFACE

From 1976 to 1979 the Organisation for Economic Co-operation and Development (OECD) carried out a research project on "The Future Development of Advanced Industrial Societies in Harmony with that of Developing Countries." The research team which was established within the Secretariat for this specific purpose was called INTERFU-TURES and published its final report, "Facing the Future: Mastering the Probable and Managing the Unpredictable," in July 1979.

This research was founded on several basic studies, one of which is the report which constitutes Part I of this book. From the point of view of the INTERFUTURES Report, therefore, this study is a kind of intermediate product; but at the same time, it is the report of an independent research project which was supported by The Toyota Foundation.

The object of this study is the interaction between the superstructure—i.e., culture and polity—and the substructure—i.e., economy and technology—of societies. Marx and Parsons assume that the one dominates the other: economists assume that they can be entirely separated. But the reality may be more complex than either extreme.

First, this report deals with the contradictions of advanced industrial societies, particularly structural unemployment, and stresses that dichotomies such as economy/non-economy, demand/supply, needs/wants, etc., cannot elucidate their real causes. Then it provides and compares four scenarios of the future of advanced industrial societies which are based on the assumption that the activities for satisfying human demands are carried out through either the formal sector—i.e., market and state—or the informal sector—i.e., self, family, regional community, etc.

The articles in Part II formed the basis of the above report, but each of them has its own value and status.

The chapter on "The Japanese and Their Economic Development," which has been newly written on the occasion of publishing this book, analyzes the economic and social development of Japan by applying the above-mentioned way of thinking.

I am very grateful to the OECD and The Toyota Foundation for agreeing to and assisting with the public release of this set of documents.

June 1982   YOSHIHIRO KOGANE
Tokyo

Part I
RESEARCH PROJECT REPORT

CHANGING VALUE PATTERNS AND THEIR IMPACT ON ECONOMIC STRUCTURE

YOSHIHIRO KOGANE

The purpose of this study is to examine the interactions between sub-structure (technology and economy) and superstructure (culture and polity) in industrial society. The need to examine these interactions becomes self-evident when we abandon the hypothesis that either one or both of them are invariable or autonomous.

A comparison can be made with the physical sciences, which long ago abandoned the hypothesis that atoms are the invariable and final units of the material world. In this case, hypotheses concerning the structure and transformation of the nucleus could be formulated, tested, and revised on the basis of controlled experiments. Since such experiments are impossible in the social sciences, there is always the danger that dogmatic and unrealistic rationalizations could result from an examination of the interactions among value patterns on the one hand and economic structure on the other. A dogmatic product would have no utility, in spite of being an excellent intellectual exercise.

The aim of this research—and that of the OECD INTERFUTURES project of which it formed a part—was not to draw a map of unknown territory, i.e., the development mechanism of human society in general, but rather to explore the paths of development of advanced industrial societies in order to identify the feasible options for the coming decades. Bearing these considerations in mind, the basic assumptions of the research—the epistemological part—were made as explicit as possible so that anyone could easily reconstruct or modify the whole process of thinking according to his or her own perceptions.

In short, this study was to be the temporary basis from which several alternative scenarios for the future of advanced industrial societies could be explored.

Section 1 of this report questions the validity of the commonly drawn distinctions between "wants" (to be perceived subjectively and treated personally) and "needs" (to be perceived objectively and treated

3

collectively), between private and public sector, and between individuals and the state. These dichotomies seem to arise from the dualistic Western view of the world which divides it into spirit and matter, soul and body, subject and object, man and nature, etc. Such distinctions may have been strong weapons for dealing with reality, but they also ran the risk of becoming unrealistic or obsolete as the real world came to seem more chaotic or complex.

Section 2 examines the recent achievement of the market-based institutions and Welfare State mechanisms of advanced industrial societies. Various disequilibria which cannot be explained by the previously described dualistic hypotheses are highlighted.

Section 3, based on the study of "new demands," introduces several hypotheses about the mechanism of production, about well-being, and about changes in demands: (1) In addition to the transfer from the *formal* sector (market-based and Welfare State institutions), people also produce their own well-being in the *informal* sector (self, family, local community, etc.). (2) Not only changes in world-view and values, but also changes in living environment (e.g. increase in average income) can bring forth changes in demands.

Section 4 provides two blocks of material for constructing long-term scenarios on the basis of the preceding work. The first describes an end-state for industrial society; its important aspect is the division of labor between the formal sector and the informal sector, between the production of goods and the production of services, etc. The second block of material—i.e., boundary conditions for mid-term trends—is composed, internally, of people's attitudes toward the role of the formal sector in industrial countries and, internationally, of the development of formal sectors in developing countries.

Section 5 describes mid-term trend scenarios. These fall into two major groups: "activist" and "passivist" scenarios, which differ with respect to the role of material production in total production. Two sub-scenarios are developed, based on positive or negative attitudes toward immigration, government intervention, and so on.

Section 6, as a conclusion, notes the discontinuity and inconsistency between the mid-term trends and the end-state; what seems important is that the changes in demands relative to the value changes are missing from the trend scenarios. The danger in applying deterministic hypotheses to the relation between economic and cultural development is pointed out, and the importance of looking for probabilistic hypotheses and of collecting information in the informal sector is stressed.

Dualistic Perception of Demands and Their Satisfaction

It is often considered rational that there are two kinds of demands, and that a person's demands are divided between needs and wants; one's "needs" can be recognized objectively, but "wants" can only be subjectively known by one's self. This distinction has an important meaning for individuals, since whether or not they can expect societal support for satisfying their demands often depends on whether or not these demands are regarded as arising from human "needs."

In Western (especially libertarian) societies, individuals can pursue their objectives freely whether they are concerned with "needs" or "wants." Problems arise when people begin to consider that they are entitled by society to satisfy their wants, or, in other words, that the ultimate aim of society should be to enable its members to satisfy their wants. Such a political view presupposes that society should try to promote individuals' happiness, which is, in this case, assumed to depend on the degree of satisfaction of their wants and accordingly affected by subjective standards of well-being.

However, if the "subjective" elements of individuals' well-being were to be restricted to ones which are completely irrelevant to those of others, policies based on the above belief would not be successful for several reasons. First, society will never be able to know what the wants of individuals are, making it difficult to find the appropriate measures for their satisfaction. Second, even if these wants could be known, it is not certain whether the satisfaction of wants would improve the wanters' well-being. For example, people could find the meaning of life in the struggle to attain certain wants, or, on the contrary, they could be liberated from mental pressure only by abandoning such wants; in both cases, helping individuals to satisfy their wants would not improve their well-being in spite of the huge cost which would have to be borne by all members of the society.

In contrast, policies aimed at satisfaction of "needs" seem to be feasible insofar as society is supposed to know what the needs of individuals are and how to satisfy them in order to improve general well-being. Thus the legitimacy of needs-satisfaction policies—which are usually called welfare policies—not only is based on an ethical belief that all people are equally entitled to obtain what they need, but also is formulated in such a way that the burden of these policies does not exceed the limit bearable for the society as a whole.

In fact, however, the objective nature of needs—i.e., the essential part of this "safety valve"—depends to a great extent on the condition that social values and the latent world-views are invariable anywhere and at any time. Even biological needs such as food and shelter tend to be heavily affected by the traditions and culture of the society concerned; thus, it is natural that most of the needs—or what people perceive as needs—for economic and social life are under the influence of social values and world-views. This means that the burden of welfare policies in advanced industrial societies could increase infinitely if social values were to become more and more diversified and unstable.

These problems are important, despite their apparent irrelevance to people's daily life and/or government policies, since many of the present difficulties of developed countries—which have not been treated effectively by business-as-usual policy measures—are thought to arise from mismatches between the ways of conceiving the nature of people's demands and the reality.

This seems to be related to the dualistic world-view which is characteristic of Western industrial society. That is, there are individual persons, each of them perceiving him(her)self *subjectively*, yet linked to each other by some inner principle or value system which more or less produces the same way of perceiving the things outside the self *objectively*.

When this dualistic view is applied to economic thoughts, individuals are only recognized as producer-consumers and the national economy is regarded as the aggregate of their activities, ignoring the existence and production/consumption function of intermediate groups, which usually compose society but are neither so indivisibly unified as to become solid entities nor easily dismembered to individuals.

Such a view would not have gone so far if there had not been a historical process of eliminating intermediate groups. The traditional groups such as extended families, medieval communities, and guilds were extinguished deliberately, by new institutions, and/or spontaneously, by competition. Small families and local communities could survive, but their productive functions were increasingly transferred to enterprises, which try to maximize their economic gains, or to governments, which are designated the proxy of the total society.

These two institutions shape the *formal* sector of advanced industrial societies which channels the major proportion of human endeavor to satisfying peoples' demands, following the rules of the market and/or state. Compared to this, other important groups such as trade unions, political parties, and various pressure groups play a minor role.

According to this perception of industrial society, support is given to individuals to satisfy certain demands which are directly necessary for the maintenance of the society, whereas the satisfaction of the other demands is left to the capacity and willingness of each individual. The first type of demand is considered to be invariable for all individuals and hence is recognized objectively; whereas the second type of demand is variable from person to person and hence is recognized only subjectively. When this objectivity/subjectivity dichotomy—which corresponds to the needs/wants dichtomy—is applied to the division of labor between existing institutions, the market sector seems to respond to "wants," the Welfare State to "needs."

Historically speaking, the role of the market may have started as a response to the "needs" for material goods for the subsistence of ordinary people, which were considered to be more or less stable under a certain physical environment. But industrialization and the accompanying diversification of people's demands seem to have changed the market so that it responds to the "wants" of people, since the existence of needs is less relevant given the capacity or willingness to pay.

In fact, this distinction is irrelevant to that between objectively recognizable needs and non-recognizable wants. Then, the State or public sector—a proxy of the total—could be responsible for helping people to satisfy needs not satisfied by the market. The assumed role of this sector is thus to redistribute income and/or opportunity for gainful work as well as produce and distribute "public" goods and services, irrespective of individuals' capacity or willingness to pay.

Another possibility is assuming that the market sector is still responding to various important "needs." We would assume that the *formal* sector—composed of the market sector and the Welfare State—responds to needs, leaving the treatment of wants completely to the *informal* sector: self, family, local community, etc.

Although these dichotomies may have been useful for analyzing the reality of industrial society, they could become unrealistic or obsolete. The real world is too chaotic an entity to be portrayed in dualistic terms. The rationality of the institutions founded on such a vision does or will not hold in another society or another period. In Japan, for example, the functioning of enterprises and government agencies has been considerably different from that of Western countries; in many developing countries, the formal sector finds it increasingly difficult to cope with people's demands so that institutional changes become inevitable. If the difficulties of advanced industrial societies were to arise from misconceptions about demands, it would be useless to blame the people operating the existing institutions.

Problems of Market and State in Advanced Industrial Societies

Some people still believe that the market is efficient and is becoming more efficient in responding to people's needs and wants. Even supposing that wants are no longer of societal concern and that needs in advanced industrial societies are less and less satisfied by the market sector directly, the latter should be able to provide sufficient resources to enable the Welfare State to complement or replace the market sector in improving people's well-being. Up to the early 1970s, the achievements of market-economy industrial countries seemed to verify such a conjecture, when assessed in terms of GNP growth rates, especially in comparison with the historical past.

Table 1.   GNP and Per-capita GNP (yearly growth rates)

| | 1870–1913 | | 1960–1973 | |
	GNP	GNP/capita	GNP	GNP/capita
Japan	3.3	2.2	10.5	9.9
USA	4.3	2.2	4.3	3.1
FRG	2.9	1.7	4.6	3.7
France	1.6	1.4	5.7	4.7
Italy	1.4	0.7	5.0	4.3
UK	2.2	1.3	2.9	2.4

Sources: S. Kuznets, *Modern Economic Growth*, 1966, Table 9; 1975 World Bank Atlas.

However, an increasingly prevalent thesis is that market-based economic institutions will be less and less able to meet three kinds of challenges: (i) utilization of available factors—e.g. natural resources, capital, labor—in the right proportions; (ii) coping with the growth of obstacles to the efficient functioning of the market, e.g. slowdown of increases in tangible and intangible investments, increases in social cost accompanying the enlargement of optimal size of productive units, change of values and attitudes toward work and consumption, the increasing influence of government on the market sector; and (iii) a decline in welfare content of what the market is most able to provide—i.e., material goods, a decline in marginal utility suggested by the saturation of demand, an increase of inequalities and negative externalities, etc.

Although it is difficult to verify these arguments on an empirical basis, the increasing weight of the public sector in GNP in advanced market-economy countries seems to support the view that the role of the market sector tends to decline either due to its obsolescence or because there is an ever-increasing demand for the benefits supplied through the Welfare State.

Table 2. Share of Government Purchases of
Goods and Services in GDP*

	1960	1975
USA	20.8%	21.5%
Japan	13.5	17.3
Germany, FR	16.7	25.1
UK	19.8	27.0
France	15.2	18.2
Italy	15.2	16.8
Sweden	20.0	29.1

Source: OECD, "National Accounts of OECD
Countries."
* If the reduction of the share of expenditure
on defense and the increase of income transfer
through the government is taken into account,
this tendency of increase becomes even more
dramatic.

If the role of the Welfare State is to satisfy people's "needs," it would
be natural for the weight of the public sector to increase with a growth
of awareness that the market sector places greater stress on "wants"
and less on the "needs" of people in advanced industrial societies. But
the reality of the Welfare State since the beginning of the 1950s has
shown that it no longer guarantees a minimum to each individual (or
group) but covers demands whose common incentive is to obtain benefit
in cash or kind, financed by public funds. This may mean that the nature
of needs tends to become less and less objective in accordance with the
tendency of social values to become more and more diversified and unstable.

Moreover, subjectivity or personal differences in "wants"—i.e., individual necessities which are supposedly not of societal concern—seems
to be diminishing. This is because of the increased "standardization"
of information and opportunity available to people and improvements in the "efficiency" of the creation, distribution, and/or utilization of goods and services to respond to their wants. In other words,
people in advanced industrial societies are more or less compelled—
often unconsciously—to have standardized wants in order to adapt
to their living environment.

If, in this way, the needs/wants dichotomy is not to hold now, the
Welfare State could become bankrupt since it does not have a brake
comparable to that of the market sector, which does not supply those
who lack the capacity or willingness to pay. From an economic point of
view, two types of comments can be made about this process. First, insofar as the workers in the market sector do not accept a continuing decline of their share of consumption, productive investment will decline

and the surplus in this sector will decrease, thus checking the expansion of the Welfare State. Second, the method of supply and the complexity of social systems often create distortions between the objectives of the Welfare State and the real effects of its interventions.

Let us assume two cases where the needs/wants dichotomy could arise. First, if needs were recognized objectively by the market, they would be satisfied most efficiently by market-based institutions with the minimum of State intervention, leaving the treatment of "wants" completely outside, to individuals, family members, clubs, and so on. This is not the current situation in advanced industrial societies. Second, if this capacity of the market were declining—through, for example, diversification of values and attitudes—and that of the Welfare State were increasing—through, for example, progress of human science and improvement of information systems—the mixture of the market sector (with a decreasing weight) and the Welfare State (with an increasing weight) would be efficient for needs satisfaction; this seems to be the case in the advanced industrial societies.

Assuming that this is partially valid—that is, that the weight of the market sector is declining and that of the Welfare State is increasing but its achievements are disappointing—what could be a plausible explanation? We should not forget that the assumed capability of these sectors is based not on empirical facts common to different countries in different periods but partly on the experience of certain countries in certain periods and partly on dualistic ideas for classifying demands and the means of their satisfaction.

Economic Growth and Structural Changes in the Labor Market

The preceding arguments could be the starting point for reconsidering the widespread belief in and reliance on the growth of the formal sector—the market sector and the Welfare State—of advanced industrial societies. But this may not be sufficient since, as we have noted, the basic criteria for measuring well-being, such as objectivity/subjectivity, welfare/happiness, needs/wants, are becoming more uncertain so that assessment of the achievements of society and economy tends to become more and more difficult.

Restructuring the conceptual framework is, however, not so easy a task, unless the discrepancies between the new reality (what is) and the old norm (what should be) are made explicit; in other words, conceptualization requires concrete facts in order to be of practical use. In this sense, it seems useful to reconsider the achievements of the market sector and the Welfare State in the full utilization of human capacities since this is supposed to be one of the most important goals of advanced industrial societies and hence legitimizes their policies and institutions.

We may begin with the examination of the instrumental meaning of full employment in the ordinary sense, focusing on two aspects.

First, full employment should maximize the volume of production (and hence consumption) at a given level of available human resources and savings. Second, it should maximize the part of production to be paid as wages under the prevailing labor market. Both aspects have been important elements of industrial society.

With respect to the first aspect, however, it should be stressed that the maximization of production (of goods and services) measured at market prices or of consumption is not necessarily the optimal response to the demands of advanced industrial societies. Moreover, as a result of technological and economic improvement of the conditions surrounding workers/consumers, the "full" utilization of human capacity—which had a more concrete meaning near to the physical and absolute maximum in previous times—is changing into a more and more metaphysical and comparative concept.

With respect to the second aspect, it still seems difficult to find a substitute for the labor market since the Welfare State has been unable to resolve the problem of rising entitlements. So we may conclude that the labor market in advanced industrial societies will not be replaced by another system of distribution in the next few decades.

Nevertheless, the present and future dependence on the labor market as a means for distribution is not sufficient justification for the classical full employment target and the supporting measures. Let us examine what has been happening in the process of pursuing the classical full employment target and how—contrary to the expectations of the people concerned—it is accumulating strains in advanced industrial societies.

Looking at the various "facts" recently observed in many OECD countries, we may suspect that continuous high economic growth tends to curtail the supply of certain kinds of jobs and to increase demand for others, without any mechanism of spontaneous adjustment—e.g. through the evolution of wages and prices, of education and training systems—of people's capacities and/or preferences so as to conform to the changes in living environment generated by the economic growth of advanced industrial societies.

Simply assuming that unemployment rates represent the gap between job-demand and job-supply in national economies, Table 3 suggests that many OECD countries have experienced upward movement of this gap during the recent cycles.

Table 3. Unemployment Rates at Cyclical Peak Years in Nine OECD Countries

	1960–65		1966–70		1971–76	
USA			(1966)	3.6	(1973)	4.7
Canada			(1966)	3.5	(1973)	5.6
France	(1964)	1.1	(1969)	1.6	(1973)	2.0
Germany, FR	(1965)	0.5	(1970)	0.6	(1973)	1.0
Italy	(1962)	2.9	(1970)	3.1	(1973)	3.4
UK	(1964)	1.4			(1973)	2.3
Netherlands	(1965)	0.8	(1969)	1.4	(1973)	2.4
Belgium	(1965)	1.7	(1970)	1.8	(1973)	2.2
Sweden	(1964)	1.6	(1970)	1.5	(1974)	2.0

Source: OECD Labour Force Statistics.

Furthermore, when we compare the peaks and troughs of past business fluctuations, there are upward trends of unfilled vacancies per unemployed worker and of unemployment at a constant level of capital utilization. This may mean that it has become increasingly difficult to maintain full employment in a classical sense owing to an increase in mismatches between jobs demanded and jobs supplied. Demographic factors, which are of course important in deciding demand-supply relations of labor, do not seem to explain the techno-economic and socio-cultural changes taking place in the labor market.

The recent increase of employment in OECD countries has shown remarkable biases toward tertiary industry, service-oriented (professional, technical, and clerical) occupations, and part-time work.

This seems to emerge from changes in the situation on the producers' (job-suppliers') side, and is especially related to their immediate technological and/or economic necessities rather than to speculation about the future evolution of manpower requirements.

Table 4. Sectoral Contributions to Employment Growth in OECD

Average annual rate of growth (percent)	1965–75	1965–70	1970–75
Civilian employment	0.9	1.1	0.8
Contribution of			
Agriculture	−0.5	−0.5	−0.5
Industry	−0.2	−0.4	−0.1
Tertiary sector	1.2	1.2	1.3

Source: OECD Labour Force Statistics.

Today's job-seekers often prefer, for example, services rather than manufacturing, white-collar work rather than blue-collar work, part-time contracts rather than full-time contracts (especially in the case of housewives). These preferences may also have prevailed previously, but such jobs were much fewer than they are today. In other words, such jobs may have been demanded but were not available in old times.

Producers now have to change the mode of manpower utilization, reacting against the changed technological and/or economic requirements: rising demand for services and declining or leveling off of demand for material goods, high potential for increasing labor productivity in manufacturing, increasing scarcity of software to respond to the reinforcement of hardware, etc.; these trends are also liable to be closely related to part-time or fixed-term contracts rather than full-time or permanent contracts.

Looking from the supply side of labor, the most remarkable phenomenon is the increased participation of housewives in many OECD countries which is reflected in the recent increase of females in working populations (Table 5). The increase in size of the college-educated labor force is also an important fact.

Table 5. Females as Percentage of the Labor Force

	Average 1965–70	Average 1970–75
Canada	30.4	33.5
USA	35.4	37.8
Germany, FR	36.1	36.4
Italy	26.8	27.2
UK	34.7	36.4
Australia	30.3	33.0
France	—	35.9
Finland	42.9	44.8
Sweden	38.1	40.9
Japan	39.6	38.2

Source: OECD Labour Force Statistics.

These two features seem to arise from changes on the consumers' (job-seekers') side, particularly in their long-term and cultural motivations, rather than reactions to physical necessities.

Even if the job-suppliers offer jobs suitable to females, youths, and college graduates—e.g. services, part-time work, professional work, respectively—at wage rates feasible from the business management point of view, they will not be met by "effective" demand unless there are housewives, young adults (especially female), and college graduates ready to take these jobs.

The motivation of such newcomers, and hence the increase in their demand for jobs, is no longer related to their economic hazards (e.g. lack of nutrition, clothing, or shelter for coping with biological needs), which are generally taken care of by either the earnings of household heads or the income transfer systems of the State.

In the case of female job-seekers (especially housewives and young girls), what is demanded may be relative economic independence from the traditional nuclear family or more direct participation in social activities. In the case of college graduates, what is demanded may be the future promotion of their professional careers or development and display of their potentialities.

The major cause of this increase in the number of job-seekers may be economic development itself, which has decreased tremendously the labor inputs required for domestic household work and created substantial resources for higher education, although there must have been dynamic interactions between economic development and cultural evolution which have changed the image of family and of vocation, the male/female role dichotomy, the elite/mass dichotomy, and so on.

Contradictions between the Aims of Policies and the Mechanisms of Social and Economic Development

The foregoing discussion suggests that the key factor determining the long-term development of demand-supply relationships in the labor market is not the trend of exogenous variables such as population, inventory of natural resources, and technological innovation, but the evolution of people's demands and its impact on social and economic development. In fact, most of the past developments of alleged exogenous variables such as those mentioned above have been, in the longer run, nothing but the manifestation of techno-economic and/or socio-cultural changes stemming from the demands of the people in advanced industrial societies.

Of course, external factors such as the development of socialist countries and the Third World could become more important, but these influences would also not be a one-way force. Repercussions or feedback between country-groups should not be ignored, but the one-way influence of an individual country such as the USSR or a country-group such as OPEC on the development of the market-economy advanced industrial countries should not be exaggerated.

Considering the above, we may infer that important discontinuities would only emerge with the appearance of "new" demands within advanced industrial societies. But what are new demands? Before defining this concept, it seems convenient to define what "old'" demands are. This distinction will have to be made on the basis of the "facts" prevailing in today's world.

Hence, the nature of people's demands and their influences on the development of society are to be assumed in a value-neutral way. That is, the people in advanced industrial societies—or, more broadly speaking, human beings in any society—"demand" either as individuals or as groups anything which they think valuable and to which they perceive themselves to be entitled; these demands, being heavily affected by the world-views and social values prevailing in the society concerned, stimulate individual or group actions which bring forth techno-economic and socio-cultural developments; there is again feedback between such developments, the demands, latent world-views, and social values.

When past development is considered in this way, it is undeniable that the central feature of old demands has been the increase of per capita (personal or collective) consumption and hence production of material goods and the realization (or maintenance) of full employment. Moreover, these two have often been combined so that a high rate of economic growth tends to be regarded as the only feasible solution to the problem of responding to the people's demands in advanced industrial societies.

This thesis, which equates greater consumption with improved quality of life, is increasingly questioned, and consequently some people prefer full employment under low productivity growth (and hence low growth of per capita consumption) from the distributive point of view. Indeed, one may argue that the lower the productivity growth, the easier the attainment of full employment, giving a certain rate of increase of total production (and hence consumption) and labor supply.

Lower growth of productivity could also be compatible with a change in the content of production, since shifts of demand from material goods to human services, from private sector to public sector, or from blue-collar work to white-collar work generally make it difficult to increase productivity by additions to physical capital. Needless to say, such a development would be realized by extrapolating the past trend.

If this means that equilibrium would be recovered by a spontaneous reduction of productivity generated by changes in the content of production which match changes in demand, such changes might not be identified as the emergence of new demands. What is demanded—i.e., full employment under low growth and the change of content of production—could be attained by extrapolating past trends.

But the preceding observations suggest that supply/demand mismatches for jobs have been increasing, accumulating strains in the labor market which could result in the breaking down of the equilibrium assumed by extrapolating past trends.

The dynamic mechanism whereby unemployment may often coexist with a labor shortage is summarized below as an example of one of the various contradictions between the aims of policies and the development mechanism of advanced industrial societies.

Difficulty of Dissolving the Core of Structural Unemployment. The first contradiction is the mismatch between jobs created by today's economic growth and those demanded by unemployed workers in traditional sectors. The "core" of structural unemployment in most developed countries is so far composed of skilled or semi-skilled workers in the manufacturing sector in which domestic demand for its products is leveling off and where the increase of labor productivity tends to accelerate. The conventional view is that a high level of economic growth is needed to dissolve this core.

However, most jobs currently created by economic growth are concentrated in services and are offered either to new employees from outside the ranks of the unemployed (housewives, youths, immigrants) or to specially trained intellectual workers. If such jobs are not matched by the characteristics of the newcomers, economic growth could—instead of rapidly solving structural unemployment—trigger wage-price inflation and balance of payments deficits due to a labor shortage coexisting with unemployment.

Expansionary Measures and Inflation. The second contradiction is that the presently available expansionary policy measures are vulnerable to cost-push inflation which threatens the economic security of the weak—e.g. old people. Due to the characteristics of the pattern of economic growth of today's developed countries, expansionary measures—especially those having job-creating effects—have to rely on service sectors in which wages but not productivity usually increase as fast as in the manufacturing sector.

Thus, instead of increasing efficiency of factor utilization so as to realize price stabilization, expansionary measures may tend to stimulate cost-push inflation. As a result, many governments of developed countries are often compelled to repeat "stop—go" policies, especially when the inflationary pressure is easily changed into balance of payments difficulties. Such developments inevitably add to the structural and cyclical unemployment complex.

Emergence of a "Secondary" Labor Market. The third contradiction is the increase in the number of "peripheral" workers who are vulnerable to cyclical unemployment. They are mainly composed of housewives and young adults engaging in services and part-time work which are created by policies aiming at economic growth, increase of employment, etc.; their number tends to increase following the improvement of unemployment benefits. They might have left the labor market in a period of recession in previous times, but today they want to stay in the labor market in order to get unemployment benefits and expect to recover their jobs even if unemployment tends to be of long duration.

Thus the appearance of a "dual economy" or "secondary" labor force—which could be the outcome of the new pattern of economic development—is subject to contradiction between equality and adjustability.

Labor Cost as a Quasi-fixed Cost for Employers. The fourth contradiction is that market-based institutions are compelled to favor the segmentation of the labor market. That is, a shift toward professional, technical, and clerical work tends to increase on-the-job training costs, which—accompanied by the increase of demand for job security from employees and hence the rise in inhibitions and difficulties in laying off workers—makes labor cost a quasi-fixed cost for employers.

Consequently, in order to maintain flexibility, management has to promote the substitution of lower priced, fixed-term, and/or part-time labor for higher priced, permanent, and/or full-time (male) labor as much as possible. The increase of employment share in the public sector—which is not usually subject to the rule of competitiveness—could check this tendency to some extent; but it would increase the tax burden.

Decline of Work Satisfaction. The fifth contradiction is the dissatisfaction with work which is seemingly accompanying the increase of employment. Although it is difficult to verify, we may infer that the symptoms observed in working places such as productivity decline, absenteeism, work stoppages, and continuous demand for reduction of working hours, must be the manifestation of work dissatisfaction. It is also difficult to prove that the new pattern of economic growth has caused increased dissatisfaction, but the analysis of this relationship is important since the aim of economic growth should be not only to increase the amount of gainful work but also to increase satisfaction or prevent dissatisfaction with work.

Increased dissatisfaction—assuming that it exists—could also impair the healthy functioning of the labor market or, in other words, make it more difficult to diminish mismatches between supply of and demand for jobs due to the qualitative difference between the jobs supplied and those demanded.

International Dispersion of Contradictions. The sixth contradiction is the intensification and international dispersion of the above contradictions. Should there be a dynamic mechanism of reproducing unemployment, inflation, inequality, labor shortage, and worker dissatisfaction within the system of maintaining growth of production and employment and related government policies, this would mean that equilibrium would be unattainable either spontaneously or deliberately (i.e., through policy measures available to governments).

If the pursuit of such a (currently absent) equilibrium is to be intensified and diffused internationally, contradictions could also be enlarged and diffused internationally so that trade wars could take place in which individual nation-states and/or their groups try to pursue their equilibrium to the detriment of the equilibrium of others.

All the above comments are not to justify leaving (and worsening) the present inequilibrium. What is indispensable is to question the feasibility of policy measures founded on the classical belief about the existence of equilibrium or the alleged consistency between development toward a service–welfare–information-oriented society and the return to full employment in the classical sense. This could mark the starting point of the search for "better" utilization of the potential of human and natural resources for improving people's well-being.

What Are "New Demands"?

Basic Hypotheses Concerning New Demands

If new demands are emerging in advanced industrial societies and causing discontinuities from past trends, they have to be identified and appraised systematically to infer the way in which they may evolve over time. This is difficult not because of the lack of observations, but because of the inadequacy of available theories or systematic hypotheses to sort out the observed "facts" to distinguish "authentic" new demands from "spurious" ones, which are not so deep-rooted as to lead to fundamental and irreversible changes in people's attitudes and values.

The study of new demands is neither a survey of new or spurious new demands in developed countries nor a list of theories. It proposes a set of hypotheses as a basis for sorting out observations and as a possible explanation of the relation between new demands and the change in development patterns of advanced industrial societies. The basic ones are: (i) individual persons produce their own well-being, and (ii) both changes in values and changes in options could be a source of new demands.

Self-production of Well-being. We are accustomed to characterize the situation of a person by his (her) income and hence consumption. In fact, this view is unnatural and destined to become obsolete in the long run since, according to it, the supply of labor and the demand for goods and services cannot be treated within the same framework. In other words, human activity is separated into two parts, labor generating income through the labor market and consumption generated by expenditure in the goods and services market. We may compare the former to the "export" of time to "unknown" people and the latter to the "import" of time from unknown but different people. In this sense, imports are often dependent on exports; therefore housewives or non-workers as importers often have to depend on husbands or workers as exporters within the family or the society.

The Welfare State does not fundamentally change this dualistic view of human life since the Welfare State neither creates income other than labor income nor produces goods and services different from those provided by the market-based use of human time.[1] Practically speaking, therefore, a Welfare State ignoring this dualism would finally go into bankruptcy.

The study of New Demands discriminates explicitly between the formal sector and the informal sector in the production of the well-being of individuals, the former being market-based institutions and the Welfare State and the latter being self, family, local community, etc. This means that the work/leisure option—to produce or not to produce—is replaceable by the option of allocation of time—to produce one's well-being directly in the informal sector or indirectly through the medium of the formal sector; in other words, there will only be a problem of choice for the same purpose, satisfaction of demands, instead of a duel between two values. From a policy point of view, it may mean that a substantial part of the role assigned to the formal sector of advanced industrial societies could be transferred to the informal sector, particularly when the latter can satisfy people's demands more efficiently, and there is decreasing demand for participation in the formal sector.

[1] The actual division of labor between the private sector and the public sector is not that characterized by the dualistic world-view mentioned on pp. 5–7 above. Most public goods—water supply, electricity and gas, education, health care—can be produced and distributed as private goods.

Such a change of perception does not justify a decline in the efficiency of the formal sector of advanced industrial societies. On the contrary, it is expected to prevent the further increase of its diseconomies of scale by removing the excessive expectations of its role. Furthermore, this would be more compatible with the emerging social concern about the increase of options for the use of time, compared to the fixed idea of regarding the formal sector as the unique source of well-being.[2]

Changes in Values and Options as the Sources of New Demands. Discussions of new demands are often confused because various heterogeneous realms are mixed up in the same kind of treatment. In order to avoid such confusion, the study of New Demands has proposed the conceptualization in Figure 1. Here, individual persons are separated from the physical and social environment and man-made material goods, and moreover, their demands are separated between "above-the-line" and "below-the-line" areas, the former stemming from values or latent world-views, the latter being constrained by the options available for doing (or not doing) something at a given moment.

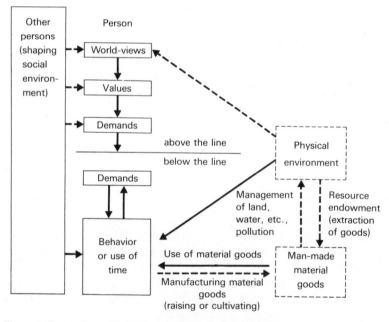

Figure 1. Perception of the realms related to human behavior.

[2] "Flexibility in Working Life," Archibald A. Evans, OECD, 1973; "Lifelong Allocation of Time," OECD, 1976.

Assuming that individuals produce their own well-being, then their values and options as the basis for decision-making could differ from person to person and from time to time. But as far as the life of an individual is affected by other people, the "personal" conditions of "average" people could not be free from the effects of changes by others, i.e., changes in the social environment. Or, the "individual attitude" is affected by the "aggregate attitude" and this produces feedback on the latter. Thus we may distinguish two types of new demands. The first type arises from a change in the values and/or latent world-views possessed by most of the people in the society, whereas the second type arises from change in the number or nature of options available for average people.

The examples of the first case may be found, historically, in the emergence of ascetic values such as Puritanism and militaristic nationalism or of prodigal values to stimulate consumption competition. They must cause a fundamental change in behavior since they change the existential meaning of human life.

A typical example of the second case may be the long-lasting increase in average real incomes. This causes a deep-rooted change in people's behavior by gradually changing their living environment; or it may eventually transform their values and world-views. New demands emerge as the symptoms of change in values and world-views.

The above hypothesis for discriminating between two types of new demands seems useful for making a framework for analyzing the long-term development of society and economy in terms broader than the usual hypotheses, according to which new demands are assumed to be the products of either change in values (caused by e.g. ideological innovations) or change in options (caused by e.g. technological innovations).

When we admit the discontinuities in the past trends of advanced industrial societies, we are inclined to infer that they have been caused by a change in values. But we must also admit that we cannot find there any innovative systems of thought—religious, political, or scientific—comparable to those during the periods of Renaissance, Reform, Enlightenment, etc., which could form the foundation for new values.

Consequently, economic rationality in the form of the maximization of production and consumption—whether private or public—might still be the central demand of today and possibly tomorrow, contrary to the first rather intuitive impression that discontinuities are taking place. But if we were to presume that new demands could emerge through a continuous change of living environment under relatively stable social values, we could better explain the change in people's behavior in recent times.

The above does not ignore the possibility that under more or less similar techno-economic development, i.e., evolution of available options for average people, new values may emerge which differ from country to country according to differences in cultural tradition. In other words, differences in cultural tradition could lead to different patterns of economic growth through variations in the nature of emerging new values.

Choice between Work and Leisure

The forecast change in preference between work and leisure in the conventional sense—which could be the essential factor determining the future of economic growth and employment—is prone to error due to the lack of understanding about the relation between people's behavior and the production of well-being proposed by the study of New Demands.

For example, looking at the past trend toward reduction in working hours, we often conjecture that people would prefer less work and more leisure if they had enough income; this is because work is painful, boring, and/or alienating whereas leisure is the opposite, and the necessity of working would decrease if workers' incomes were to increase substantially. However, this simplistic understanding of the detriments of work and the benefits of goods and services exchanged for labor income does not explain why the new entry of housewives into the labor market has increased in many developed countries when their husbands' real incomes have been increasing. This has resulted in the increase of housewives' working hours in paid employment cancelling out the decrease in their husbands' working hours.

Moreover, this tendency has been conspicuous in higher income countries and now is spreading to Japan where per capita incomes have arrived only recently at the levels prevailing in Western Europe. Indeed it is doubtful that the working hours per family will decline when the income per capita increases,[3] especially if we are to take into account the increase in part-time work of housewives and students, the tendency of accepting secondary jobs (called "moonlighting" or "black work"[4]) which often accompany the reduction of normal working hours, etc.

The answer to this question cannot be obtained by comparing the welfare content of "money income" with that of "freedom," "partici-

[3] Working hours are generally measured at the place of work by worker and not by household, making it difficult to estimate working hours per family (or group of people sharing the same consumption pattern).
[4] "Flexibility in Working Life," p. 44.

pation," "self-realization," etc., since these are centered on different value concepts. In comparing the welfare content of time used in the formal sector with that in the informal sector, the study of New Demands demonstrates that whether a reduction of working time increases or decreases the welfare of a person depends on his personal situation.

Furthermore, there seems to be a widespread conviction about the detriment of work or time spent in the formal sector: that irrespective of the content of their work, the people participating in the formal sector will generally be "alienated" in exchange for money income, whereas those staying in the informal sector (housewives, retired people, children) are "not alienated." However, many people have friendly relations with colleagues at work but not necessarily at home or in the local community. The extreme case may be found in Japanese male workers in big organizations; most of them have very few friends outside those that they have made at work.

If so, a person might prefer work to leisure at a wage rate which another person would reject; in this case, the "one-price-to-one-good or one-wage-to-one-hour's-work" principle would no longer hold for this worker, since the same working hour could contain more well-being for him than for another worker.

All the above may not be contradictory to workers' claim for more time "off" since the welfare content of the time spent in the formal sector is supposed to depend on an individual's situation and is not subject to a general law. A real contradiction would appear if a person were to fill up the increased time "off" not by products of the informal sector but by those of the formal sector; in other words, to increase leisure activities heavily dependent on the products of market-based institutions or of the Welfare State.

This person either would need more work and more leisure at the same time, resulting in heavy pressure on his available time—which is 24 hours a day for everyone—or would have to exploit other people's time spent in the formal sector, by increasing his (her) wages, profits, or transfer income, decreasing tax burden, etc., regardless of how much he (she) produced in the formal sector.

If everyone did this, it could cause, under certain conditions, an extraordinarily rapid increase in productivity and per capita consumption, i.e., high economic growth and price stability. However, under different conditions, it could also cause a decline of productivity and a price rise through the rejection of the rules of industrial society (e.g. absenteeism, work stoppages, tax evasion, etc.), resulting in unintentional zero or minus growth under inflation.

Should the latter situation materialize, the present stagflation could

become a chronic disease since policy attitudes founded on the work/
leisure dichotomy do not seem to work well in advanced industrial societies. A serious examination of the flexible allocation of time between
the formal sector and the informal sector could provide a feasible
alternative, insofar as both activities produce well-being and do not
promote confrontations between production/consumption, diligence/
idleness, money/satisfaction, subordination/autonomy, alienation/self-
realization, etc.

Change in Industrial Structure and in Institutions

*From Goods to Services, from Informal Production to Formal Produc-
tion.* Why has the growth of service production been faster than that of
material production? Economists may try to attribute it to the income
elasticities of demand for services, which are assumed larger than those
for material goods. But the numerical values of elasticity derived from
statistical data are not comparable to the data in controlled experiments.
That is, they are simply the outcomes of past development in which
social and economic conditions were determined from time to time
endogenously. Thus, the high elasticities of demand for services are
better understood as the "results" of a specific pattern of social and
economic development rather than as its "determinants."

Furthermore, the increase of employment in the service industries
seems to be faster than that of production in those industries. Economists may try to explain it by saying that it is more difficult to replace
human labor with physical capital in service production than in material
production. This also is not very persuasive, since we could make a long
list of services—transportation, entertainment, commerce, education,
health care—which have so far substantially "economized" on human
labor by standardization, mechanization, automation, computerization,
and so on.

This inadequacy of current theory in explaining the rapid increase of
demand for labor in service industries and service-oriented work may
be overcome to some extent by utilizing the distinction between the
formal sector and the informal sector for producing people's well-being,
which is the concept employed in the preceding section.

In advanced industrial societies, the production of most material
goods, e.g. vegetables, has shifted from the informal sector to the
formal sector. Therefore, in recent decades, most of the increase of
material production has been generated by the increase in demand for
the products of the formal sector.

With respect to services, the situation is different, since the informal sector still meets a substantial part of the demand for services. Thus the demand for services is met by both the formal and the informal sectors. Let us refer to the former as "formal production" and the latter as "informal production" of services, both of which may meet the same demand.[5] Given the above conditions, however, it seems that there has been a substantial shift from informal production to formal production of services in recent years.

Thus, the growth of the formal production of services recorded in statistical data could have stemmed from two factors, one being the growth of demand for formal production *per se*, and the other being the shift from informal to formal production—which was compulsory rather than voluntary—owing to the decline of supply capacity in the informal sector. If the second factor were more important, the growth of productivity in the service-producing sector would tend to be slower —and hence employment would increase faster—since such a shift could take place irrespective of the increase of productivity in the formal sector.

Assuming that the above conjecture is valid, there may still be some important questions; for example: Why was that shift restricted to the one-way movement from informal production to formal production? Will it continue in the future, level off, or reverse?

Traditional Division of Labor between Goods and Services.   In order to answer the above questions, it seems useful to reconsider the distinction between goods and services which was evident in the early period of industrial society but is now becoming more and more vague.

In pre-industrial society, almost all kinds of human achievements were either embedded in material entities as material goods or utilized instantly as services. For example, the work of a fisherman is embedded in the fish he catches, whereas that of a soldier is only realized when he is fighting against an enemy. This does not mean that the benefit brought forth by the latter disappears instantly. On the contrary, fish may rot in a few days, but the independence secured by soldiers could last for centuries. What is different is that the usefulness of the former is visible in a physical form, whereas that of the latter is invisible and can only be visualized through symbols or signs such as decorations.

Under such conditions, the growth of production in the formal sector—especially market-based institutions—was centered around supply-oriented material goods. The word "supply-oriented" refers to an

---

[5] For example, a meal may be served either by a professional cook as formal production or by a wife as informal production. But this is not usually the case with respect to the production of beef or vegetables, which is normally carried out in the formal sector.

indifference toward the specific demand arising from the specific situation of the user. For example, a unit of supply-oriented foodstuff may simply slake the user's appetite or—speaking more scientifically—supply a suitable number of calories. Personal preferences are dealt with either by alternative modes of utilization or by the self-production of demand-oriented goods or services, e.g. the preparation and cooking of food.

In fact, the core of the formal sector—especially the market sector—of industrial society is composed of institutions which evolved or were designed in order to deal with identifiable and quantifiable—or "standardized"—demands of people which are to be satisfied by goods and services that are indifferent to the specific conditions of the users. A "one-price-to-one-good" principle should and could be the foundation of the rules of the game under such a condition.

Another important part of the formal sector is occupied by institutions such as banks, transport, and administrative services which are needed to maintain or organize other goods- or service-producing institutions.

The above may more or less be applied to the Welfare State, whose main role is to produce services such as education and health care. Its products are usually more demand-oriented than those of the market sector since they are concerned more with inferred users' "needs" than with speculated producers' "profits." But they are still supply-oriented insofar as conjectures have to be made on the suppliers' side, based on information and values held by suppliers.

Rapid increase in production of supply-oriented goods was welcomed by users, especially in the beginning of industrialization, since there was ample labor or human capacity in the informal sector to utilize the output of the formal sector. That is, there was no fear about the capacity of services to utilize the increased supply of foods, textiles, tools, etc.; for example, the supply of cooking, sewing, transporting, and distribution services in either the informal sector—e.g. housewives—or the formal sector—e.g. cooks, dressmakers, transporters, merchants—was supposed infinite or at least elastic. What was lacking—or perceived so —was the quantity and quality of supply-oriented goods. If any shortage were to appear in the production of the above-mentioned services, instrumental material goods would have been invented and produced to fill the gap.

Similar considerations apply to the relation between "public" services and their users. For example, there was no fear about the utilization of the output of school education. The human capacity reserved in the informal sector was abundant. Furthermore, the service-producing market sector and the Welfare State could use the "surplus" material goods for increasing the efficiency of their production. In other words, there was a certain synergy between the growth of material goods production and that of service production.

Appearance of Obstacles and the Trial of Adaptation. The classical expansion of the formal sector crashed against the obstacle of over-production and unemployment. If it was assumed that only the formal sector is or should be responsible for producing the goods and services demanded for people's well-being, the following rationalization could hold: people wanted to increase their real income or production in order to improve their well-being, but were faced by increased unemployment and a resultant decrease in real income because of a shortage in the demand for their products.

This logic is, however, insufficient since it does not explain why there could be a shortage of demand for the products which—according to the first premise—must improve people's well-being. So it has to depend on exogenous factors such as market failure or—in other words—bad maneuvers of employer-producers or ignorance of worker-consumers. Therefore, it seems better to replace it with the following rationalization: First, a steady increase of supply-oriented goods tended to cause redundancy of those goods which do not fit individual demands. Second, the expansion of the formal sector increasingly absorbed the productive capacity of those goods and services in the informal sector which are indispensable for utilizing or supplementing the products of the formal sector.[6]

As a result, the demand for real income, which is a proxy for formal sector production, increased in order to cope with the reduction of productive capacity in the informal sector, but it was obstructed by the fact that the formal sector had already been suffering from redundancy of its products.

The formal sector adapted to this situation in two ways.

Differentiation of Material Goods Production. The first was the differentiation of the production of supply-oriented market goods to respond better to the different conditions of users. From the business management point of view, this may be understood as efforts to exploit effective demand. It is also expressed in the increase and differentiation of instrumental material goods for improving the efficiency of informal production: sewing machines, electric appliances, passenger cars, etc. Many new products created demand for skills and/or experience. As a

---

[6] This may still be valid today in many developing countries where many kinds of products in the formal sector do not fit the needs of the users.

result, the formal sector needed more professional and part-time service workers.

One of the detrimental effects of this trend may have been the acceleration of inflation under the tremendous increase in demand for material goods which should theoretically suppress the rise of prices; however, it may be that the more the people are absorbed by the formal sector, the higher become the prices of services which were very low when most of them were produced in the informal sector. This also may be the reason why the general price level of developed countries is much higher—despite the flood of material goods and the high efficiency of service industries—than that of less developed countries where most of the services are produced in the informal sector.

It may be argued that the maximum differentiation of material goods —i.e., giving everyone every kind of finished good—would end this development, but this means an extreme waste of natural and human resources. In fact, the recent development of the United States and Japan has led to a tremendous increase of negative externalities: pollution, congestion, waste of natural resources, etc.

Growth of the Welfare State.   The second type of adaptation was the growth of the products of the Welfare State which are distributed regardless of the users' capacity for formal production. This may have compensated for the loss of productive capacity in the informal sector since most of people's "needs" would be satisfied by the products of the public sector. In other words, the Welfare State was expected—in place of maximizing the activities of the material goods-producing market sector and the related service-producing sector—to replace substantially the earlier production in the informal sector.

As this development would not stimulate the growth of the material goods-producing market sector compared to the first type of adaptation, the contradictions stemming from its excessive growth needed to be mitigated in some way. Thus, the human capacities which were not absorbed by the service-producing market sector were utilized by the Welfare State.

In spite of these comparative advantages, this type of adaptation tended to result in ever-increasing claims on the State, resulting either in economic catastrophe or in the increase of government intervention. The cause of this increase in claims is the discrepancy between objectively recognized "needs" and the users' demands arising from their situation; this was combined with supply shortages caused by the lack of stimulation of the material goods-producing sector and its related service-producing market sector.

The above two types of adaptation not only were effective in coping with the classical difficulties of industrial society but also expanded its formal sector by absorbing at an increasing speed the human capacity located in the informal sector. Thus, the problems in advanced industrial societies have changed from classical ones to new ones; as the old obstacles disappeared and new ones appeared, new types of adaptation had to be found.

Toward a More Demand-oriented Production. The preceding arguments suggest that the crucial point is how to make the production activities of advanced industrial societies more appropriate for satisfying changes in peoples' demands. In some respects, the market sector is becoming increasingly skilled at producing demand-oriented products. One example is the production of foods for specific requirements other than the simple demand for calories: saving time, emergency food, refreshment. Formerly, it was impossible for the formal sector to respond readily to such demands.

For example, *mochi* or rice-cake—one of the traditional foods of Japan—possesses the exactly same characteristics as today's instant foods, but had to be produced mostly in the informal sector—i.e., by families or local communities. During the course of industrialization, the production of many kinds of such demand-oriented goods in the informal sector declined, reflecting the decrease of productive capacity. But the production of instant foods (including rice-cake produced and packed in the modern way) is now one of the most rapidly growing activities of the formal sector of advanced industrial societies.

A second example is the package tour which is different from the traditional group tour that aimed at transporting passengers to a certain destination at the lowest cost. This could never be produced without consciousness of the specific demands of the passengers for visiting scenic or historical spots, sports, shopping, attending conferences, etc. Thus, in demand-oriented production, it does not matter whether the products are goods or services, and this was a characteristic of the informal production in pre-industrial societies.

The demand for physical goods like instant food depends less on the physical nature of the material and more on the know-how of experts on dietetics, seasoning, conservation, etc., and their integration as in the case of professional cooks or experienced housewives. In contrast, the demand for services like package tours depends less on what the producer does and more on the existence of various material goods such as transportation equipment, hotels, and communication networks, the use of which was formerly organized separately.

We may refer, in such cases, to material goods as hardware and to know-how as software; then we may define instant food as software integrated in hardware, whereas package tours are hardware integrated in software.

The key factor in combining various elements of hardware and software to produce demand-oriented products is the storage, retrieval, processing, and transmission of information. It would be impossible for the informal sector to do such jobs because they require special knowledge and the skill of intellectual workers. Therefore, the future development of the formal sector will be centered around the production of hardware such as computers and communication equipment and related software as well as research and development, since this is the way of utilizing its comparative advantages over the informal sector.

In spite of such a development in the formal (especially market) sector, however, there could be a gap between potential formal production and what is demanded. The ultimate source of this gap may be the dualistic structure of industrial society: producer and consumer, employer and employee, work and leisure, labor and capital, individuality and collectivity, man and nature, and so on. The gap may cause consumer dissatisfaction and waste as well as underemployment of natural and human resources. Thus we may want to reconsider the implications of production in the informal sector where there cannot be such a mismatch.

This dualistic structure—or internal distortion—of industrial society could have been the source of extraordinary energy for increasing and maintaining the comparative advantages of its formal sector over the informal sector with respect to productivity. But it seems that a considerable change is now taking place; the time may have come to question the belief that formal production will always be more efficient than informal production in responding to people's demands. Indeed, some symptoms suggesting the decline of the absolute advantage of the formal sector are apparent.

The first is the appearance of the do-it-yourself industry, which should be regarded as more than a leisure industry; it should be understood as a sign that the material goods-producing sector has discovered the necessity or desirability of cooperating with (rather than substituting for) production activities in the informal sector.

The second symptom is resistance against further expansion of the Welfare State. Although effective production in the informal sector needs appropriate physical and social conditions which the Welfare State could provide, this does not mean that only the Welfare State should and could produce the individual or collective well-being— whether individual or collective—of the people.

Thus the belief that the formal sector will always be more efficient than the informal sector seems to have become somewhat out of date. There is the potential increase of productive capacity in the informal sector, which has been provided by the ever-increasing efforts of the formal sector, whether material capital or intellectual capital. And there is the comparative decline of the formal sector, which has been caused by its own negative externalities—loss of freedom, degeneration of the work ethic—brought forth by the domination of instrumentalism.

The production of services and some goods "directly" aiming at the satisfaction of demands could be gradually returning to the informal sector due to the restoration of its comparative advantages over the formal sector. Such a development may remove some of the dissatisfaction of consumers and taxpayers. It may also lower unemployment and the alienation of those who desire to work for self-realization and/or for the well-being of other people. Indeed, if more people were engaged in informal production in the future, the demand for jobs in the formal sector would decrease.

Tools for Constructing Scenarios

The evaluation and choice of policy objectives and/or measures which have long-term effects—whether intended or unintended—should be based on forecasts of the long-term effects of the options open to advanced industrial societies, particularly their effects on internal developments. This means that the policy-maker should consider several alternative scenarios describing the possible future developments of the economy and society according to each of today's policy options.

However, assessing the possible path of development following the introduction of certain policy measures is a difficult task, because they bring about complex interactions among society members, who pursue their ends individually or collectively through the available measures. Moreover, the effects of such interactions are not short-lived, but continue to exert dynamic influences on the subsequent development paths of society and the economy.

Therefore, the writer of such scenarios has to rely on fairly simplified assumptions about the internal dynamic mechanism, otherwise it would be difficult to distinguish the changes caused by alternative policies. In this connection, current theories simply say that economic regulators such as income, prices, wages, interest rates, and exchange rates will constantly work so as to equilibrate people's demands and the response of their society and economy.

But this can hardly explain why the "theoretically" feasible and desirable policies may not achieve their objectives, especially the recovery of equilibrium in supply-demand relationships among labor, money, commodities, foreign currencies, etc. Nor can they explain why most of the developed countries are suffering from common (though the degree and attitude are different from country to country) contradictions such as the lack of effective demand in an inflationary environment, rejection of more efficient technology without any proof of its ill effects, the negative attitude of employers in face of the remarkable increase in unemployment, and the decline in work satisfaction under physically favorable working conditions.

What is important in this connection is that they are, on the one hand, of a purely socio-cultural nature but, on the other hand, must be related to the past techno-economic developments and the present economic difficulties of developed countries.

The preceding part of this report has been devoted to proposing a conceptual framework which can take account of these contradictions and provide a consistent method for long-term projection. The aim is to shed light on the interplay between techno-economic development and socio-cultural development, which—parallel with the emergence of the Third World—may have a critical influence on the future course of advanced industrial societies.

As yet the output of this approach has been insufficient to provide a "hard" tool for long-term forecasting comparable to mathematical models. However, it seems possible to derive from it a tentative logical framework for sorting out several possible patterns of internal and international division of labor between the formal sector and the informal sector and between material goods and human services.

Nevertheless, the present state of our empirical knowledge is still deficient for proposing either new values to be the normative foundation for desirable and feasible end-states of our economy and society at the end of a projection period—i.e., around the year 2000—or new methodologies to analyze the dynamic responses to certain policies or the systematic interaction of structural changes.[7] Even whether or not there could or should be such values or methodologies is difficult to judge from the preceding arguments.

This consciousness of the weakness of our tools has led us to propose "incomplete" scenarios which have heads and tails but lack bodies.

[7] Here the term "structural changes" means the non-conjunctural and seemingly irreversible changes occurring in various areas of advanced industrial societies, e.g. people's attitudes toward work and leisure, demographic trends in the labor market, the speed and direction of technological progress, the relation between public sector and private sector, the use of energy and raw materials, inter-industrial relations, international division of labor.

They have a common end-state far into the future, possibly after the middle of the 21st century; their different development paths start from the present and end before the end of the century. Thus the link between the end-state and the initial trend is missing in any scenario.

Such scenarios may have no value in themselves as futures studies due to their incompleteness—which is not the case with most of the other long-term projections of world development—and hence they have to be utilized as the means for testing the feasibility of other scenarios elaborated elsewhere, including the INTERFUTURES scenarios.

Classification of Countries by Stage of Industrial Development

In order to develop scenarios capable of treating international problems, it is necessary to distinguish countries or country-groups according to their geographical location and stage of industrial development. The difference between "free market" economy and "centrally planned" economy does not seem very important since the significance of this distinction is declining as a means of identifying economic conditions country by country; in fact, socialist countries are increasingly dependent (even if implicitly) on market forces, whereas capitalist countries are strengthening government intervention into the market mechanisms.

Of course the political significance of differences in regime is and will remain large, but what is more relevant in this study is the differences in the stage of techno-economic development among various countries. Therefore, we may resort to the usual classification of countries, discriminating among advanced industrial countries (AICs), newly industrializing countries (NICs), and less developed countries (LDCs).

There may be no problem about including North America, Japan, northwestern Europe, and Australia-New Zealand in the AICs; but the treatment of some other countries may be difficult because, for example, they have high income per capita but low production and employment in secondary industry (e.g. some OPEC countries) or low income per capita but a relatively large industrial sector (e.g. some Asian countries). Thus it may be useful to have two criteria for measuring the degree of "industrialization." One is the weight of production and employment in secondary industry, and another is the weight of production and employment in the formal sector.

The process of industrialization has been characterized by the growth of production in secondary industry and the decline of employment in primary industry. It may also be regarded as the process by which human resources are moved from the informal sector (subsistence farming, domestic services, handicrafts) to the formal sector (market-oriented agriculture, commercial services, modern manufacturing). During this process people's lives have been increasingly integrated into the market sector and the Welfare State.

Therefore, the so-called high income countries not only have high productivity in their material goods-producing industries but also generally have a high proportion of people whose production activities are integrated in the formal sector, resulting in higher money incomes and price levels compared to "less industrialized" countries, especially in the case of "free market" economies.

According to the above, an AIC must have a high weight of production and employment in secondary industry as well as a high income per capita. OPEC countries could not be classified as AICs under this definition. Similarly the NICs with low incomes per capita may not be placed in the AIC category, even if they have considerable production capacity in their modern industrial sector. We may notice the importance of the rising industrialization in some less developed countries such as the Republic of Korea, Taiwan, Hong Kong, Singapore, India, Indonesia, Iran, Brazil, Mexico, Algeria, and Nigeria. According to the second criterion, however, it seems difficult to classify all of these countries as NICs, the intermediate group between LDCs and AICs, since some of them still seem to depend substantially on the informal production of goods and services which are related to people's routine lives, even though they have a considerable production capacity for certain industrial goods competing with those of AICs. In contrast, some countries in Europe and Latin America, which still have a high weight of production in primary industry but have already integrated a substantial part of production into the formal sector, may be classified as NICs, even if some of them have centrally planned economic systems.

As our work does not need a detailed classification of individual countries or country-groups, it would be sufficient to point out that some of the countries listed above, some OECD countries, and some socialist countries may be included in the NICs according to our definition. As a consequence, most of the countries which belong neither to the AICs nor the NICs are classified as LDCs in the following discussion.

End-state of the Relation between the Formal Sector and the Informal Sector

The nature of the end-state assumed here for the AICs is different from the geopolitical relations among AICs and LDCs which are mentioned in the report of INTERFUTURES, "Facing the Future."[8] The end-state scenarios proposed in that report refer to the end of the projection period—around 2000—and are supposed to be the means of reference for the analysis of the social dynamic process. It is considered that the dynamic analysis of changing patterns of relationships and balance of forces and of conflicting strategies should be considerably eased by a prior "knowledge," however imperfect, of potential end-state international environments, understood as defining the range of possible (or preferred) futures for this environment.

Thus the alternative end-states of geopolitical relationships among AICs and LDCs are assumed to be logically consistent with the paths of evolution of such relationships in the method proposed by the IN-TERFUTURES. But in the present document the end-state of the division of labor between the formal sector and the informal sector is irrelevant to the process of evolution since it uses a special notion about the mechanism of production of goods and services as an input for the well-being of human beings. We assume the historical process of the increase and then possible decrease in the weight of the formal sector of industrial society, following the way of thinking employed in the preceding section.

There are neither theoretical nor empirical grounds for speculating that, in post-industrial society, production activities will be carried out half through the formal sector and half through the informal sector. On the contrary, people may gravitate toward one of the following two extreme cases.

Case A. Almost all production activities are carried out on an informal basis: people obtain what they demand through their own efforts and by cooperation among family or community members. Institutions for capitalistic as well as bureaucratic control of individuals disappear since there is no longer scarcity of goods and services, and the alienation, suppression, pollution, unemployment, etc., brought about by the activities of the formal sector of industrial society are gone.

This end-state, which may appeal to the so-called "decentralists," seems to ignore the "fact" that most people in AICs tend to prefer the visible benefits (even if they involve substantial social costs) offered by the formal sector rather than run the risk of losing all the heritage of the past industrialization process.

Case B. Almost all production activities are carried out on a formal basis; people receive all the "parts" necessary for their life from either

[8] OECD, 1979.

the market sector or the Welfare State, and assemble them so as to satisfy their demands. These parts may include "services" for the inter-mediate assembly of more crude goods and services. The production of parts is not in general an amusing task since they do not directly satisfy the producers' demands. In order to minimize the amount of such "input" per output, the formal sector has to pursue rigorously its specialization, systematization, automation, computerization, etc.

This end-state may appeal to the orthodox economist-sociologist, but it seems to overlook the fact that human beings can find it difficult to manage large complicated systems, especially when they involve a large number of human beings. Sophisticated instruments are not sufficient.

Thus the 50–50 composition seems to be a "neutral" point between the two poles. The purpose of assuming such an end-state is not the "harmonization" between decentralist and economist-sociologist—which seems almost impossible—but setting an immovable goal at a distant place in the future to be the guide for trend scenarios. Such a goal does not necessarily have a normative meaning, although Case A or Case B may be a highly normative description of the future state of individual AICs.

Another important aspect of the end-state of AICs is the future state of today's developing countries. The AICs will not arrive at the stage of post-industrial society without affecting or being affected by the development of the present NICs and LDCs. Thus it seems necessary to consider what are the feasible goals for the NICs and LDCs com-parable to the AICs case. This is important not only from the point of view of possible interactions between these country-groups but also from the point of view of the general applicability of the above hypoth-eses about the development mechanism of AICs.

Considering the above problem, the latent hypotheses behind Table 6, which summarizes historical production patterns, may be stated in the following manner, and could be referred to when the mid-term trend scenarios are examined.

Hypothesis (1): All AICs have arrived at the full formalization of production of goods, and have embarked on the process of formali-zation of services. But full formalization of service production is impossible.

Hypothesis (2): It will often become impossible to discriminate good production from service production in post-industrial society; moreover, the system of production will have become very much different from that of today even in the formal sector.

Hypothesis (3): It is impossible to specify the techno-economic struc-

Table 6.   Historical Production Patterns

| | Production | | Stage of development of country-group |
	Material goods	Services	
Pre-industrial society	Half formal Half informal	Informal	LDC NIC
Industrial society			
Initial stage	Quasi-formal	Half formal Half informal	NIC
Present stage	Formal	Quasi-formal	AIC
Future stage (transition)	: Do-it-yourself industry : Diversified combination of hardware/ software : Transformation of public sector : Flexible working time (day, week, season, year) : Dual labor market		
Post-industrial society	Half formal Half informal		

ture at the end-state or the organization of future formal and informal sectors. Institutions will emerge and formalize rather spontaneously according to the evolution of social values and people's attitudes as well as social structure. They will not be designed and constructed on the basis of specific knowledge and values established in the preceding period.[9]

Hypothesis (4): It is improbable that all NICs and LDCs will follow the same path of development as the AICs. Not only have they their own values and attitudes determining their course of development, but also the values and attitudes of AICs will change so that the international environment may not be suitable for the widespread reproduction of the industrialization process followed by today's AICs. What is more fundamental is that the latecomer countries do not have to follow the same paths as their predecessors, especially when it involves a large loss of human and natural resources which could better be utilized for improving the well-being of their people.

Hypothesis (5): The above means that post-industrial society will

[9] Consider the difficulty of designing the institutions of feudal society in the period of ancient empire, or those of industrial society during the feudal period.

not necessarily be composed of today's AICs. Some AICs may remain in their present stage or in a transition stage; and some NICs or even LDCs may have arrived at post-industrial status by skipping some part of the process of formalization of production and employment. Furthermore, it is possible that today's nation-state-oriented country classification will no longer hold.

Boundary Conditions for Initial AIC Trends—Internal and International Environment

Starting from the supposition that the end-state of industrial society has been set (by an invisible hand) as mentioned above, it is unlikely that many AICs would immediately begin to evolve in that direction since it has not yet been perceived by the general public or their leaders. On the contrary, movement toward such a goal would probably be a cumulative process of trial-and-error, and therefore the initial movements of AICs could deviate very much from the shortest path to the end-state.

Given the nature of recent political thinking, it is probable that such initial trends will be affected substantially by realistic considerations of the internal and international environment rather than by transcendental beliefs about the aims of AICs. Thus, to be useful the scenarios need explicit and realistic assumptions about such boundary conditions, including how people justify or rationalize their adaptation to their new environment.

If the boundary conditions for the initial trends of the AICs follow from their past development, including their impact on NICs and LDCs, the following assumptions could be derived from the historical process of development of the formal sector in industrial society.

Internal Environment. Most people believe that expansion and sophistication of the activities of the formal sector could and should be the only feasible means for treating the present "structural" problems. This belief determines the basic attitude toward attempts to adapt to the new environment, because in the short run there is no way of organizing the informal sector to cope with such problems.

But further "formalization" of production in the AICs as a means of adaptation could intensify problems such as redundancy of material goods and/or unemployment of human capacity in the formal sector, waste of raw materials and/or environmental disruption, shortage of human capacity in the informal sector, and cost-push inflation. The validity of this inference depends on the earlier conjecture about the long-term development mechanism of industrial society, according to which many of today's structural problems have their roots in the over-formalization of production activities.

International Environment (a). The NICs have almost finished the formalization of material goods production, and are likely to accelerate the expansion of formal sector activities. This conjecture is based on the experiences of AICs concerning the advantages of the formal—especially market—sector in the production of goods and services, and assumes that there are considerable reserves of human capacity in the informal sectors of NICs and LDCs. Moreover, the forecast increase of capital and technology transfer from AICs is likely to favor the expansion of the formal sectors of Third World countries, and especially those of NICs.

Thus the NICs and some LDCs could amplify the contradictions of the AICs by, for example, making competition more severe in the market sector which is engaged in traditional production. They could also be the source of increasing demand for the products of the formal sector of AICs, since the expansion of the formal sector needs various instrumental goods and services which are difficult to produce domestically and hence often have to be imported.

International Environment (b). Other LDCs may find it difficult to formalize the production of material goods, for two reasons. First, the production of goods in the formal sector—whether market-based or centrally planned—does not function well. This may be due to mismatches in the capacity or supply of workers, managers, engineers, or physical capital, or mismatches between assumed demands—mostly based on life in Western societies—and actual demands based on traditional life-styles. Consequently, the informal sector tends to function better, or more efficiently. Second, the formal sector may be oriented to the international market, to serve the demands of industrialized countries rather than indigenous demand. This would cause a lack of dynamism in the formal sector, since it would fail to utilize the demand and supply factors which are potentially available from the informal sector.

Some people in AICs may consider this phenomenon to be favorable in that a large part of the non-AIC world could absorb the surplus capacity of the material goods-producing market sector of AICs. But it is doubtful whether AICs will have the vitality to respond to the demand, especially if the competition from the material goods-producing sector of NICs is to be taken into account. Moreover, difficulties in the LDCs could increase protests that the AICs are making insufficient contributions to the development of the LDCs, which would inevitably exacerbate the international environment.

Alternative Mid-term Trends

Alternative Basic Attitudes to Adaptation

The above described internal and international environment would narrow the options of the AICs, insofar as most of their strategies depend on the expansion and sophistication of their formal sector. This would be difficult without rather immediate feedback internally on their informal sector and/or internationally on the economies of NICs and LDCs.

Such factors can be considered in the development of scenarios to explore the possible adaptation of the AICs to their new environment. These scenarios do not aim at linking past development with the end-state of industrial society nor at proposing feasible paths and relevant policies during the transition period in long-term evolution. The aim is to clarify various gaps between the real world and its perception in some current theories; an exposition of these gaps should provoke fundamental but realistic arguments about what could and should be important in future society.

When the purpose of scenarios is of this form, less importance is attached to the probability of actual occurrences and more importance to the consistency between the basic attitudes of the people and the consequent evolution brought forth by them.

Moreover, such scenarios become more realistic if they are based on the assumption that the people of the AICs—not only the decentralist minority but also most of those with "common" sense—are already conscious of the discrepancies between the myths of the market/ Welfare State and the reality. ("Myths" often include considerable truth as well, of course, since they are confronted every day with the real world.)

Thus, two contrasting attitudes of the people of AICs toward the immediate future of the goods-producing sector, i.e., "activeness" and "passiveness," can be identified. This should be distinguished from the high growth/low growth controversy. In contrast to the concept of economic growth—i.e., increase of GDP at constant market prices—it is assumed here that there are dynamic interactions between the national economy—or goods and services produced and distributed through the medium of market and state—and the human activities carried out domestically but outside the framework of the former.

More precisely, the concerns of the "optimist" or the "pessimist" about economic growth are mostly related to the future trends of "exogenous variables" or "structural parameters" which are not immediately affected by the evolution of incomes and prices (of goods, capital, labor, etc.).[10] These variables and parameters, in the activist/passivist dichotomy discussed here, are to be determined "endogenously" within the longer-term and wider framework of techno-economic and socio-political development.

Consequently the criteria for distinguishing the activist from the passivist may arise from the difference between activeness and passiveness at a rather normative level of thinking about the necessity and inevitability[11] of expansion and sophistication of the material goods-producing market sector of AICs in the near future. Furthermore, such a comparison may be insufficient to distinguish between the alternative policy attitudes corresponding to the goals of activists and passivists. Therefore activist and passivist scenarios need to be divided into sub-scenarios, according to the identifiable policy attitudes, compatible with their aims and with the logic of dynamism assumed here.

Contrasting Activist and Passivist Scenarios

Group I: Activist Scenarios. Activists include those people who believe in the necessity and inevitability of continuing a high growth of production in the material goods sector.

They consider that the "limits" to growth, such as supply of energy and minerals, accumulation of pollutants, etc., will not cause serious problems in the longer run. Technological progress can take care of those of a technical nature as in the long history of the AICs. They foresee that the demand for participation in formal production will continue to increase (among females particularly) or to persist (among old males particularly), explicitly or implicitly, and that such a demand could be met by jobs offered by the service-producing market sector and the Welfare State.

At the same time, they infer that only the growth of the material goods sector could create sufficient jobs for professional, technical, and clerical work either directly or secondarily in the formal services sector. They also rationalize that the growth of the service-producing market sector and the Welfare State, without the growth in material goods production, would only make ordinary people suffer from inflation and/ or heavy taxes, since the production of services has to consume material goods directly or indirectly.

---

[10] Examples may be demographic trends of working age population, speed of technological progress, natural resource endowments, level of education, people's attitude to work, and saving.

[11] In the case of normative thinking, "should be" and "is" are often mixed up and perceived as a voice from Heaven.

The major weakness of this argument is that there may be insufficient effective demand in the AICs for a major expansion of the material goods sector. This is because the production of material goods is completely carried out in the formal sector in which the producer and the user are not usually the same person. Moreover they belong to different social groups, and hence the more the producer tries to satisfy the demands of the user, the more he produces extras which often miss full and/or proper utilization.

The fact that the "central planning" system in socialist countries has been unable to completely replace the "wild" adjustment mechanism of the market is not surprising, since the above dualism is common in any industrial society. Empirically speaking, the judgment of the market seems to have usually been "healthy"—at least compared with that of technocrats sitting in planning agencies—with respect to the production and distribution of material goods. The major exception is the difficulty of treating the mismatches arising from the intrinsic nature of the system, i.e., the separation between producers and final users. Thus the available technical and/or economic measures for treating excess supply—which must emerge under the conditions favorable for activist scenarios—are subject to severe constraints. Moreover these exert secondary but amplified negative effects on the intermediate demand for instrumental goods, e.g. productive equipment, semi-finished goods such as primary metals, textiles, chemicals, etc., which are needed by the intermediate users of material goods.

Of course the people who can utilize the material goods produced by the market sector of the AICs are not limited to their circle. There must be a large number of potential users of such products, especially among those who have not had access to them.

A similar idea emerged in the earlier period of industrial society when it was suffering from over-production of supply-oriented goods and unemployment of blue-collar workers. It yielded the classical concept of international division of labor. This concept was simplistic and static insofar as it divided the production of material goods into primary goods and secondary goods, and assigned the production and export of the former to non-industrial countries and the latter to industrial countries.

Such a dualism did not endorse the expansion of the formal sector of non-industrial countries since it was to correspond to the dichotomy of developed country/undeveloped country, ignoring the fact that there could and should be internal dynamics within non-industrial countries. Furthermore, under such an international division of labor, there could be little dynamic interaction between the exports of industrial countries and those of non-industrial countries since both of them were subject to the convenience of the material goods-producing sector of industrial countries; that is, the main role of AIC export was the disposal of its surplus production, whereas the role of LDC exports was to supply raw materials.

Consequently, the "activist" of today admits that the dynamism of the material goods-producing sector of AICs would not recover through the classical international division of labor in which the formalization of production activities of non-industrial countries is partial and static, or that, in other words, it isolates and then integrates a part of their society into the marginal part of the formal sector of industrial countries. Thus the idea of making the growth of material goods production the driving force of the internal development of AICs would naturally be linked with active attitudes towards the integration of the informal sector of non-industrial countries into the formal sector of AICs.

We may then discriminate between two policy attitudes for stimulating the activities of the material goods-producing market sector of AICs. The first may be called the "direct" integration of the people of NICs and LDCs into the formal sector of AICs through immigration. The second may be called "indirect" integration through the expansion of material goods exports which are to be the instruments for the growth of the formal sectors of NICs and some LCDs.

Group II: Passivist Scenarios. The purpose of proposing the "passivist" scenarios is to define the inverse of the "activist" group above, and to highlight the possible variants in basic attitudes toward the goods-producing market sector. Therefore, there should be no difference between the two in the way of perceiving the ultimate reality, for such a difference would in general result in sterile disputes between different dimensions. The difference is concerned with the way of selecting and assessing the facts widely observed in the present world.

The people who favor the passivist scenarios hold more or less the same views as those who favor the activist scenarios. For example, they hold similar views on the technological solutions to limits to growth, people's demands for participation in formal production, and the absorptive capacity of the market sector and the Welfare State for such demands. They are skeptical, however, about the necessity and inevitability of maintaining high growth in the material goods-producing market sector in order to satisfy people's demands and about the realization of individual potentialities. That is, their perception is different from that of activists concerning the benefits (e.g. satisfaction of biological and/or psychological demands) and costs (e.g. sacrifice of biological and/or psychological demands) of the growth of production of material goods. They infer that the opportunities for those who want to realize their capacity would become increasingly distant from the production of material goods and related services.

According to this perception, the satisfaction of people's demands does not necessarily require the increase of material goods production. In other words, production and employment in the service-producing market sector and the Welfare State are supposed to grow, with a substantially slower growth of the material goods sector, in contrast with the basic assumption of the activist scenarios.

In the passivist scenarios, the problem of outlets for the surplus production of material goods—which is the central concern of the activist scenarios—is not of great importance since the growth of production is substantially slower than in the activist scenarios. But the passivist does not ignore the dualistic nature of the system of industrial society which cannot treat the mismatches between the goods supplied and those demanded. This means that if the total production were not so large as to yield excesses, there would remain substantial demands which are not satisfied because of the inappropriate "quality" of the goods supplied.

Then the passivist scenarios would suggest the following. If the people are to continue to look for the goods which directly or indirectly satisfy their demands among the products of the formal sector instead of producing the goods themselves, this could easily stimulate wage-price inflation. In this sense, the passivist shares the activist's fear of inflation and/or heavy taxes with low growth of material production, both of which injure the economically or politically weak. Moreover, with a decline of surplus material production, exports would tend to decrease and imports to increase, resulting in increased balance-of-payments deficits.

Thus, there could be a shortage of foreign currency to import essential instrumental goods and services. Moreover, a substantial number of jobs could be lost because of the unexpected reduction of production, thereby obstructing the people's demand for participation in the activities of the formal sector. This difficulty would be particularly severe if other AICs pursued activist scenarios and many NICs successfully expanded their formal sectors.

As the passivists are aware of this danger, they would not like to have zero growth in the material goods-producing market sector. In fact, zero growth would be very difficult to maintain, particularly intentionally. Furthermore, the scenarists in this group are not so optimistic as to assume that internal as well as international equilibrium can be brought forth spontaneously by the market mechanism under conditions of feeble growth of material production.

We may then discriminate between two policy attitudes towards intervening in the distribution mechanism of production factors and material goods. The first is a positive attitude towards the intervention of the power of the state in internal and international markets; the second is a negative one which prefers to modify policies suspected of generating shortages of material production.

Sub-scenarios and Corresponding Policy Attitudes

The purpose of the following sub-scenarios is to illustrate the differences between several alternative policy attitudes; the probability of their actual occurrence is not important.

Case I — 1: Stimulation of Immigration from Developing Countries. This scenario is only conceivable if the difficulties of the AICs are perceived to have arisen from declining internal demand for material goods and from the exhaustion of the human capacities formerly abundant in the informal sector. Immigration from less industrialized societies could mitigate both conditions. In fact, this type of international migration never took place in the earlier period of industrialization. Migration was limited to that from densely populated areas to "unexploited" or "undeveloped" areas.

Although many NICs and LDCs would favor the adoption of this scenario by AICs, it is unlikely. Immigration from developing countries has generally been regarded as a "necessary evil" which is only acceptable when there are labor shortages in the formal service sector. The favorable aspect of increased effective demand for the excess products of the material goods sector is generally ignored. Unless there is a change in the general public's perception of the nature of the difficulties of AICs, the merits of this scenario could not outweigh its political and cultural cost; political and/or cultural barriers are usually far more difficult to surmount than technological and/or economic ones. Worker immigration could result in the formation of new minorities or inequalities and hence cause additional strains within AICs. Moreover, a considerable level of immigration would be needed to revive the vitality of the material goods market sector in order to dissolve the core of structural unemployment. If the scale of operation were too restricted, unemployment could increase rather than decrease, and the immigrants might be blamed for it.

The important factor may be a country's geographical and economic ability to accept a substantial number of immigrants within a rather short period. This immigration would not be accompanied by a rapid increase of exports, since that mainly depends on internal demand and supply factors. Considering that high growth in material goods production would usually cause a rapid increase in consumption of raw materials, a rapid increase in domestic production of primary goods would be required to avoid balance-of-payments difficulties.

Such considerations suggest that the only possible candidates for this increased-immigration scenario are North America and Australia-New Zealand, and political obstacles make it unlikely even for these countries.

Case I — 2: Stimulation of Exports to Developing Countries. In this scenario, AIC exports of capital goods, e.g. productive equipment and intermediate goods, increase rapidly to support the expansion of production and employment in the formal sector of NICs and some LDCs. For many years the growth of intra-AIC material goods exports has been a source of dynamism for the formal sector of AICs as a whole. However, its effect is of the same nature as the increase of internal demand for formal production, and it is destined to level off when the formalization of productive activities arrives at a certain point of saturation.

A dynamic interaction between the AIC exports of manufactured goods to weakly industrialized LDCs and these LDCs' exports of primary goods may not emerge. In order to secure basic material goods, it could be essential for these LDCs to import more than their capacity to export, because of their rapid population growth and scarce capacity for formal production. Of course it would not be so difficult for AICs to provide such basic material goods in spite of LDC balance-of-payments deficits. But the continuation of this kind of aid would not directly lead to the dynamism of the world economy.

Dynamism in the international economy would emerge only when AICs played the role of supplier of capital goods for the expansion of the formal sector of NICs and their candidates. With regard to the other LDCs, the import of such capital goods would often result in a simple accumulation of their borrowing from AICs, since they would not lead to import substitution or to increases in exports, because of lack of internal dynamism in the formal sector of these LDCs.

Superficially this scenario seems to be universally feasible, but actually its feasibility would be limited to a very small number of economically "competitive" AICs.

If there are only a small number of NICs dynamic enough to absorb the AICs' export capacity of capital goods, the export competition among AICs could be so severe that only a limited number of producers could survive. Should the number of such NICs be large, the competition between AICs and NICs could quickly accelerate in both domestic and international markets, at first for finished goods and later for capital goods. It is technically possible and economically desirable for NICs to do this in order to increase the inflow and/or decrease the outflow of foreign currency to finance the growth of capital goods imports and raw materials for the growth of their formal sectors.

Germany, Japan, and the United States, with their particular advantages, may be the candidates for such international competition. This scenario—which may appeal to the neo-classical liberalist—would raise questions about the meaning of such competition, particularly if we were to abandon the view that only severe competition among producers in the formal sector can lead to optimal economic development of all countries. And provided that this scenario were successful, there would be no guarantee that the contradictions of the AICs would not diffuse all over the world, with more radical disruption of the physical environment, waste of human and natural resources, inflation, unemployment, etc.

Case II — 1: Intervention in Wage-price Formation and International Trade. This is the case where the state intervenes in the formation of wages and prices in the internal market and in the trade of goods and services in the international market. The intervention is to avoid or contain the detrimental effects of the growth of the service-producing market sector and the Welfare State, which tend to cause domestic inflation, balance-of-payments deficits, and unemployment given feeble growth of material production.

Whether or not dirigist protectionist policies would be unfavorable for the growth of the formal production of AICs—which is the concern of economists—is not a relevant problem here since the latent view behind this scenario does not consider such growth the important policy objective. Nor is the scenario concerned with the question of whether or not protectionism would depress industrialization of NICs and some LDCs, since the AICs willing to adopt these measures must have lost confidence in the international competitiveness of their products. In other words, these measures should be of a defensive nature and not aimed at destroying the emerging industries of NICs and some LDCs.

Although this scenario may appeal to the classical dirigist-protectionist, it must be a neo-dirigist-protectionist scenario since the perception of the goal to be pursued should be different from those of the former. That is, the purpose of this scenario is not to limit the function of the market but to improve the well-being of the people of AICs. Thus the merit of this scenario has to be assessed in terms of the suppression and containment of various imbalances such as unemployment, inflation, and balance of payments deficits, without seriously injuring other welfare components.

In this connection, there are several worries about the achievements of this scenario. Apart from the possible inefficiency of dirigist policy measures, they could have detrimental effects on the welfare components which they are supposed, implicitly or explicitly, to serve. For example, new inequalities could appear and grow up between those who are near the power of state and those who are not; institutions for controlling wages could be incompatible with increases in flexibility for the allocation of time to work and leisure; change of content of national products to a more demand-oriented one could be obstructed by lack of enforcement by the market mechanism.

As the openness of the economy—and hence friendly relations with other countries—has to be sacrificed to some extent, the feasibility of this scenario could be limited to these AICs which either have ample natural resources or can exert special cultural and political influence on resource-rich countries.

Considering the above—and the recent tendency toward price stability and balance-of-payments surplus—Germany, Japan, and several small countries in Europe would have to be excluded as candidates for this scenario. It would be difficult to implement this scenario for other AICs without allied countries having common interests and values as well as mutually complementary resources.

Case II — 2: Removal of the Excesses of Welfare Policies. The people who like Case II — 1, except for the classical dirigist-protectionists, may take it for granted that the service-producing market sector and the Welfare State will continue to grow at high speed, in spite of a slowdown in the growth of material production, in order to maintain full employment and improve the "quality of life." Thus they might resemble the people who advocate a change in the content or the quality of GDP; meanwhile, the people who like Case I — 2 might be expected to stick to the continuation of the high growth of GDP with traditional content. But, in fact, the distinction between I — 2 and II — 1 is irrelevant in terms of the dichotomies of quantity/quality, traditional/new, private/public, export oriented/welfare oriented, etc.; it is composed of two different kinds of attitude.

The first is the attitude toward the method of forecasting the growth of material production, which has led to the distinction between Group I and Group II. The second is the attitude toward the way of forecasting the weight to be attached to the freedom of production activities against the power of the State, which is larger in $I - 1$ and $I - 2$ then in $II - 1$. The reason why Group I does not have a sub-scenario assuming a smaller weight of freedom than in others is that such a policy attitude toward stimulating the growth of material production is not conceivable in the AICS, although it might have been feasible in the past—in wartime or during the emergence of industrial Japan—or could be in some NICs and LDCs.

We may then have a sub-scenario attaching less importance to material production than in Group I and more importance to freedom of production than in Case $II - 1$, obtaining Case $II - 2$:

	Less freedom	More freedom
More goods		$I - 1, I - 2$
Fewer goods	$II - 1$	$II - 2$

This passivist scenario shares the view of the activist about the danger involved in the unbalanced growth of the service-producing market sector and the Welfare State with a slow growth of material production, namely, the danger of provoking internal and international inequilibrium. Then, should it reject dirigist policy measures for preventing or removing such imbalances, it would inevitably adopt the reverse policy attitude, that is, to suppress the growth of the sector favored in Case $II - 1$ by removing or freezing the policies which are suspected to be stimulating the unbalanced growth of that sector.

Because of its openness to the international market, this scenario does not seem to cause political difficulties—especially concerning natural resources—such as those mentioned with respect to Case $II - 1$, nor would it suffer from the various rigidities which normally accompany dirigist policy measures. Consequently, its feasibility would depend on whether or not it is possible to identify and eliminate the policy measures which are playing only a marginal role in responding to people's demands: for example, to supply jobs which are neither attractive for workers nor appreciated by consumers. If it were possible, a slower growth of the service-producing market sector and the Welfare State than in Case $II - 1$ would be sufficient to realize the same increase in people's well-being with less internal and international friction.

Although this scenario may appeal to the classical liberalist, it must be considered a neo-liberalist scenario since it is based on the new conditions and attitudes prevailing in today's world. Even if the observations and judgments about these conditions were appropriate, it would be impossible to legitimize such a policy attitude without an important change in public opinion about the dynamic interactions between the pursuit of welfare society and the increase of various imbalances, including the skewness caused by government intervention.

In addition to this difficult task of changing people's awareness, there would be a more direct and immediate obstacle to the realization of this scenario: the increase of unemployment which would be more striking, at least in the early period of implementation, than that in Case II–1. This is because most marginal workers depend on the service-producing market sector and the Welfare State, which are to be directly hit by the change in policies. Consequently, unless some kind of shock-absorber was designed and implemented in the initial period, this scenario would practically make no sense.

This scenario seems potentially feasible with respect to all AICs, and particularly attractive for those having scarce natural resources or who prefer reconciliation and stability to competition and powerfulness and attach importance to the freedom of production activities, but so far it seems that there is no candidate among the AICs.

Change in Demands Which May Emerge from Value Changes

The mid-term trend scenarios may be able to distinguish several possible patterns of development of the AICs, on the basis of alternative norms concerning the role of material production in total production and of freedom in production activities; both would have to be taken into account by the people of AICs, in order to improve their adaptation to the new internal and international environment.

But the trend scenarios mentioned above suggest that none of them follows the direct path toward the goal which was first set as the end-state of industrial society. If pursued persistently, supposing that this goal is feasible from the longer-term point of view, they would either fail due to technological and/or economic contradictions or be abandoned because of the great political risk involved.

Such a discontinuity between the development paths and the end-state of industrial society is not an unexpected one. It was predicted or even intended in the construction of the scenarios. Even so, the constructor of such incomplete scenarios might be obliged to guess what could be done to extend the trend scenarios in order to arrive at the end-state. In this sense, attention must be paid to an important factor which is missing in the trend scenarios and could be utilized for completing the whole picture.

This factor is the change in people's demands, which may emerge from changes in deep-seated values and attitudes rather than from superficial changes in income, prices, or technology. The impact of such a change in demands was not considered one of the determinants of mid-term trends in the preceding scenarios. But this does not mean that it was discarded because of its irrelevance to either individual daily life or the macro-economic development of AICs. On the contrary, the more we examine the contradictions of AICs, the stronger becomes the suspicion that they could not be elucidated without admitting the existence of dynamic interactions between the change in demands generated by techno-economic changes and the more deep-seated one related to the cultural change in industrial society.

Thus the significance of the study of New Demands may be found in preparing a hypothetical framework for analyzing the interplay betwen techno-economic demand changes and socio-cultural demand changes, by employing dualistic terms such as change of option/change of values, formal production/informal production, goods-producing sector/service-producing sector, etc.

But at the same time, this study has highlighted the importance of discriminating between the change in demands and that in values, since discussion of new demands without this consciousness becomes easily confused. If deterministic hypotheses about the relationship between such change and techno-economic development were adopted in the construction of trend scenarios, it could be very misleading for all scenarios.

If such a change in demands were introduced in the classification of sub-scenarios, it would add another dimension to the two, i.e., weight of material production and that of freedom, mentioned before. But our conclusions are that it is impossible to identify the interactions between such a change and the evolution of production and distribution of goods and services; nor is it certain that there would or could be fixed relationships between them.

Differences in attitudes about more or fewer goods concern the problem of efficiency for a better life; differences in attitudes about more or less freedom concern, on the one hand, the problem of expressive value but, on the other hand, that of the efficiency of dirigist policies intervening in production activities.

Compared to these two dimensions which have been utilized earlier to distinguish four sub-scenarios, differences in attitude about more or less equality concern the problem of expressive value which is neutral with respect to the efficiency of policies or institutions aiming at, e.g. growth, price stability, or balance-of-payments equilibrium. Different attitudes regarding more or less leisure would also concern the problem of expressive value, if its direct relation with GDP—i.e., more (less) leisure means less (more) GDP—were omitted in order to avoid redundant thinking.

Most of the arguments about new demands in AICs stress that (a) people would increasingly prefer a more equal distribution of GDP to its increase, and (b) they would increasingly prefer more leisure than work. The first inference seems to be derived from two completely different speculations about the evolution of facts and that of values. That is, economic growth increases inequality of distribution of GDP and, hence, egalitarian values *should* become prevalent if the implications of such a trend in the AICs are to be prevented; or, economic growth reduces the number of people suffering from shortage of income, and hence egalitarian values *would* become prevalent inasmuch as the people would lose their passion for expanding their share of the pie.

The second inference is intimately related to the first since less leisure (more work) would *ceteris paribus* result in higher economic growth and vice versa, and, moreover, more equal distribution of GDP would be desirable from the point of view of the norm generally accepted in AICs. In other words, the same conclusion—i.e., (b)—could be drawn from two forecasts which are mutually contradictory. In one, economic growth is undesirable because of the increase of inequality, and hence values against the classical work ethic *should* become prevalent in order to check it; in another, as the number of poor people who have to work hard declines due to economic growth, values conforming to more leisure *would* become prevalent.

The factual—i.e., not normative—basis of these arguments seems to be that there is a fixed relation between the increase of GDP and its distribution. That is, if the society and economy of AICs are managed appropriately, the increase of GDP per capita would make its distribution more unequal but, at the same time, decrease the number of "deprived" people. This may seem a plausible forecast looking from the past experience of AICs, but such an interpretation of their past development must be said to be a tricky combination of intuitive judgment and statistical evidence.

In order to prepare common ground between the "intuitionist" and the "positivist," let us resort to the dualism of formal production/informal production, according to which GDP is the proxy for the products of the formal sector. Then we may obtain the following theses:

(i) The past economic growth of AICs has *not* made the distribution of the products of the formal sector more unequal than before as far as intertemporal and interregional comparisons of available statistical data are concerned.

(ii) It *may* have made the distribution of total welfare as the mixed product of the formal and informal sectors more unequal than before, by rigorously and at random exploiting human time and physical resources which were formerly at the disposal of informal production.

(iii) It *has* almost eliminated the people who are forced to increase formal production in order to subsist.

(iv) It may *not* have decreased the number of people who are suffering from the shortage of welfare, because of a decline of available products of the informal sector.

The earlier interpretation of the consequences of past economic growth of AICs—i.e., the combination of (a) and (b) described on the foregoing pages—may be derived from the combination of (ii) and (iii); a reverse conclusion could then be derived on the basis of a combination of (i) and (iv). That is, (a') people would become less interested in the equalization of income distribution, either because it would be spontaneously realized through economic growth or because they would still be more concerned with the increase of income; and (b') they would be less concerned with increase of leisure time, either because economic growth—i.e., more work—would have desirable effects on income distribution or because the number of people who need more income would increase. In fact, there are several phenomena suggesting the validity of this conclusion; examples are the resistance against further expansion of the Welfare State and the persistent increase of female participation in the work force.

However, a contest between the (a)–(b) combination and the (a')–(b') combination would hardly make sense if the reality were to be perceived more clearly by taking into account all four factors, or by looking from a more comprehensive point of view than usual.

If factors (i) to (iv) were all to be taken into consideration, they would support the judgment about the danger of adopting deterministic hypotheses on the relations between economic development and cultural development before establishing probabilistic theories accompanied by empirical data comparable to modern science—i.e., post-classical physical science.

Consequently, the following measures may help to extend the trend scenarios: (I) to wait until some signs of definite new demands—i.e., not "spurious" new demands—appear, and (II) to collect and analyze information about the present and (if possible) past development of the informal sector of the AICs as well as its relation with the formal sector, in order to improve our understanding of the relationship between cultural change and the direction of changes in demands.

Part II

SUPPORTING AND SUPPLEMENTARY PAPERS

OVERVIEW OF NEW DEMANDS
IN "END-OF-CENTURY" FRANCE

BERNARD CAZES

We shall begin by postulating that in addition to "hard" data such as the number of inhabitants, the rate and direction of technological progress, the development of international trade, and so on, the "soft" data constituted by a country's social and cultural characteristics also form an essential component of any future-oriented scenario, inasmuch as they generate constraints and opportunities that are bound to affect the capacity of governments to act.

As a related assumption, we shall say that in any pluralist society there is a dominant culture[1] co-existing with "secondary" cultures of varying vitality which may perhaps include tomorrow's "dominant" culture. To say that there is a crisis of civilization would therefore mean that a time has been reached when the foremost cultural model has lost its credibility without an alternative model having as yet supplanted it.

By the same token, it becomes feasible to study the new demands that everybody is busy identifying in the advanced industrial societies, taking care not to consider them in a Manichean and unilinear manner. The term "Manichean" is used here to mean the process of arbitrarily defining the structure of these demands by attributing to the group supposedly in the mainstream of history all the values considered positive by the observer and by attributing to the group which is losing momentum all the values considered to be on the decline and retrograde. (Table 1 gives an outline of the type of facile dichotomy found in a great deal of writing on the future.) There are, however, reasons for thinking that cultural changes do not occur in such a clear-cut way and, in particular, that the culture which could be predominant in France

---

[1] Defined as "the model accorded most value by the prevailing culture, transmitted and taught most energetically by the mass media, advertising, schools and political discourse, and perceived as desirable by the majority of the population" (Cathelat, 1977, p. 237).

towards the end of the century will be somewhat less "modern" than might have been hoped (or feared). Likewise, if it is accepted that, while it has lost some of its hold, the dominant cultural model is far from moribund (in short, that it is probably not in the position of paganism relative to Christianity after the death of Julian the Apostate), it will be concluded that the content of the new demands of the "end-of-century" French will not inevitably emerge in a unilinear movement; at the very least, two future trends can be envisaged—one where the culture which still has supremacy finds renewed vigor, the other where its rival succeeds in gaining the upper hand for good (or rather for a few decades).

Table 1. Changing Values in France

Rising values	Declining values
Permissiveness	Authoritarianism
Egalitarianism	Elitism
Frugality	Wastefulness
Solidarity	Egoism
Ecological awareness	Exploitation of nature
Fulfilling work	Instrumental work
Active leisure	Passive leisure
Transparent relationships	Exaggerated attachment to material possessions

Two (or Three) Cultural Models in France

Compared with economic or sociological studies, analyses of socio-cultural change suffer from a major handicap in that the statistical material available for the purpose is extremely limited.

Admittedly the psycho-sociological surveys which enable changes in values and attitudes to be detected are relatively numerous, but they are carried out by many different institutions working separately. The questions asked are rarely repeated from one year to the next, so that the information collected is not cumulative, and when it is it emanates from profit-making bodies which give their subscribers first access to their longitudinal analyses.

Luckily, however, there is a recent overall study for France which focuses more on the results than on the methodology used (Cathelat, 1977). This, therefore, is what we shall be drawing on, while at the same time remembering that the data base used is obviously very narrow in relation to the ambitiousness of the subject.

On the basis of a typological analysis of the replies to a series of surveys carried out since 1970, Cathelat has established the coexistence of three socio-cultural profiles which he calls "Utilitarian" France, "Adventurous" France, and "Centripetal" France.[2]

"Utilitarian" France: The Legacy of a Pre-industrial Past

It will be recalled first of all that France's psycho-sociological geography as revealed by the survey data is defined here by means of two axes which connect and oppose four poles: horizontally, the values of Order and Movement, and vertically, the values of Positivism and Sensualism (see Appendix I).

In relation to these axes, so-called "Utilitarian" France is located in the South-East quadrant very near the values of Order and Positivism. The ten million French involved are characterized by their support for a set of *nine values*:

—Monolithism ($\neq$ Mosaic): uniformity and sacro-sanctity of the social rules of conduct and of legal norms.

—Individualism ($\neq$ Integration): desire to be entirely self-dependent and to prevent any encroachment from outside (whether by neighbors or by the state).

—Permanence ($\neq$ Metamorphosis): attachment to traditions and precedents, distrust of change as a matter of principle.

—Functionalism ($\neq$ Hedonism): pre-eminence accorded to the practical value of objects.

—Otherworldliness ($\neq$ Mundaneness): conviction that lofty principles exist which are of lasting value and which justify sacrifices.

—Discipline ($\neq$ Permissiveness): control over individual passions and appetites, rejection of out-of-norm behavior.

—Passiveness ($\neq$ Achievement): belief in knowing how to keep one's place and not seeking to rise above it.

—Hierarchy ($\neq$ Co-operation): acceptance of the pyramidal organization of levels of command without argument.

—Materialism ($\neq$ Being oneself): seeking personal identity in material possessions.

This "basic personality," which is in some respects reminiscent of the bureaucratic society model brilliantly analyzed by Michel Crozier (1963), is a declining phenomenon among individuals since it is

[2] It should be said right away that this book, like all books on psycho-sociological topics, employs a *sui generis* terminology which does not facilitate discussion. In particular, the word "Utilitarian" is obviously not to be taken in the Benthamite sense.

characteristic of populations of a low economic and cultural level. On the other hand, it is still of considerable sociological importance in that it continues to influence the functioning of institutions, and particularly government.

"Adventurous" France: The Alliance between Innovators and Pleasure-seekers

The "adventurous" state is now "the dominant attitudinal and behavioral model in which 38 per cent of Frenchmen recognize themselves today (as against 42 percent in 1974)," according to Cathelat.[3]

The defeat of 1940 played a decisive role in that connection inasmuch as it thoroughly loosened the hold of the "Utilitarian" model and enabled alternative values, largely brought in from outside, to take over. Another crucial factor may have been the active presence of General de Gaulle, who carried on and expanded the work of Jean Monnet by "gallicising"[4] a certain number of North American values, thereby encouraging them to take root in the French cultural seedbed that had long been hostile to them (cf. G. Duhamel).

It may be noted in passing that the current of so-called optimistic progress, which brings together the typical values of the Adventurous mentality, has the peculiarity of extending over the North-West and South-West quadrants (Appendix 1); in other words it comprises fairly heterogeneous components in that "the progressives dominate the traditionalists and conservatives," while at the same time the "pleasure-seekers" outnumber the "hard workers."

This duality is unfortunately not perceptible in the list of some twelve values specific to the Adventurous mentality, and we have tried, at our own risk, to reflect it by distinguishing more or less arbitrarily between the values of Rationality and the values of Self-Fulfilment.[5]

(a) Values of Rationality

—Integration ($\neq$ Individualism): the individual must disregard his own particular tendencies in order to enjoy the advantages of mass production.

—Mundaneness ($\neq$ Otherworldliness): emptiness of lofty principles compared with problems described as concrete.

---

[3] In what follows, otherwise unidentified quoted passages are from Cathelat (1977).

[4] In the same way that he gallicised the supersonic aircraft, nuclear weaponry, and the presidential regime.

[5] In a more detailed analysis, one would have to ask whether this distinction is not fairly closely linked with what Daniel Bell (1976) calls the disjunction between the social structure and the cultural sphere.

—Achievement ($\neq$ Passiveness): desire for self-assertion through success in strenuous competition (cf. D. McClelland's (1961) "need for achievement").

—Outward-reaching attitude ($\neq$ Centripetal attitude): there are constantly new challenges to be taken up and new demands to be satisfied.

—Technology ($\neq$ Nature): confidence in the ability of scientific knowledge and its technological applications to solve the problems of society as they arise.

—Realism ($\neq$ Symbolism): pre-eminence accorded to the intellect, to rational knowledge, and to objectively measureable reality.

(b) Values of Self-fulfilment

—Mosaic ($\neq$ Monolithism): individual demand for an independent and non-stereotypical identity, and desire to adopt a variety of social roles.

—Metamorphosis ($\neq$ Permanence): value attached to change and the ephemeral.

—Hedonism ($\neq$ Functionalism): quest for immediate pleasure and desire to enjoy life.

—Permissiveness ($\neq$ Discipline): laxity with regard to social norms.

—Being oneself ($\neq$ Materialism): people are defined not so much by their personal possessions as by their intrinsic characteristics.

While 38 percent of the French population recognizes itself in this dominant model, this mental structure is more common among professional persons, employers, and managers than among manual workers, clerical staff, and farmers. Similarly, those in the 16–35 age bracket incline to it more than do older people.

"Centripetal" France: The Alliance between "Petits Bourgeois" and the Defectors from "Adventure"

The "centripetal" model is a full-fledged socio-cultural model in its own right, whose historical origins antedate the appearance of the "Adventure" mentality since they correspond to the establishment in France of a middle class composed of well-to-do small property owners whose outlook was "ostentatious but conformist, reforming but prudent, pleasure-seeking but thrifty, comfort-loving but puritan, outgoing but egocentric."

This current has however been enriched by "modern" values thanks to inputs from wealthier and better-educated social classes, whose members are disappointed by the currently dominant model, so that it constitutes in the author's view a credible alternative to "Adventurous" France.

It can be seen that this outline contains two values—Materialism and Passiveness—taken from "Utilitarian" France and also four specific values, the first three of which are in contradiction with the "Adventure" mentality, while the fourth—the value of Cooperation—runs counter to the "Utilitarian" mentality.

—Nature ($\neq$ Technology): distrust of science and technology, respect for the ecological environment, and a liking for what is "natural."

—Centripetal attitude ($\neq$ Outward-reaching attitude): "anything for a quiet life."

—Symbolism ($\neq$ Realism): demand for the right to be subjective, intuitive, and irrational.

—Cooperation ($\neq$ Hierarchy): attachment to human-sized communities where relations are personalized and participatory.

This lifestyle is the one least strongly correlated with a social category, an age bracket, or a particular region. It encompasses 42 percent of the French population, but its sociological influence is less in that the major institutions continue to favor the other two rival cultural models.

Alternative Possible Courses

The "Explosive" France Scenario

The number of alternative courses which together form the full range of those possible obviously depends on the number of cultural models to choose from and their respective dynamism. In the case of France, the data drawn upon show clearly that the "Utilitarian" lifestyle is continuing to lose its hold and cannot therefore be a serious contender for cultural hegemony in France between now and the end of the century. The choice therefore lies between the other two cultural models whose degree of ascendancy is more or less the same at present, "Adventurous" France and "Centripetal" France; this means that two socio-cultural development scenarios can be identified up to 1990 with one or the other of the two models asserting its domination. The first scenario would represent a complete reversal of the decline of the "Adventure" mentality, which would become rejuvenated (the "Explosive" France scenario), while the second would reflect the continued growing ascendancy of the "Centripetal" mentality since the end of the 1960s ("Implosive" France scenario).

The two divergent courses open to the French resemble fairly closely the two versions of post-industrial society recently expounded by Michael Marien (1977), in which he sees "the pole of the dominant ideological debate in forthcoming decades," namely, on the one hand a technological, affluent, service society, and on the other "a decentralized agrarian economy following in the wake of a failed industrialism." There is, however, an important difference in that Daniel Bell (1973; 1976) and Herman Kahn (1976), for example, concentrate mainly on the development of social structures in the *broad sense*, and seek to associate with it a certain cultural dynamic which they consider, moreover, to be in profound contradiction with the logic of the post-industrial society they are analyzing. Cathelat is apparently of the opinion that the social structure has a certain pliancy and will end by adjusting to this dynamic, but that this adaptation is likely to be less traumatic and more lasting in the case of an "Implosion" scenario.

The "Explosive" France scenario with which we shall begin is based on an extrapolation of the cultural trend observed in France since World War II, and it is therefore assumed that the "Adventurous" mentality is still the predominant lifestyle, with its two axiological directions designated earlier by the values of Rationality and Self-fulfilment. Compared with the post-industrial society described by Daniel Bell, the specificity of this model is two-fold. First, it accommodates to some extent the lower or intermediate social categories which are still attached to the "Utilitarian" mentality but want to enjoy comfort, consumption, and pleasure in living in line with the currently dominant "Adventure" model, whereas the American sociologist does not seem to assign much importance to them.[6] Second, the two more or less contradictory tendencies which make up the "Adventurous" mentality are embodied according to Bell in opposing social groups, the scientists and engineers versus the intellectuals of the *adversary culture*, between which the "Polity" have the difficult task of arbitrating. According to Cathelat, these tendencies are to a large degree interiorized by the same individuals, who are simultaneously motivated by competitive efficiency and the narcissistic cult of their Ego. This is no doubt one of the reasons for the explosive quality of this indeed rather unstable compound; the other, probably more fundamental, reason is that this scenario is

---

[6] Unlike the Bergers (1971), whose article "The Blueing of America" can, I think, be interpreted as a scenario of the revitalization of the dominant/declining cultural model through the support of social classes still little affected by the "Centripetal" cultural change.

based expressly on the radicalization of the characteristic values of the "Adventure" mentality, and carries to an extreme the "unconstrained satisfaction of individualities in the anarchy of powers, leaving each person or social group to his own objectives and his own capacities."

The main components of the "Explosion" scenario will be presented under two headings: personal life and working life. We shall then attempt to show what they imply in terms of goods and services and forms of social organization.

The Content of Personal Life.   As the fundamental cell of society, the family is tending to give way to the individual, an elementary social unit which can if necessary adopt a temporarily family way of life. Couples will consist of partners anxious to preserve their mutual independence and inclined, therefore, to replace stable marriage with free temporary unions.

Children,[7] who will be few in number, will escape the influence of the community and their education will be directed towards self-fulfilment rather than centered on a cultural norm. As a result, a "parallel education" will emerge whose object will be to correct official education and help to shape an original and independent personality. So more than ever adolescent marginality will be a fact that has to be lived with.

Relations between individuals will be manifold but not very lasting because of frequent changes in job and place of residence—whence a greater readiness to accept a "transit habitat" in which home life will be of less importance than outside activities, occupational and other, and to put up with dense and anonymous urban surroundings[8] in which the disadvantages will be offset by "the proximity of places of leisure and work, the prestige of the center-city and thriving commerce." The number and superficial nature of these relations will also encourage the use of audiovisual systems for distance communication (video

---

[7] The population problem is only lightly touched on by Cathelat, and the little that is said does not allow any clear distinction to be made between the two scenarios; in "Explosive" France the birthrate "will be low and will in time pose a serious problem with regard to the equilibrium of the age categories," while in "Implosive" France "the birthrate will not increase; a birthrate of two children will be deemed sufficient to maintain the stability of the French population."

[8] This point will be returned to later because it is not obvious that the megalopolis is the only urban form congruous with an "Explosive" lifestyle. It could be argued that having a tertiary job that could be done at home by using a telecomputer would eliminate daily trips to and from work and make it possible to practice a hyper-individualistic lifestyle in what would be urban "surroundings" as opposed to an urban "environment."

telephone and telecopiers), which will remove the need for face-to-face physical contacts.

Nature will be looked upon as a force to be subjugated in order to realize human ends, and will be experienced as "an exotic and rare spectacle for a primarily urban and mechanized society." Journeys will be more frequent and over longer distances. In a hyper-individualistic culture independent transport will be highly valued, to the maximum advantage of small cars, helicopters, and private aircraft, so that towns will become departure areas rather than "havens of retreat."

A feature of consumption will be the frequent changes in centers of interest and the desire not to be encumbered with heavy equipment which might impede the mobility of one's way of life. Renting will become common practice "as the most economical and easiest way always to have the most up-to-date things." From this point of view services, being immaterial, are perhaps better suited than goods to an emotional investment which is at once intense and temporary.[9] There will therefore be an increase in the supply of those services aimed at customers' deep-seated psychological needs.

Working Life. The foregoing suggests that educational establishments will hand over most of their cultural and moral training responsibilities to parents or parallel educational bodies. They will therefore have to concentrate on preparation for working life, taking care to select the most productive elements on the basis of meritocratic criteria. This efficiency-oriented approach will also be a feature of adult retraining because of the intense competition which will characterize working life.

Efficiency will be the overriding concern in working life, the result being very marked labor mobility and a strong link between pay and output. Apart from this, the desire for variety and independence will be met by frequent changes of job, temporary work, or an increase in the number of independent activities of the "quaternary" type. Physical and repetitive tasks will be eliminated by automation so that human work can concentrate on creative activities.[10] Correspondingly, manual work will be much less highly rated.

Lastly, in this socio-cultural model the contrast between work and

---

[9] One should not forget that there is a very clear tendency in advanced industrial societies for services to be replaced by electrical engineering or electronic goods (Gershuny, 1977).

[10] Or on non-occupational activities because of shorter working hours. In this case, we should have the dualistic universe of the *Player Piano* (Vonnegut, 1972), in which a minority composed of highly skilled scientists and technicians operate an efficient productive apparatus whose products are consumed by a majority composed of idlers or disguised unemployed.

leisure will be less marked than in the past, either because mixed activities will be engaged in (training courses, study trips) or because work and leisure will be governed by identical criteria as regards intellectual or sensory stimulation and competition, and will also require sophisticated equipment.

Implications in Terms of Goods and Services and Modes of Social Organization. The only recent long-term projection concerning the French economy covers the period 1970–1990 (CGP, 1975). It comprises a "high" hypothesis where household consumption increases over this period by a factor of 2.5 (annual growth 4.6 percent) and a "moderate" hypothesis where the same aggregate doubles (annual growth 3.4 percent). Unfortunately, the breakdown of the projected trend of households' consumption is by industry so that it cannot be related to the usual breakdown by final use. It is, however, possible to gain a very approximate idea of the structure of consumption in 1990 by extrapolating the trends for the period 1970–1980, as calculated for the purposes of the VIIth Plan, on the assumption that aggregate consumption will continue to grow at the same rate of 4.6 percent per year (INSEE, 1976). As might be expected, the results, shown in Table 2, give a fairly wide range of growth rates by category.

Overall, it would seem that the "high" hypothesis is more consistent with the socio-cultural scenario of an "Explosive" France, and this for two reasons which are moreover very complementary. In the first place, a context of strong growth could be said to provide an "objective"

Table 2. Structure of Consumption in France, 1970 and 1990: High Increase Model

	Relative share (%)	
	1970	1990
Hygiene and health (increase 4.7 times)	12.6	22
Transport and telecommunications (increase 4.7 times)	10	17.5
Culture, leisure activities (increase 3 times) and more especially the sub-categories Radio-TV-record players (7.6), Cameras and cine cameras (3.0), Sports and toys (3.5)	5.7	9.5
Housing (increase 2.7 times)	21	22
Hotels, cafes, restaurants (increase 2.15 times)	0.6	7.5
Food (increase 1.6 times)	28	16
Clothing (increase 1.5 times)	9.8	5.5
Certain sub-categories under Culture and Leisure activities (Entertainment, 1.6; and Books, magazines and newspapers, 1.8)		

justification for the relevance of the "Adventure" model and to positively reinforce (in the Skinnerian sense) the attitudes and behavior consistent with this model. Correspondingly, adherence to the values of rationality and self-fulfilment creates a psycho-sociological environment which fosters economic growth in that the mentalities underlying this axiological orientation are more receptive to innovation and mobility, more open to exchanges with the outside, and more prepared to practice a lifestyle in which market-provided goods and services feature prominently.

We shall therefore assume that the realization of this first socio-cultural scenario would concur with those global Interfutures scenarios which postulate fairly rapid growth based, in particular, on successful industrialization of the dynamic part of the LDCs. In a sense it will be "traditional" growth, if this is taken to mean a style of development involving continuous technological change, the quest for micro-economic efficiency, and the use of willingness-to-pay as a guide to consumer preferences. At the same time, however, it is no less evident that future economic growth, if it is strong enough, will continue to be, as Schumpeter put it, a process of creative destruction. If, for example, one considers the implications of the "Explosive" scenario for the structure of household consumption, one can see that, if that scenario materialized, its influence on consumer choices would pull in two directions. There would be an increase in the growth of certain items of consumption which are already very dynamic, i.e., (private) expenditure on hygiene and health,[11] transport, and equipment for leisure activities. Also, there would be renewed growth of certain items of consumption which are not very dynamic, such as expenditure on entertainment[12] and expenditure under the heading "Hotels, cafes, restaurants."

On the other hand, it does not seem that expenditure on housing would be very much affected, nor, for that matter, purchases of food and clothing.

However, the new demands emanating from French households will not be confined to the nature of the goods and services that they wish to consume. It may therefore be useful to broaden the scope of the above remarks by trying to identify the collective behavior of these households which seems consistent with this first socio-cultural scenario, and which could generate a social demand to which enterprises

[11] For example, services on the borderline between psychotherapy and religious experience, whose rapid growth in California is recounted by the geographer Peter Hall (1977), and which can moreover result in sales of material goods.

[12] In this connection, the same article instances the success of the historical recreations organized by a private association, the Living History Center.

and general government would be forced to provide an answer. These types of behavior will be discussed as they are related to allocation of time, use of space, and people's expectations as regards the market and the non-market sectors.

Allocation of time. The few indications given in Cathelat's book sug- gest that there is no downward trend in working hours inherent in this socio-cultural movement, apart of course from the time devoted recur- rently to occupational retraining. Curiously enough, no mention is made of the ending of working life. The most probable characteristic of leisure time is that it will mainly be spent outside the home, but it does not seem to be particularly highly valued in relation to work.

Use of space is characterized in this model by the contented accep- tance of a "megalopolitan" lifestyle involving frequent changes of residence, rental of accommodation rather than ownership (including, no doubt, secondary residences), and frequent travel to foreign countries for tourism or occupational activities. The scant attention given to nat- ural surroundings and the confidence placed in technology suggest that there would be less hostility towards nuclear energy in the context of an "Adventure" scenario.

Collective attitudes will be favorable towards *the market,* not be- cause of any doctrinal attachment to capitalism, but because the private sector is better able to meet a very varied and constantly changing de- mand. Also, the enterprises which will be called upon in "Explosive" France will extend well beyond the national frontiers.

With this scenario, the Welfare State will not have to intervene so frequently since "the community's responsibility for individuals will be reduced to a minimum." The Welfare State will be expected not to hinder the functioning of the organizations set up alongside the public establishments to serve a clientele seeking less uniform services, and it may even be required to satisfy demands for efficiency in those areas for which it will continue to assume responsibility.

Social organization relates to the direct consequences of Scenario 1 as seen from the point of view of enterprises and general government; we shall attempt to define what the new demands on them might be.

As far as enterprises are concerned, we shall not dwell on the demand aspect proper, which has already been discussed, except to say that the new markets would doubtless be increasingly representative of the non- material requirements of the population, whether these concern uncon- ventional forms of education for young people or the organization of "trips" (in the broad sense) in space or in time.

There are important implications as regards enterprises' production functions.[13] Enterprises will probably be less likely to see their production costs increase because of social insurance charges, protection of the environment, or the necessities of geographic decentralization. On the other hand, they will have to place special emphasis on innovation in order to introduce efficient methods of production in tertiary-type activities (Levitt, 1976), given that those activities are expected to represent an increasing share of GNP. They will also have to be more active than in the past in periodically updating the knowledge and skills of their personnel, and even in organizing training prior to working life.

Government role. Little mention is made of general government in Cathelat's book, but I think it is possible to outline the social demands which it would have to meet for the purpose of Scenario 1, differentiating as before between areas of activity and production functions.

As regards the State's areas of activity, there would be an increase in infrastructure expenditure (road and air transport, urban capital equipment) and a relative decrease in transfers (to enterprises and households)[14] and also in expenditure on education and training, which would be in marked contrast with the trend observed in France since the beginning of the 1960s (OECD, 1977, Table 2). Correspondingly, the respective shares of taxes and social security contributions would change to the detriment of the latter—again in contrast with what has happened over the last 15 years. Overall, it is reasonable to suppose that the percentage of public expenditure in the French GNP (average for 1973–1975: 40 percent) would not be very different.

General government production functions would also inevitably be affected by the socio-cultural trend. Not only would capital expenditure be given priority over operating expenditure, but the administrative staff used would be managed from the standpoint of efficiency rather than that of public service. Efficiency itself would be sought in recourse to *exit* in preference to *voice*, to use the famous distinction made by Hirschman, in the sense that the adjustment between supply and demand would be effected through the stimulus of competition among a great many private and public organizations; the latter being compensated on the basis of the results obtained. Lastly, there is reason to think that this scenario would provide a fairly favorable climate for the introduction of negative income tax and public consumption vouchers.

---

[13] It should be emphasized that the "new demands" do not concern only the composition of national output, but also the way in which it is obtained.

[14] Except for those transfers which result from the acceptance of intense competition.

"Implosive" France Scenario

We saw earlier that there is a third France, the so-called "Centri-petal" France, which has its own constellation of values and is characterized by widely differing social groups, some belonging to the independent middle classes and others coming from the well-off salaried categories who wish to repudiate the old socio-cultural model to which they or their parents used to subscribe. According to Cathelat, this particular France is gaining influence all the time.

The scenario which goes with the progressive strengthening of this hold, and whose main features we shall describe below according to the same arrangement of ideas as before, leaves a curious impression in that some of the attitudes and behavior patterns it incorporates undoubtedly reflect the preferences of the "silent majority," while others belong on the contrary to what Michael Marien (1977) calls a decentralized agrarian post-industrial society. But perhaps this heterogeneity is the price that has to be paid before a constellation of values finally acquires the status of a dominant cultural model.

The Content of Personal Life. The "Implosive" cultural trend is distinguished first of all by the triumphant return of the family as the elementary social cell and basis of individual identity, even though this concept of the family hinges not so much on blood ties as on "affective co-optation" whereby the home proper is enlarged to include "a broader community of friends and relations with many shared activities." Marriage will also be rated higher, but it will imply affective rather than material solidarity between husband and wife.

Children, again few in number, will receive a stricter education with more active parental participation as a reaction against the permissiveness and lack of guidance of the 1960s.

Personal relations will be at once more intense within culturally circumscribed and socially homogeneous communities, and more limited —even to the point of distrust and hostility—vis-à-vis territorially distant groups, especially if they are foreigners.

The mode of housing will be defined negatively by repudiation of the megalopolis and positively by a preference for urban areas of limited size which are symbolically appropriable and encourage human communications. Detached houses will more than ever be the ideal for the vast majority of French people, but they will be looked at as a means of balancing the desire for *privacy* and the desire to take root in a friendly and protective community; this will give rise to such conceptions as "new villages" composed of private houses grouped around communal cultural and sports facilities, accompanied by services used on a shared-time basis (TV, washing machines). At the same time, there will be a strong current of alienation from large towns which could, in extreme cases, take the form of "townspeople's uprisings."

Nature will be a dominant value in the "Implosive" culture both as a vital component of people's surroundings and as a beneficial force expected to provide solutions to the problems of the world; there will be an *a priori* bias against technology. The need to take root will combine with technophobia to make journeys less frequent and shorten the average distances covered, particularly as far as international travel is concerned. The means of transport used will also be affected in the sense that restrictions on the use of private cars in urban areas will find increasing support among the public. However, public transport will have to adjust to the demand of a clientele which, not pleased by the need to travel, will demand a high quality of service and will refuse to be treated as a captive market.

Lastly, consumers will give priority to capital goods and items for the home which increase the quantity of "services" provided by the dwelling, while purchases motivated by fashion, the desire to be different, or whim will tend to decline. At the same time, the durability of equipment will be more appreciated than in the past for complex reasons encompassing the upward trend in the relative prices of manufactured goods, ecological considerations, and a changing psychological relationship with objects. This latter factor will moreover foster "a renewed preference for ownership rather than rental."

Working Life. The school and university system will probably undergo two major changes which would have the effect of integrating it more fully in the local environment and of reducing the gap between educational and socio-economic life. As a reaction against Parisian centralism, schools and universities will be more receptive to social demand formulated at the local level, which will have the effect of diversifying them and bringing them more under "community control" in its various forms. In addition, the priority given by education to the acquisition of knowledge and mastery of the abstract will be replaced by a desire to help young people to gain better control over the superabundant information they receive via the mass media. In addition, emphasis on the narcissistic objective of individual improvement will appear less essential than the training of a human being who is productive and responsible, capable of organizing or executing a task and able to assume responsibility for the consequences of his action (Coleman, 1973).

Work itself will be looked upon less as "an inevitability or an aim in itself," and it will no longer be so systematically equated with the holding of a full-time paid job. Non-occupational activities will also acquire social prestige, although the number of adults in good health who voluntarily withdraw from the labor market will remain very small. The jobs considered satisfactory will be those which simultaneously offer regular pay, proximity to the place of residence, the flexibility that will make it easier to reconcile occupational and private commitments (whence the probable attraction of part-time work), and, lastly, warmth of personal relations (whence the repudiation of large and very hierarchical production units, undifferentiated rules, and routine tasks programmed from on high).

Implications in Terms of Goods and Services and Modes of Social Organization. For the same period, 1970–1990, we shall take a "low" hypothesis whereby consumption increases by 2 percent per year (in francs at constant prices, as in the "high" alternative), which corresponds to an increase by a factor of 1.5. To assess the structure of household consumption in 1990, we shall use the projection drawn up recently by Claude Quin for the period 1975–1985, extrapolating it by five years, which will provide a few approximate orders of magnitude (Quin, 1977).

Compared with the strong growth hypothesis, the changes in the relative shares of the different items of consumption tend in the same direction, but the upward or downward movements are more moderate, as shown in Table 3.

Also, this "low" alternative would appear to correspond fairly closely to the socio-cultural scenario of an "Implosive" France for reasons similar to those given on with reference to the previous scenario. The persistence of a sluggish economic situation would tend to prevent the "Adventure" values from developing and would, on the contrary, tend

Table 3. Structure of Household Consumption in France, 1970 and 1990: Low Increase Model

| | Relative share (%) | |
	1970	1980
Hygiene and health (increase 1.8 times)	14	17
Transport and telecommunications (increase 1.7 times)	11	13
Culture, leisure activities (increase 1.6 times)	9.5	10
Housing (increase 1.6 times)	23.5	25
Clothing (1.3 times)	11	10
Food (1.2 times)	31	25

to validate the rival socio-cultural model. Conversely, this latter model is probably less likely to foster economic dynamism since it favors non-mobility and distrust of technical innovation, strengthens the protective role of the State, and results in lifestyles in which the relationship between paid work, earnings, and consumer purchases will be less predominant.

Our hypothesis is therefore that the realization of the "Implosion" scenario would concur with those global Interfutures scenarios which imply economic growth which is less rapid and differs in content from that in scenarios with traditional growth patterns. In this respect, some items in the household consumption breakdown ought probably to be adjusted to allow for changes in values and attitudes,[15] but it is doubtful that these adjustments would be on a very significant scale compared with the structural distortions that can be attributed to the slowdown in the rate of growth. This means that a large proportion of the consequences of redirected growth could very well go unnoticed if one considered only the household budget.

This is why we shall proceed in the same way as for the previous scenario and consider the collective behavior patterns of households which appear consistent with the "Implosion" scenario, using the same headings: allocation of time; use of space; expectations with regard to the market and the non-market.

Cathelat makes very little reference to the allocation of time. It may be supposed that employment difficulties coupled with slower economic growth will result in an above-trend reduction in working hours, and that this reduction will be favorably received in the new socio-cultural context characterized by considerable emotional investment in the family sphere and the local environment.[16] The same logic suggests that the reduction of time worked will result not so much in longer annual holidays as in a shorter working day or week.

It is moreover perfectly possible—and this is one of the difficulties of socio-cultural futures research—that the same quantitative changes could occur with equal probability in either scenario, but that they would result in practice in very different types of behavior outside working life. It can be argued, for example, that Gösta Rehn's (1977)

---

[15] These changes would tend logically to increase the share of "Housing," reduce that of "Transport and telecommunications," and alter the structure of "Culture and leisure activities."

[16] However, one should be wary of idyllic visions in which the entire French population would eagerly engage in friendly conviviality and disinterested service for the public weal.

suggestions concerning the creation of drawing rights on a "time bank" are compatible with highly contrasted cultural models and that the difference lies in the use made of these rights.

The desire to maintain stable and strong interpersonal relations, to live in pleasant surroundings (contact with nature, intolerance of urban disamenities), and to secure safer conditions for people and possessions should increase the attraction exerted by medium-sized towns, where it would seem possible to obtain a more satisfactory trade-off between the opposing demands of amenity and accessibility (Hall, 1970), and therefore to reduce the cost in journey-time for a given level of services. At the same time there may be a slowdown in the growth of international tourist traffic to the advantage of intranational traffic, which would make it possible to reconcile balance-of-payments difficulties and "Centripetal" values. Also, it was seen earlier that private cars will be used less for town travel—that is, assuming that behavior is consistent with advertised values; after all, Cathelat's book shows clearly that the car has changed as a symbol and that it is now advertised by means of arguments very different from those used in the 1960s, so that it is very easy to imagine the driver of the 1980s using the language of "Implosive" France to defend in all good faith his right to drive in towns. Lastly, ecological considerations and technophobia will no doubt give rise to hostile or, at the very least, reticent attitudes towards nuclear energy.

Market expectations are diametrically opposite to those which are a feature of the previous scenario. This is due not so much to changes in the political sphere (although a prolonged period with the Left in power would naturally contribute to this) as to the actual orientation of the cultural model which would be dominant in this case. In the first place, enterprises will be seen as potential sources of serious disamenities and/or innovations which are non-essential and may even be dangerous to the environment and health. Secondly, the Welfare State will be responsible for the economic (and physical) safety of the population and for ensuring greater equality of access to public services—this equality being assessed more in terms of socio-occupational or socio-demographic groups (women, old people) than by reference to abstract criteria such as the interquintile gap or the Gini coefficient (this point would have to be clarified, moreover, because since we have very few ideas as to what the prevailing concept of social justice is today, it is difficult to anticipate what it may become twenty years hence).

In speaking of modes of social organization, once again, the object is to define the new demands which society might make on enterprises and general government, demands which can affect either the composition of production or the way in which it is created.

1. In the context of the second scenario, enterprises' new markets seem likely to relate in large measure to the housing function and, more especially, to the renovation and maintenance of old dwellings; repairs to household appliances which their owners would like to last longer, both because the notion of durability will be socially more highly esteemed and because the trend of relative prices will make it less attractive to renew appliances at frequent intervals; new non-polluting forms of transport; "reasoned" innovations such as "modular objects" which lend themselves to partial improvements without having to be completely replaced; and energy saving in culinary activities.[17]

Two questions remain unanswered. One concerns opportunities for sales of professional equipment adapted to the requirements of individuals wishing to produce their own goods in the home (making bread, furniture, etc.), along the lines of the "dual society" outlined by J. Gershuny (1977). The other concerns "counter-taylorism technologies" (Dalle and Bounine, 1976), i.e., mini-computers and numerically controlled machine tools which, in the view of some specialists, should facilitate the arrival of more flexible and decentralized forms of organization of the productive system (industrial and tertiary), and would therefore be quite consistent with the socio-cultural climate of the "Implosion" scenario.

This use of new technologies will be coupled with a "return to less cumbersome structures" via the decentralization of large firms and the creation of many small or medium-sized firms, which will permit better adjustment to a more uncertain economic context, shorten decision-making channels, and lessen the weight of hierarchy. The enterprise will no longer be judged solely on the traditional elements of its activity (wages paid, prices, attractiveness of its products), but also on its "ecological awareness," the working conditions enjoyed by its staff, and the degree of consistency between what it claims for its products and how they actually perform.

2. General government will obviously play a more active role than in the previous scenario. Cathelat predicts that "the community will take paternalistic care of an increasingly large number of personal problems," and concludes that "the assisted person mentality" which will develop will lead to an "inflation of public services." More specifically,

---

[17] In France, domestic culinary tasks are estimated to absorb 18 percent of the primary energy consumed by the French agri-food system.

it can be inferred from the preceding observations that the State's activity will tend to move away from prestige investment and concentrate instead on transfers to households[18] and financial assistance designed to promote the growth of medium-sized towns, more extensive use of public transport, pollution control, renovation of old dwellings, and, generally speaking, the quality of urban life. This financial assistance will be accompanied by stringent regulations designed to modify the behavior of enterprises[19] and households in order to save energy and raw materials, preserve the natural environment, protect public health, etc.

But since some of the values underlying the "Implosion" scenario lead logically to a demand for increased participation in collective decisions, particularly when these have a direct impact on day-to-day conditions of living, there could well be, it seems to me, an accentuation of the already perceptible contradiction between the centralizing tendencies inherent in any effort to correct negative externalities and the decentralizing trend towards maximum respect for the freedom of choice of infra-State communities. This contradiction will be joined by another, relating this time to the dynamics of "informal" democracy and characterized by the existence of voluntary organizations (associations of residents, parents, public service users) which assert that they embody the real needs of their members, and thus find themselves in some cases taking a stand against both locally elected representatives of the people and State technocrats.

Lastly, at the international level the trend will probably be towards the creation in France of a "new isolationism," quite indifferent to any grand policy of spreading French culture through the world, and concerned with reducing the permanent source of insecurity represented by interdependence between nations. This "passive nationalism" will tolerate the European Community inasmuch as it can be looked upon as a means of insulating France, like some cocoon, from the areas of turbulence associated with the functioning of the world economy. According to Cathelat, the European idea will only make progress in "Implosive" France if its image accords with the fragmentation into micro-cultures

---

[18] This obviously refers, as in the case of "inflation of public services," to what is implied by the logic of the scenario and not to what the situation of the economy will permit.

[19] Here we have an interesting difference as between this view and that of Daniel Bell (1976). He considers that post-industrial society is characterized culturally by the coexistence of moral permissiveness and economic dirigisme, while according to Cathelat the latter would be accompanied by a return to "stricter and more repressive moral standards" (p. 268).

and the inner-looking stance which are typical of the new dominant cultural model. However, the danger is that this Europe of regions would then witness increased confrontations between economically competing national regions (French vine-growers versus Italian vine-growers) more sensitive to divergence of interests than to the attraction of campaigning together against the central power of their respective nation-states.[20]

Conclusion: From New Demands to New Policies

A whole range of considerations prompt one to regard the "Implosion" scenario as the more probable: the feeling that the old socio-cultural model has had its day, the attraction of some of the values underlying "Centripetal" France, skepticism with regard to any long-term scenario which does no more than postulate a prolonged status quo. At the same time, however, it is clear that the non-socio-cultural factors do not by any means constitute a simple dependent variable which will sooner or later adjust itself—as this paper might suggest—but in fact possess their own dynamism. Moreover, Cathelat reminds us at the end of his book that it would be naive to base a prognosis solely on psycho-sociological data since "economic, scientific and political factors are bound to correct, modify or counteract this trend."

We endeavored to take these interrelations into account, and we considered that the "Explosion" scenario squared better with fairly rapid economic growth, whereas the "Implosion" scenario would go with slower economic growth (see Fig. 1). This is also what is suggested by the global Interfutures scenarios in their present state, and it has to be recognized that the work done by McClelland (1961) tends to corroborate the connection thus established between an achievement-oriented cultural model and good economic performance.

It would seem premature, however, to take for granted the one-to-one correspondence illustrated in Figure 1, and to assimilate socio-cultural change with a lasting slowdown of economic growth as if the two automatically went together. After all, Japan's economic history shows that the relationship between the two is by no means as simple as that, and there is nothing to say that the last two decades of the twentieth century will not call our present ideas into question.

In other words, while in the case of France we are inclined to concentrate our attention on the "Implosion" scenario (i.e., the right-hand

[20] The latter is the scenario favored by Denis de Rougemont in his latest book (Rougemont, 1977).

	"Explosion"	"Implosion"
Rather low	−	+
Rather high	+	−

Figure 1. Socio-cultural evolution.

column), we also believe that it is wise to consider both of the cases covered in the diagram, i.e., congruence (+) and non-congruence (−) between economic and socio-cultural trends. This we shall do by way of conclusion.

1. *The congruence hypothesis* ought itself to break down into two sub-hypotheses in the sense that there can be *universal* compatibility if the whole of the Western world grows slowly, or *limited* compatibility if the slowdown is confined to France. Rightly or wrongly, the first sub-hypothesis seems improbable (moreover, it is not incorporated in the global Interfutures scenarios); besides, if it were to materialize, it would be for reasons which had little to do with the future socio-cultural movement of the OECD countries.

Accepting the second sub-hypothesis would mean that France would form a sort of enclave where "Centripetal" values would be coupled with a persistently depressed economic context. This combination might be the result of a deliberate choice whereby the French would collectively decide that fulfilment of the new demands induced by "Centripetal" values implies, *inter alia*, much more moderate economic growth compensated for by other satisfactions not accounted for in GNP, in which case it would be better to speak not of slow growth but of "soft" growth, or some other such euphemism.

The above combination may also be involuntary and stem from an inadequately controlled process at the end of which France fails to become integrated in an international environment which has recovered its dynamism. It is naturally difficult to say exactly how this failure might occur. There are, for example, policies of "false new growth" whereby employment is supported by means of palliatives such as "work sharing" or increasing the number of public sector jobs not corresponding to services actually wanted by the population. This would indeed reduce the efficiency of the productive system so that anything gained by propping up domestic demand would be lost on the external demand side. Similarly, radicalizing "Centripetal" values would result in more extensive marginalization of young middle class people abandoning the "Establishment" in order to raise sheep in the Ariège.

2. *The non-congruence hypothesis* implies that the French "Implosion" scenario unfolds in an international economic context which is distinctly growth-oriented. At first sight this hypothesis does not seem to raise any serious problems. In fact, we believe that this is not at all the case, because in the first place a dynamic world economy will check the spread of the "Centripetal" model in that it will cause people to think that this model is not so squarely in the mainstream of history as its supporters believe, and, secondly, the values peculiar to this model can handicap the French economy in its efforts to adapt to the new international deal in ways similar to those described in the previous paragraph.

Deciding what action to take will be fairly delicate since it will after all be a question of seeking economic efficiency in a cultural ambience not particularly favorable to this purpose. As a first approximation, one can say that action would probably have to be directed along three lines:

A. *Search for new combinations of factors of production* (or consumption), using biological processes and skilled manpower rather than non-renewable and/or imported natural resources. The following may be instanced by way of illustration:

—Agricultural production methods which substitute soil and controlled biological processes for energy and raw material inputs;

—Increasing the real life span of household appliances, which implies, among other things, a change in the relative costs of replacement and repairs;

—Increasing the share of public transport in urban traffic, etc.

These active policies, designed to reconcile economic rationality and certain so-called quality-of-life values,[21] will be all the more necessary in the event of massive and relentless opposition to nuclear energy.

B. *The reorganization of productive activities* designed simultaneously to make paid activity more compatible with the expectations specific to the "Centripetal" cultural model, and to alleviate the pressures put on the labor market by job applicants.

The first line of action suggested is consistent with a complex and

[21] This reconciliation will necessarily be imperfect since public policies at the State level (e.g. public transport) will run counter to the desire to make the basic communities more autonomous, unless one boldly supposes, like de Rougemont, that a regional authority is ipso facto more courageous and more ecology-minded than the nation-state.

apparently well-established cultural trend which rejects both "piecemeal work" and vast, impersonal organizations with rigid hierarchical structures. The satisfaction of these preferences will have to fit in with the exigencies of competitiveness or, if another phrasing is preferred, not be too costly in terms of living standards. This could be achieved by re-organizing production tasks in such a way as to give operatives greater scope for initiative; here, the "intermediate technologies" referred to earlier would seem capable of making a valuable contribution which would extend, moreover, to improvements in the efficiency of small enterprises.

However, the creation of numerous small *and* highly efficient firms in the still little-industrialized French provinces also seems necessary in order that young and innovative people may exercise their entrepreneurial talents without having to bow to the organizational constraints (cumbersome hierarchical systems) and geographic imperatives (being in the Paris area) characteristic of very large enterprises.

The forms that government action may take here are less obvious than in the previous instance. Possible examples of such action would be the systematic use of physical planning policies in favor of medium-sized towns, expanded access to business schools, removal of bureaucratic obstacles to the establishment of enterprises, redirection of certain government R & D programs towards counter-taylorist technologies, etc.

The second approach proposed can be justified by two kinds of consideration. One argument, which is economic, is that even if economic growth regains its former momentum, the combination of strong female demand for jobs and labor-saving technical progress will tend to push up structural unemployment. Non-market activities in the home sector must therefore be made as attractive as full-time dependent employment, which will divert some of the potential work force from the labor market. (This is, by the way, the type of reasoning developed by Gershuny, [1977].)

Another argument, which is non-economic in essence, is that it is not a good thing for paid work to be placed so high on the scale of social values, and that other roles deserve to be collectively more highly rated. What is more, individuals ought to be offered a broader range of alternatives than the rigid choice between the status of full-time worker and that of full-time unemployed. It may be added that this notion of people withdrawing from the labor market is not just wishful thinking (or, as with Cathelat, based on qualitative data which are very difficult to interpret), but can be exemplified by the drop in participation rates for men aged between 25 and 54 (see, in the case of the United States, *Business Week*, 1977). It is true also that the real significance of this phenomenon may be distorted by the existence of widespread unde-clared labor, and it will be recalled that Professor Fuà (1976) con-vincingly demonstrated the misleading nature of the low male partici-pation rates in Italy.

In both cases, it would appear that the final result can be character-ized by the expression *dual economy* (Gershuny, 1977), which indicates that in the future there would be two sectors existing side by side: en-terprises which would function according to the traditional rules of the economic game (productivity and profitability), and households, or rather certain households, characterized by continued abandonment of the labor market and the practice of goods- and service-producing activities (non-market) which could moreover give rise to purchases of inputs from enterprises.

Three institutions, of which only the first two exist as yet, could serve to sustain this dual economy:

—part-time work, which is less widespread in France than in most other countries;

—transfer incomes,[22] such as early retirement pensions and partial disability pensions, not counting the internal transfer constituted by the wage of the spouse;

—the system of drawing rights on a time bank (Rehn, 1977), where-by all wage-earners would enjoy very considerable latitude throughout working life to combine the various allocations of paid non-working time (holidays, continuing training) to which they are entitled, so that they would be able to withdraw temporarily from working life at inter-vals.

C. It would be very convenient if one could derive from the current socio-cultural changes a fairly clear picture of the "new" community services best able to satisfy the aspirations for qualitatively different growth. Unfortunately, things are not so simple, because this is an area where it is particularly tempting and easy to make sample surveys say what one wants them to say. Special care must be taken not to equate expansion of the public non-market sector with satisfaction of the qualitative demands of the second scenario, for this would be to invite serious setbacks if the majority of economic transactors were not to ratify, through the non-inflationary price and wage increases they accept, the compulsory levies that correspond to the additional "social income" distributed.

---

[22] It is known that those opposed to negative income tax are afraid that it will accentuate this trend among able-bodied adults. Despite (or because of?) this risk, Gershuny advocates introducing a minimum guaranteed income as means of moving closer to a dual economy.

All that can reasonably be submitted in this connection is that in order to move towards "Centripetal" values, community services should be freer from central supervision in Paris, provided in establishments sized on a human scale, more receptive to the requirements voiced by users, and (this is more by way of conjecture) less discrimination against the poorer segments of the population. None of this is very original, and basically it all boils down to the simple idea that there should be more effective feedback of demand on supply.

The remedies that can be envisaged are well known, moreover. They come down essentially to three types of reform which are in no way mutually exclusive:

—creation of competing markets or quasi-markets,[23] where the penalty for inadequacy of the service supplied is loss of clientele;

—decentralization of public decisions, giving freer rein to the mechanisms of political competition;

—"grass-roots" participation by users ("grass-roots" can be very near the top in the case of a very centralized service such as the telephone). This is the solution which is usually considered, rightly or wrongly, as the most innovative from the point of view of breaking with old habits.

Discussing the respective merits of each formula would take us too far, and we shall do no more than note that they raise two problems of compatibility with economic exigencies. It has already been pointed out that political decentralization may make it more difficult for the state authority to internalize external costs. The second problem arises with regard to participation, in that participating in the management of a community service or the preparation of a collective decision takes time. This may therefore constitute an extra-economic argument for reducing daily (rather than weekly) working hours.

References

Bell, Daniel. *The Coming of Post-Industrial Society*. New York: Basic Books, 1973
Bell, Daniel. *The Cultural Contradictions of Capitalism*. New York: Basic Books, 1976.
Berger, Peter and Brigitte (1971), "The Blueing of America." *New Republic*, April 3, 1971.
Business Week. "The Great Male Cop-Out from the Work Ethic." November 14, 1977.

[23] *Vouchers* are the most creative example of a quasi-market for community services (such as education), but the drawing rights mentioned come into the same category, except for the fact that the exchange is not between individuals but takes place within the life-cycle of each individual.

Cathelat, Bernard. *Les styles de vie des Français, 1978–1998*. Paris: Editions Stanké, 1977.

Coleman, James S. "Education in Modern Society," *in* Martin Greenberger (Ed.), *Computers, Communication and the Public Interest*, Baltimore: Johns Hopkins University Press, 1973.

CGP (Commissariat Général du Plan) (1975), Perspectives de développement économique à long terme (1990), mimeo, 8th January.

Crozier, Michel. *Le phénomène bureaucratique*. Paris: Le Seuil, 1963.

Dalle, F., Thiéry, N. (sous la direction de). *Dynamique de l'autoréforme de l'entreprise*. Paris: Masson, 1976.

Fua, Giorgio. *Occupazione e Capacità Produttive: la realtà italiana*. Bologna: Il Mulino, 1976.

Gershuny, J. "The Self-Service Economy." *New Universities Quarterly*, Winter 1977.

Hall, Peter. "The Search for Environment." *New Society*, 16 April 1970.

Hall, Peter. "The Sunbelt Industries." *New Society*, 6 October 1977.

INSEE. Article by A. Fouquet, "La Consommation des ménages en 1980," *Economie et Statistique*, December 1976.

Kahn, Herman. *The Next Two Hundred Years*, New York: William Morrow, 1976.

Levitt, Theodore. "Management and the Post-Industrial Society." *The Public Interest*, summer 1976.

Marien, Michael. "The Two Visions of Post-Industrial Society." *Futures*, October 1977.

McClelland, David C. *The Achieving Society*, New York: Free Press, 1961.

OECD. Public Expenditure Trends. CPE/WP2(77)1, mimeo, 1977.

Quin, Claude. "La consommation des ménages en 1985." *Cahiers de l'AFEDE*, March 1976.

Rehn, Gösta. Towards a Society of Free Choice. OECD, SME/DEC/77.17, mimeo, 1977.

Rougemont, Denis de. *L'avenir est entre nos mains*. Paris: Stock, 1977.

Vonnegut, Kurt, Jr. *Player Piano*. New York: Dell Publishing Co., 1972.

Appendix 1

Using factor analysis of the replies to the surveys carried out by Cathelat since 1970, the underlying values can be grouped along two axes

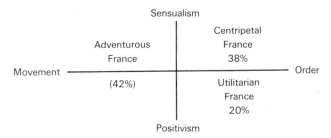

Figure A 1. Axial grouping of values.

as shown in Figure A1: a horizontal axis which opposes the values of *Order* to those of *Movement*, and relates mainly to socio-economic stratification; and a vertical axis which opposes the values of *Positivism* to those of *Sensualism*, and is associated more with differences in life-style.

THE JAPANESE AND THEIR ECONOMIC DEVELOPMENT

YOSHIHIRO KOGANE

The Importance of Human Elements in Economic Development

Professor Fosco Maraini describes the relationship between Japan's economic development and its human—i.e., non-economic—elements as follows:

> It is clear from the outset that the human factor has paramount importance in the spectacular development of modern Japan. When, however, one looks at things from closer quarters one runs up against a wall; Japanese society appears immediately to be so different that traditional explanations give results which are far from satisfactory. Some authors dismiss these differences as superficial or scarcely significant, and consider them rather like optical illusions which take shape when general theories are applied incorrectly to individual cases. Others adopt a more radical view: *the system of classical economics developed in Britain and the United States*—says Professor De Vos—*must be seen, to some extent at least, as ethno-economics with an implicit ethno-psychology as a motivational base. Its emphasis on the source of human motivation . . . is too much dependent on a view of human nature as individualistically motivated and solely instrumental.* The author of the present paper tends to agree with the latter point of view.[1]

Maraini would also be of the same opinion if he were to apply *general* economic theories to analysis of the unsatisfactory economic achievements of the South. Most economists had to admit that their theories could not very well fit the reality in the South, but they tended to justify themselves by predicting that the situation would change after a certain stage of development. Now such an argument would be regarded as a

[1] Maraini, 1975, pp. 15–16.

form of ethnocentrism inasmuch as it presupposes that American or European rationalism would hold anywhere if the residents were advanced enough.

The Danger of Determinism and the Utility of a More Probabilistic Approach in the Social Sciences

In fact, it is impossible to neglect the non-economic realm in formulating economic theories. Thus the externalities appear in economic models either as exogenous variables (e.g. change in tastes of consumers) or as structural coefficients (e.g. propensity to save) which more or less depends on the ascetic or hedonistic values held by the people.

Therefore, the problem is not the exclusion of non-economic factors from economic analysis, but it could be the inadequacy of their treatment. Economics assumes that the interactions between economic variables could take place without interdependence with non-economic variables, that the relation of exogenous variables with endogenous variables is a one-way causal link, that the structural coefficients—including lag-structure—are invariable. It also assumes that *structural* changes may occur but does not explicitly formulate such cases.

Then, according to a set of values of exogenous variables, only one set of the values of endogenous variables is given by the model. Such a rationalization would be subject to the deficiencies of determinism if the empirical relations between relevant variables were not free from the effect of irrelevant (economic or non-economic) variables which may actually be relevant but are neglected by the model-builder.

This nature of the logical structure of economics may be attributed to the traditional Western world-view which assumes that each society must be structurally interrelated as a whole—like a mosaic—and guided by some inner principle. Daniel Bell (1976) describes it: "For Hegel, it was the *Geist*, or inner spirit. For Marx, it was the mode of production, which determined all other social relations. . . . The motion of the web is to be found almost everywhere. . . . It forms as it were the underlying conception of sociology, which regards society as a web of relations." But Bell does "not think that it holds any longer," and would now say that "society is not integral, but disjunctive."[2]

After dividing society, analytically, into the techno-economic structure, the polity, and the culture, Bell argues that these are not congruent with one another and have different rhythms of change, following different norms which make legitimate different—and even contrasting—types of behavior. The merit of his approach is in allowing that the rela-

[2] Bell, 1976, pp. 8–10.

tionships among these realms change irregularly in the course of time. In other words, it is more probabilistic than the classical world-view.

Should we try to consider non-economic factors such as social values, people's attitude toward technology, reserves of natural resources, etc., together with economic factors, such a probabilistic way of thinking would be indispensable; otherwise we would be trapped by the classical type of determinism.

Values and World-views

Behavioral Differences and Values

In order to analyze the economic achievements of Japan in comparison with those of Western countries, it is necessary to distinguish the differences in human factors and then elucidate them in connection with economic development without relying on stereotyped or ethnocentric views which often appear in the discussion of national character, basic personality, cultural psychology, and so on. Once this type of approach is successful, it could be applied to the analysis of economic achievements of the South where the traditional culture is very different from that of North-West Europe.

To point out the differences in *behavior* between Japanese and Westerners is itself so easy and interesting that innumerable publications called "Nihonjin-ron" (discourses, meditations, essays, theories on the Japanese) have appeared over the course of several centuries, written by both Japanese and Westerners.

On the other hand, to clarify the causes of such differences is far more difficult if the discussion of national character and the like is to be avoided. The differences in *values* held by different peoples may be useful for distinguishing the behavioral characteristics of different nations at different times. But, what are values? The INTERFUTURES group within OECD defined them as follows:

Values express underlying preferences, such as those possessed by an individual as a result of his personality, the particular society in which he lives, and the interactions between the two. But also, because of social cohesion, they often constitute an archetype held desirable by a particular social group.[3]

In a given society, the values held by individuals may differ from

[3] Organisation for Economic Co-operation and Development, 1979, p. 99.

person to person, differentiating their choice among available options. From a more macro point of view, however, individual societies may have different archetypes of value system which differentiate the behavioral characteristics of peoples. In this case, the term *values* refers to general conceptions of the good which refer to the ideas about how people should live and satisfy their hopes and aspirations. A network of shared values binds a society together and helps make acceptable the rules which give it solidarity and unity.

In most civilized societies, such as those of China, India, the Arab nations, and Europe, people are supposed to have their own value systems which are more or less stable and revealed. They judge the actions and intentions of the people around them as good or bad; thus the rules become consistent with the value system so as to integrate various social groups with different interests.

In Japan, however, "ethics are not based on universal principles—as it is the case in the West—but have an *atomic* character. . . . They function in circles, or phases, one independent from the other. . . . In Japan proper behaviour depends on circumstances and may change when moving from one circle to the other" (Maraini, 1975, p. 42). What is important is, therefore, not the difference in archetype of values (i.e., Catholicism, Protestantism, Buddhism, Confucianism, Shintoism, materialism, post-materialism, and the like), but the difference in the nature of values. They are *globalistic and categorical* in the West, whereas in Japan they are *particularistic and situational* (Benedict, 1949).

Thus the differences in values between Japan and the West may not be the only key for elucidating the behavioral differences between Japanese and Westerners.

Monistic vs. Dualistic World-view

Maraini stresses the importance of the way of perceiving ultimate reality—which may be called the world-view—as the deep-seated determinant of people's behavior:

The basic assumptions that any group of human beings, large or small, entertains about the world around us and its nature, about the universe and its hidden mechanisms, have subtle and powerful influences permeating the structure of personality and the sphere of action: they percolate continuously to the level of circumscribed values and attitudes justifying ordinary motivation, organizing daily activities. Aspects of ultimate reality are abstract only when observed with the eyes of philosophic speculation: if we consider them as unexpressed assumptions embedded in myths, beliefs, conduct, they become extremely concrete entities, the invisible bones of any given society's mental frame (Maraini, 1975, p. 20).

The nature of the world-view of the Japanese is, according to Maraini, monistic, whereas that of Westerners is dualistic:

> There seems to be general and complete agreement that the Japanese do not see the world, as the West has done in the past and normally does today, in dualistic terms: spirit and matter, soul and body, creator and creation, supernatural and natural, true and false. . . . The view to which Japanese civilization has almost unanimously subscribed, as far back as records can take us, may be defined much more easily as monistic. . . . Matter and spirit flow one into the other, subject and object are often difficult to separate with a neat distinguishing line. . . . Man is not opposed to the world, but immersed in the world (p. 21).

Assuming that values refer to *should be*, we may say that world-views refer to *is*. In the latter case, too, differences between the specific world-views held by the Japanese and by Westerners are not so important: more important would be the differences in the nature of those world-views. When the dualistic world-view is applied to relationships among people, its holder would perceive him(her) self as separate from others. Those who have such an individualistic world-view would be better off holding globalistic and categorical values; otherwise the cohesion of their society would be very vulnerable. Meanwhile, the holder of the monistic world-view would perceive him(her) self as immersed in his(her) group. Those who have such a collectivistic world-view are likely to hold particularistic and situational values under which their society can function normally.

The chronic diseases of the individualistic society are "alienation" and harmful interactions among individuals trying to surmount social barriers.[4] As long as the Japanese maintain a collectivistic world-view, such diseases will not prevail in Japan. This does not mean, however, that there is no disease peculiar to the society of Japan.

---

[4] "En Occident l'homme essaie de surmonter les difficultés que créént ses rapports avec le monde, êtres et choses, en dominant ceux-ci: en triomphant des autres dans les compétitions du statut et du pouvoir, en s'affirmant, fût-ce aux dépens d'autrui, en utilisant les objects comme instruments au service de ses fins" ["Occidental man endeavors to overcome the difficulties which characterize his contacts with the world—people and objects—by dominating them; by vanquishing others in competition for status and power, he affirms himself at the expense of others, and uses them for his own ends"] (d'Iribarne, 1973, p. 112).

Basic Assumptions about the Behavioral Characteristics of the Modern Japanese

Applying a two-dimensional dualistic approach to world-views and values, we may, very roughly speaking, obtain a schematic discrimination of various types of society:

Values　World-views	Monism (East)	Dualism (West)
Globalism (empires)	Chinese	Europeans
Particularism (tribes)	Japanese	Africans

Such differences do not stem from those in the genes of human beings but are the result of a very long historical process. As such, it should be possible to specify the source and evolution process of the world-views and/or values—at least in relatively new societies such as European and Japanese—in the light of impacts from outside as well as of internal social dynamics.[5] However, we shall not enter this interesting but difficult area but will concentrate on analysis of the economic and social development of Japan.

The principal hypothesis here shall be that Japanese world-views and values had developed the above-mentioned characteristics long before the Meiji Restoration in 1868 and that even since then they have remained intrinsically unchanged in spite of the repeated shocks and changes in government, in people's way of life, in revealed world-views and values, etc. This means that the human factors in the economy of Japan have not essentially changed since the feudal age. The remarkable resilience of the economy and society which Japan has demonstrated for more than one century could only be explained by assuming the existence of such stable and continuous human factors.

The Actor

The Japanese as Individuals

Recently, a substantial number of Western authors are inclined to attribute the success of Japan's economy to the collectivistic values or *team spirit* of the workers—from the top to the bottom—in Japanese

[5] With respect to Japan, see Kogane, 1975; 1979.

firms. This seems accepted by the Japanese in general; but at the same time, it should also be kept in mind that without high quality of individual workers their aggregate capacity would not be very high.

It is obvious that the main engine of Japan's economy is the high and ever-increasing efficiency of its manufacturing industry, and the Japanese are endowed with the traits most favorable for manufacturers. First, they are pragmatic, probably more so than Westerners. Second, they are very interested in technology. Third, although they are emotional and irrational with respect to matters which are supposed to be important, they display an extraordinary capacity for rational thinking in dealing with instrumental matters.

As Japanese pragmatism is considered to stem from the monistic world-view, it could be more vital than in the West where the dualistic world-view tends to divide attention between *this* phenomenal world and *that* transcendental world: "Western pragmatism is academic, it originally took birth, as a theory, in the heads of philosophers. . . . Japanese pragmatism is something born in the thought processes of farmers, fishermen, potters, carpenters and their like" (Maraini, 1975, p. 70).

With respect to a liking for technology, there may be many others who share this taste, especially in today's industrial world. But, the Japanese are distinguished by possessing both pragmatic and rationalistic attitudes toward the objects to be treated.

Technology is a useful instrument which human beings have invented, but cannot be more than that. This has been fortunate for the Japanese, paradoxically, because rationalistic ways of thinking have been available only when the matter is not of essential importance in their lives: "The prevailing Japanese ways of thinking are essentially *intuitive and emotional*—at least at those levels which are considered valuable and significant. Within the limits of a more restricted horizon, when reasoning becomes instrumental, a useful tool in the pragmatic process, a mental technique for making or organizing things, Japanese ways of thinking can be, and have been for centuries, admirably rational" (Maraini, 1975, p. 27).

The above is a macroscopic observation which does not deny the existence of deviations of individual Japanese from the average. Nevertheless, if any sample of a group—males, females, young, old, rich, poor, mass, élite, etc.—is tested from the above-mentioned point of view, such traits will inevitably be highlighted without exception. In other words, the existence of exceptional individuals does not at all affect the nature of an average Japanese, so that the nation appears as if composed of completely homogeneous material. This may be related to the Japanese traits as elements of social groups which are discussed in the next section.

Such a unanimous and intuitive pragmatism is often regarded by neighboring nations as an immoral and barbarian vitality which causes uneasiness. Even for the Japanese, this kind of pragmatism often leads to activities without adequate consciousness of goals. Examples are the disorderly aggression of the Imperial Army before the Pacific War and the environmental destruction during the postwar high-growth period.

Instrumental rationalism coupled with liking for technology often intensifies the dominance of means over goals, bringing about confusion and disorder caused by such an imbalance. There is no internal mechanism for checking the imbalance and restoring equilibrium: the history of Japan shows that serious disequilibria have had to be removed by crashing against external forces such as the coming of the West's "black ships," defeat in the Second World War, the 1970s oil crisis, and the like.

The Japanese as Elements of Groups

The rigorously altruistic values found in the Chinese, Indian, and Judeo-Christian traditions were not domestic products but imports from foreign civilizations. Presumably, it would not have been necessary to invent such values if original beliefs had held that a group should and could be, at least socially, indivisible to individual personalities.

The imported values were based on a more categorical and syllogistic approach to reality and hence were useful for integrating dispersed groups—families, clans, tribes, etc.—into a coherent society. Through the process of integration or reconstruction, however, they were gradually but steadily transformed so as to conform to the traditional attitude of the Japanese which was based on a situational and existential approach to reality.

Thus Japanese collectivism, if may be called that, should be regarded as the outcome not of syllogistic thinking but of a more intuitive and empirical view of group life, even if it seems based on sophisticated conceptions of value. The traits of groups composed of Japanese individuals may be summarized as follows.

First, each member of a group is basically optimistic about its relation with the self or implicitly obliged to expect such a relation. For example: it will (can) not harm me; its gains will be more or less returned to me some time in the future; even if I am not appreciated in my circle, my descendants will respect me; and so on. Such optimism is probably the outcome of the fortunate past of the nation in which the continuity of culture has never been destroyed by foreigners, monistic world-views inherited from ancient times, or interactions between the two. Japanese obedience or fidelity to the groups to which they belong can be better explained by employing the theory of an intuitive and emotional expectation concerning the group-individual relationship than by relying on the theory that strict altruistic values are the basis of such an attitude on the part of individuals.

Second, a group formed by the Japanese is closed, limited, and homogeneous. This means that it is not easily open for all to join or leave on a purely contractual basis; and this is not only true for the relation between individuals and their group but also applicable to that between sub-groups and their agglomeration. As a result, Japanese complex groups—examples of which in industrial Japan may be pre-war *zaibatsu* or today's big-business conglomerates—and, in fact, the nation itself have a remarkably homogeneous structure. There is a division of labor between various sub-groups with different kinds of capacity, size, and history, but the nature of these compartments is everywhere the same, i.e., closed, limited, and homogeneous.

The famous Japanese lifetime employment system, seniority system, rules for reaching consensus, etc., have grown up in such soil and are not the intended product of deliberate design and its execution. Such segmentation or compartmentalization of homogeneous big groups could also relate to the monistic world-views and particularistic values of the Japanese. The former contribute to forming gigantic and homogeneous groups, whereas the latter allow the freedom—sometimes disobedience—of inner groups.

This may be paradoxical from the point of view of the West where the integration of liberal individual personalities is supposedly the ultimate aim. But nevertheless, the fact that the social and economic development of Japan has been satisfactory for centuries in spite of various external shocks and internal imbalances, whether short-term or mid-term, may show the remarkably resilient nature of Japanese social groups or the society of Japan itself. As such resilience could not survive in a society where contradictions prevail, Ruth Benedict must have been wrong when she said: "In Japanese life the contradictions, as they seem to us, are as deeply based in their view of life as our uniformities are in ours."

The Potential of the Techno-economic Structure of Japan

The Technology

Technological progress, with its effect on the increase of labor productivity, is not the enemy of workers. The history of human beings shows that technological progress has always been, at least in the long run, the best friend of producer, worker, and consumer. Of course, it sometimes causes nuisances such as accidents, pollution, and unemployment, and sometimes appears extremely destructive, especially in warfare. But many of these should be and/or have been finally dealt with by technological progress; with respect to the others, what is really responsible is not technology. For example, genocide existed long before the appearance of modern technology; serious unemployment prevails mainly in areas where technology cannot develop; and so on. Although technology is nothing more than an instrument of human beings, whether the potential for its development is large or small may be a matter of greater significance than whether or not a country has plenty of oil reserves.

In addition to the above-mentioned Japanese traits which are suited to modern technology, contemporary Japan is favored with the popularization of higher education, computerization, automation, etc., all of which would jointly create extremely favorable conditions for technological development. The problem is how such potential may be realized in the future as in the past.

It is true that most of the recent technological achievements of Japan were led or stimulated by imported technology. Now, however, the technological gap between Japan and the Western advanced countries in general seems to have disappeared. Technological development in future will have to depend much more on Japanese originality. It will become more and more difficult to import technological innovation; Japan will have to produce it or obtain it in exchange for its own. Should the Japanese advantage be only in copying the ideas of foreigners, this would mean that the situation has become less favorable than before.

The theory that Japanese are good imitators but do not have creative capacity is of dubious validity, especially where technology is concerned:

> Japanese swordsmiths, for example, were by the 13th century making steel of a quality never yet made in the West and describable, even in theory, only by the use of concepts developed in the 20th century. Their mastery lay in their complete control of the disposition of carbon in the sword blade they were making—a control vital to the forging of a weapon which needs an edge hard enough to be highly sharpened, a blade soft enough not to shatter, and a back rib stiff enough to prevent it from bending. Yet the Japanese swordsmith had no word for carbon and no concept of it. Refinements like this

are to be found elsewhere in early technology. They are not convincingly attributed to trial and error. The metallurgist who told me this example, the fruit of his own researches, spoke of craftsmen communing with their material in language which I should have expected from a Zen Buddhist, rather than from a Professor of metallurgy (which he in fact was).[6]

It could be reasonable to assume that contemporary Japanese engineers inherit such a creative capacity from their ancestors who were not polluted by a rationality based on Western dualism. If such an intuitive—i.e., impossible to explain by the logic of the West—technological ability is jointed with the guidance of scientific principles, there will be dynamic interaction and acceleration of the progress of both. But one cannot be optimistic about their possible results. On the contrary, there could be serious imbalances between the market sector and the non-market sector as well as between Japan and the rest of the world. In this case, Japanese technological development would either be constrained by political hazards—whether domestic or international— or control itself spontaneously in order to avoid a catastrophe.

The Market Sector

Should the relation between technological potential and a nation's economy be comparable to that between the engine and a car, production units such as families, private companies, public corporations, etc., could be compared to the parts of a car.

Japanese production units—big private firms in particular—have a world-wide reputation for their efficiency in market activities. The capacity and diligence of individual workers and a high capital intensity per worker as well as skillful management of the team must be the factors contributing to their high efficiency. But these inputs would be useless if they were not accompanied by some internal mechanism which integrates them so as to serve the purpose of the team, i.e., producing and selling goods and services.

Western economists would rationalize that this mechanism is the interaction between the desire of workers to maximize their wage income and that of the team to maximize its profit: some Japanologists may attribute it to obedience or fidelity to the mission of the team which is based on the collectivistic values peculiar to the Japanese tradition. Both approximate reality to some extent. But contemporary Japanese

[6] Vickers, 1977, p. 464.

workers are neither pure *economic men* nor *samurai* from the feudal age. Therefore, the hypothesis that they are half-breeds between these two cannot be plausible. So it seems better to distinguish three kinds of ties integrating individual workers to achieve the high efficiency of Japanese production units.

The first is the tie among individual workers, including the head, deputies, etc., in the smallest unit such as a family, subcontract factory, section or division of a big company. As the Japanese generally feel immersed within such a small group, there would be no need of special motivation for keeping such a tie except for the case in which a substantial number of the members feel they are being treated inappropriately.

The second is the tie among the nation-wide units which are supposedly different entities, e.g. Mitsui, Mitsubishi, Sony, Hitachi, and so on; this may be comparable to the chassis of a car integrating numerous parts of different size and function. It is the common acceptance of the law of the market as the basic principle. The monistic world-view held by an overwhelming majority of the Japanese regards this phenomenal world as absolute and rejects anything existing over and above the phenomenal world as abstract and unreal. Under this circumstance the rules of the market could have been useful as a substitute for general and universal norms, principles, or laws which are indispensable for integrating many complex groups, especially if the rules of physical power are considered undesirable or inefficient. Thus the more abstract and unreal ideas such as Confucianism and Buddhism—and even indigenous values such as *Bushido*—had been steadily replaced by the rationality based on market law even before the Meiji Restoration.

The third tie is that integrating the smallest units into bigger ones, which may be regional, national, or international in scale. It defines a hierarchical structure extending from the top of a core company to the bottom of its affiliated small companies. This tie is in fact the most fragile among the three in spite of the seemingly magnificent structure, because the whole system is too large to effectively integrate various subgroups which have a closed and limited nature, resembling the factions of political parties. They are finally subject to the rules of the market, so that their efficiency can be assured in the long run. But because of the existence of vertical division of labor, it is impossible to make market law function immediately. Some observers acknowledge the existence of an inner market which is only made possible with the help of the lifetime employment system. Furthermore, the above-mentioned intuitive and emotional optimism about the group-individual relationship forms a favorable condition for maintaining the stability of such a fragile hierarchical structure.

The Japanese feeling of security in a small group and their reliance on market law are not likely to change in the near future, so the relative advantages of the Japanese market sector may continue to hold for a substantially long period. Problems can only take shape in the management of several big hierarchical structures since the optimism about group-individual relations we have described has neither theoretical nor empirical validity with respect to greatly enlarged, closed, limited, and homogeneous groups.

The Non-market Sector

Let us assume that all social groups other than production units jointly form the non-market sector of the economy. According to this definition, any individual must belong to some group(s) in the non-market sector. In market-economy industrial countries, a major part of the working population belongs to the market sector, supplying their products to the non-market sector through the market, administration, direct personal relations, and so on.

The difference between these two is that the market sector sells its products and buy its necessities in the market, whereas the non-market sector only buys and does not sell. Groups in the non-market sector may support themselves: a housewife takes care of the children in the family; volunteers run their community center; ecologists manage their movement against the development projects of the government; and so on.[7]

Most of the products of the market sector are of an instrumental nature from the point of view of people's lives, whereas those of the non-market sector are generally supposed to directly serve their final aims: for example, the products of the family must be related to health, peace, love, etc.; those of a school, to wisdom; those of a hospital, to health; those of a political party, to legitimate adjustment of different interests; those of the state, to public safety and the like. They are not always free, but nevertheless they are offered because they are demanded and not because they are paid for. Economics pretends that demand unaccompanied by the receipt of payment does not exist, but this is for the convenience of equilibrating demand and supply in a (fictitious) market.

There are interactions between the market sector and the non-market sector. When the efficiency of the former is high (low), the latter is more

[7] Such activities can be defined as the products of the *informal* sector. With respect to the relation between the formal sector and the informal sector, see the papers by Kogane (beginning on p. 129) and by Gershuny in this book.

(less) easily able to satisfy people's demands than otherwise: when the function of the latter is obstructed, the efficiency of the former declines since workers' problems tend to increase, and so on. The interactions occurring in Japan in the long run seem to be very unique: as the efficiency of the market sector increases, the structure of the non-market sector becomes weaker, increasing dependence on the market sector which—rather than collapsing—tends to further increase its efficiency in order to carry the increased weight of the burden.

In the same way we analyzed the mechanism of the market sector, let us distinguish three kinds of ties binding individuals into coherent social groups in Japan now.

First, the tie among family members is intrinsically emotional and is still strong. But traditional extended families no longer exist, and the remaining nuclear families and simple three-generation families are too small to function as social units.

Second, the tie binding nuclear families and the like so as to form intermediate groups was well established in the feudal age. Its nature was also emotional, but it contained the rational aspect of accepting minimum hierarchical relations among the residents of *mura* (villages), the consciousness of which has been inherited even by the top élites of modern Japan. This kind of tie vanished, and the role of traditional intermediate groups has been mostly transferred to the market sector and organizations more or less under the control of the central government.

At the third level, there is no tie integrating intermediate groups since these scarcely exist: but in place of it there is a very strong tie integrating individuals in the nation-state. This tie is completely emotional in nature and can be explained as a product of the history of Japan, perfected by its homogeneity and its extremely well-developed information network.

The conclusion may be that the non-market sector in today's Japan is subjectively unified but objectively atomistic because of the lack of properly functioning intermediate groups. In order to cope with this situation, increasing dependence on the market sector seems to be a better choice than intensifying the control of the central government. But the imbalance between the market sector and the non-market sector cannot and should not increase infinitely. If it did so, it could cause and aggravate international conflicts, inflation and/or unemployment, pollution, congestion, etc., so that the expansion of the market sector runs up against a wall ultimately.

The key to restoring a balance between the two sectors seems to be the question of whether or not the nature of the third tie—which is strong emotionally but practically weak—in the non-market sector could change. The sentiment of national unity is a precious inheritance of the nation but not necessarily suitable for the management of the non-market sector of a gigantic civilized society, which requires openness to universal principles and to people from other cultures.

Future Prospects

Variance or Invariance of the Basic Determinants of the Japanese Attitude

The basic traits of the contemporary Japanese are considered as the outcome of a long—i.e., hundreds or even thousands of years—historical process and hence hardly changeable. It is true that the attitude of the Japanese has often astonished foreigners by shifting from one extreme to another almost overnight, for example from pacifist/isolationist to militarist/imperialist, from totalitarian/patriot to democrat/utilitarian, and so on. But this can be explained by the fact that the particularistic and situational nature of Japanese values made them subject to change quickly and unanimously when the nation's monistic emotions were stimulated by overseas countries.

If one wants insight into the future prospects for Japan, it would be better to assume that the Japanese traits as individuals which were mentioned before—pragmatic, technology-oriented, and instrumentally rational—will not change. Even if they are not inherited through genetic codes, their nature seems near to instinct. With respect to the traits as members of groups, on the other hand, these are more of an acquired nature in being obtained by discipline after maturity.

Variance or invariance in the nature of values and world-views of the Japanese is inseparably related to their future traits—as individuals or as group members—but, nevertheless, can and should be treated as a problem of different dimension. Here it seems better to assume that the monistic nature of Japanese world-views—which may be imprinted first in infancy—will not change, whereas the particularistic nature of values—which may be learned—can change.

Thus there could be two alternative futures (for example, after one or two decades). The first case is the combination of particularistic values and closed/homogeneous groups: the second is the combination of globalistic values and open/heterogeneous groups. Other combinations do not seem plausible: if values are globalistic, the groups will become open and heterogeneous; if values are particularistic, the groups will be closed and homogeneous.

The first case may be called the status quo scenario, in which the technological potential is constrained and gradually diminished due to international conflicts and isolation as well as to imbalances between the market sector and the non-market sector. The second case may be called the revolutionary scenario, in which international and domestic imbalances tend to be gradually resolved so that the technological potential is fully realized ultimately.

What is worrisome in the second case is that the change in the nature of values and hence in groups could affect the Japanese monistic world-view so as to injure the foundation of the culture and hence the personalities of individual Japanese as well as the cohesion of Japanese society. This fear may not be groundless; but, as the expected change in culture is spontaneous and continuous, the risk of destroying the heart of the nation may be far smaller than in the case of abrupt and discontinuous changes brought forth by, for example, foreign domination because of advantages in instrumentalities such as weapons and transportation capacities.

Interdependence between Japan and the Rest of the World

As far as the historical records are concerned, the relation of Japan with the rest of the world—especially the "advanced" part—has always been passive or isolated. Exceptions can be seen in a limited number of very short periods in which the Japanese were stimulated—or affected temporarily—by the globalistic values of the advanced nations and had an illusion that the Japanese world—which is actually closed and limited—could and should be extended from end to end of the outside world. Even such exceptional periods were too short, with too long intervals between, to leave a Japanese mark on the lives of people from other cultures.

The situation has now changed. This is because the techno-economic development of Japan has got out of the catching-up stage and become more and more autonomous; it is autonomous from the point of view of outsiders, but, from the Japanese point of view, there is no alternative to defending their lives against the possible shortages of physical resources and gainful employment other than working hard so as to strengthen the techno-economic structure of Japan.

There could be an alternative, if the Japanese were to have recourse to more political and/or cultural means. But, as the Japanese have never shared their lives with those having different cultures and legitimacy, it is impossible to develop such means. In other words, market law is the only universal principle on which the Japanese can rely both domestically and internationally.

Thus the export of Japanese products related to computers, robots, electronics, biotechnology, etc., combined with those of the United States, will power the transition of today's industrial world to the post-industrial age. The producers who cannot keep up with this trend—many of them could be non-Japanese—will have to withdraw from the market. From a long-term and objective point of view, this seems an unavoidable phenomenon: from a different point of view, however, such a phenomenon may seem to be a kind of epidemic.

Looking at the Japanese side, to depend solely on comparative technological advantage not only may be unwise from the political point of view but also may handicap the economy: that is, Japan may have to pay the cost of compensating for political weakness after all. If the development of Japan is directed toward the status quo scenario, internal imbalances and external constraints will interact so as to run against a wall. That was the situation before and during the Second World War. If Japan's development goes toward the revolutionary scenario, the situation will be less destructive.

With respect to the Western advanced industrial societies, the nature of the crisis seems to be substantially different. It could be a crisis of values: the people who have dualistic or individualistic world-views need globalistic values; otherwise their society will be disjointed: their social groups will have to rely on coercion and/or egoistic motivation to prevent them from breaking down.

Assuming that neither Greek-Christian tradition nor the invisible hand of the market can be the basis of general and universal norms any longer, advanced industrial societies in the West will have to invent new values suitable to the reality of today's industrial society. But it seems difficult so far: if such values are close to those in pre-industrial societies, they will not be accepted by the majority of industrial societies; if they try to conform to individual concrete situation—or become pragmatic—their nature will tend to be particularistic and situational so that the risk of collapse of social groups becomes enlarged. The breakdown of advanced industrial societies in the West would have a harmful effect on the societies in the South which are vulnerable because their foundations for industrial society have not yet been established.

Subsequently, integration of the Japanese into the rest of the world could bring forth two kinds of benefits. First, the rest of the world may have the opportunity for utilizing the Japanese genius in technology, not only in the form of manufactured goods but also as direct human services. Second, the world, especially the West, may absorb useful suggestions for modifying its world-views so as to construct the basis of new values through direct contact with the Japanese. The recent increase in concern with Japanese society may stem from an intention of imitating Japanese methods of business management, but at least a small part of it seems to originate from concern with the heart of Japanese culture on the part of Western intellectuals who have become aware of the biases of their classical world-views.

However, even if the necessity or desirability of integrating Japan into international society is agreed by both sides, a problem will still remain: the lack of immediate means for carrying it out. Therefore, efforts from both sides will be necessary in order to find and apply feasible means one by one.

References

Bell, Daniel. *The Cultural Contradictions of Capitalism.* New York: Basic Books, 1976.

Benedict, Ruth. *The Crysanthemum and the Sword: Patterns of Japanese Culture.* Boston: Houghton Mifflin, 1946; New American Library, 1967.

d'Iribarne, Philippe. *La politique du bonheur.* Paris: Editions du Seuil, 1973.

Kogane, Y. *Ninhonteki Sangyo Shakai no Kozo* [The Structure of Japan's Industrial Society]. Tokyo: Sangyo Noritsu Tanki Daigaku, 1975.

Kogane, Y. *Nihon: Daini no Kaikoku* [The Second Opening of Japan]. Tokyo: Sangyo Noritsu Tanki Daigaku, 1979.

Maraini, F. "Japan and the Future: Some Suggestions from Nihonjin-ron Literature," in *Social Structures and Economic Dynamics in Japan Up to 1980.* Milan: Institute of Economic and Social Studies for the Far East, Luigi Bocconi University, 1975.

Organisation for Economic Cooperation and Development. *Interfutures: Facing the Future.* Paris: OECD, 1979.

Vickers, Geoffrey, "The Weakness of Western Culture." *Futures,* Vol. 9, No. 6 (1977).

GOODS REPLACING SERVICES:
SOME IMPLICATIONS FOR EMPLOYMENT

JONATHAN I. GERSHUNY

The conventional wisdom, stated at its simplest, is that as technologies advance in the manufacture of particular products, and manpower productivity rises, labor is displaced in traditional industries; but with the expansion of the economy, new demands emerge, and hence new employment opportunities. Technological unemployment is to be seen as a recurrent phenomenon, perhaps locally prolonged but, in the developed economy as a whole, a transient one. Where the innovation affects a particular process within an industry which faces an elastic demand curve, the new jobs may be elsewhere in the same industry. Where the innovation affects the whole industry, or where demand for the industry's product is not elastic to price change, general economic expansion may lead to the availability of new jobs in other industries. And where, as is now the case in most developed countries, significant manpower productivity increases are to be found throughout manufacturing industry, the conventional view holds that new jobs, now and in the future, are to be found in the expanding service sector, which of its nature is subject only to minimal manpower productivity increases.

The present paper challenges this view. I have previously argued (Gershuny, 1977a; 1977b; 1978) that we cannot expect service employment to grow naturally and of its own accord. The sizeable areas of past growth in service consumption in the developed world have been in education and medicine. Other service consumption—transport, entertainment, domestic—has fallen considerably over recent decades. Rather than buy increasingly expensive services, households have preferred to buy ever cheaper goods which are used to produce approximately equivalent results—cars instead of transport services, domestic machines instead of domestic services, television instead of cinema. (A selection from the data on which this argument is based can be found in the Appendix). Rather than the service economy, we might better

103

think of the *self*-service economy. Technical and organizational innovation may in the future extend this developing pattern of provision into
medicine and education, especially in marginal areas of new provision
such as adult education. The U.K. Open University is a striking demonstration of what may be possible; the growing governmental
involvement in financing medicine and education throughout Europe
and in the U.S.A., together with resistance to higher levels of taxation,
can only encourage other such developments.

The emergence of the self-service economy can be viewed as a process of increasing manpower productivity in the conventional service
sector. Or it may be seen as a diminution of demand for the product of
that sector. Both interpretations of the argument fit the facts; neither
gives very much support to the vision of a demand-led growth of the
service sector to compensate for losses in manufacturing employment.
This paper explains the self-service economy argument and speculates
on some of its implications for the future of employment.

Services and Self-service: Some Definitional Considerations

Before going further it will be helpful to clarify some terms. A "final
service" commodity, in the sense employed here, is the provision of
some condition or sensation or circumstance to its final consumer. It
is the end of economic activity; once provided it is *literally* consumed—
it vanishes from the experience of all but the ultimate consumer. (Of
course, that ultimate consumer may consider the service consumption
to be merely a means—he may, for example, listen to music as an aid to
concentration on some other task, and Marglin (1974) cites a meal he
consumed in a smart Boston restaurant a decade ago as his best ever
investment in terms of subsequent satisfaction—but to an observer such
motives can only be insecurely inferred). The importance of this definition lies in the distinction it makes possible between services and goods;
goods are not in reality consumed, they persist over time and are used,
finally, for the provision of some service—they are not means, not ends.
Economists talk of durable goods "consumption" only because the
product of their use is normally unaccountable in money terms. Private
cars are not consumed when they are driven from the forecourt of a ga-
rage, but because nobody pays anybody for the transport services produced in private motoring, it is reasonable to exclude them from cal-
culations of quantities such as the Gross National Product.

But when considering the development of economies such exclusions may not be so reasonable. The import of the self-service economy argument is that over time, whole areas of provision for final needs are transferred out of the formal money economy. To understand the process of change in the economy it is not sufficient merely to compare, for example, the public transport industry with motor vehicle mainten- ance and manufacturing, since the transfer of production from trans- port services to transport goods involves the transfer of the labor in- volved in vehicle operation largely out of the formal economy. It is helpful to visualize the organization of production as in Figure 1.

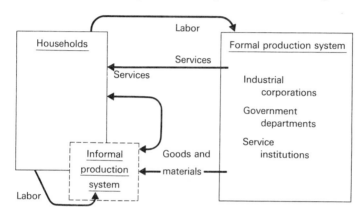

Figure 1. Formal and informal production of goods and services.

At one point in time, the formal economy produces a given range of final goods and services. The services are, by my definition, con- sumed; the transport, educational, medical, recreational, and other pro- visions are input directly into members of households. All the labor and capital required for the provision comes from the formal economy, and those receiving these formal services are essentially passive. The goods, however, are used by the members of the household as means for the achievement of final services. They are, in effect, not consumption but capital items. The domestic washing machine in a kitchen is merely an alternative locus of investment to the installation of a commercial wash- ing machine in a laundry. The ultimate service that the household re- ceives from a good will be in many cases equivalent to services bought directly from the formal economy, but its members are not passive consumers; they put their own labor into the final process of produc- tion.

As time passes, technical innovation reduces the price of consumer goods, making them increasingly versatile and decreasingly demanding of labor time and skill. Concurrently, economic growth drives real wages upwards, so that the prices of (labor-intensive) services in the formal economy increase relative to those of goods. There are thus continuous economic pressures for the transfer of consumption from the final consumption of services purchased from the formal economy towards the consumption of services produced by direct labor within the household, using consumer capital goods purchased from the formal economy. This statement is an oversimplification, but for the moment we shall leave the discussion of the self-service economy thesis and return to some further definitional issues.

There is a category of services which do not reach final consumers but which are intermediate inputs to the formal process of production. Manufacturing industry itself employs many professional, technical, managerial, and clerical workers who produce services as means to the production of material goods. The immediate effects of their

Table 1. Distribution of Occupations across Industry, U.K., 1971
(% of total workforce)

			Occupations		
			Predominantly manual		Non-manual
			Primary occupations	Secondary occupations	Tertiary occupations
			Farmers, miners	Manufacturing processes, construction, transport	Clerical, professional, admin. and sales
Products — Predominantly material	Primary industry	Food, mined products	3.4	0.6	0.3
	Secondary industry	Manufacturing production and ancilliaries (distribution, financial and some professional services[a]	0.6	34.5	27.8
Predominantly immaterial	Tertiary industry	Production of services (transport, some professional services,[b] other services, and public administration)	0.4	7.8	24.6

[a] Accounting, legal services, research.
[b] Educational, medical, social, religious, cultural.
Adapted from *Census of Population 1971*: Economic Activity, Table 19.

activities are conditions or sensations or circumstances, as opposed to material things, but these "intermediate services" have no value in themselves; they are merely *instrumental* to the production process. And outside manufacturing industry, there are other service workers—"producer services" in the term used by Greenfield (1966)—technical consultants, legal, financial, distributive and administrative workers, whose output in whole or in part goes towards the production of material goods. So the number of service workers in an economy is by no means an adequate indicator of the final consumption of services in the economy.

We have therefore to bear in mind two quite orthogonal dimensions of employment in the formal economy. One dimension relates to the nature of the final products of the various *industries*, the other relates to the nature of the *occupation* within the industry. When we distribute the working population of the U.K. (1971) across these two dimensions (Table 1), we see that the majority of workers in service occupations were in fact involved in intermediate service production.

Though more than half of the working population was employed in non-manual work, less than a third of it was involved in the production of final services. To make the point more clearly we might consider the hypothetical input/output matrix in Figure 2.

The bottom row in the diagram lists the three categories of final production: materials, goods, and services—the commodities that households actually draw from the formal economy. The arrows above them show schematically the connections between particular categories of employment. The message is a very obvious one: there is no necessary connection between the size of employment in a particular industry and the final consumption of its product. Virtually none of the output of the capital goods industry emerges as final product. Similarly most of the output of the producer services is input to manufacturing industry. The output of the producer services is input to manufacturing industry. The output of the consumer services group goes almost entirely to employment and also for around 25 percent of final output.

Bearing in mind these definitions, the simplest version of the self-service economy argument differs from the more conventional "service economy" thesis in the following respects. First, it proposes that the technical and social organization of provision for particular needs changes over time. Needs that call for service outputs from the formal economy at one date may later call for goods. Even though it may be true, following Maslow (1954), that as real income rises the remaining needs are increasingly abstract and nonmaterial in character, their effect on the formal economy may still be demands for more material

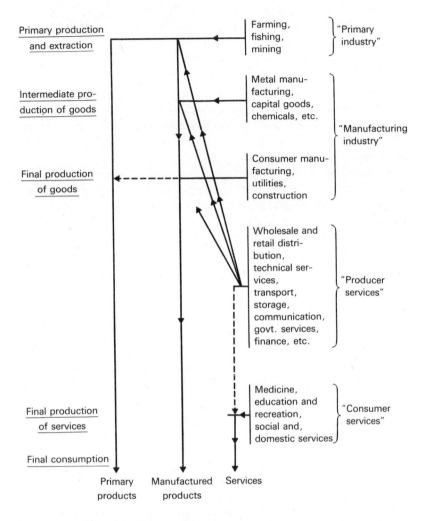

Figure 2. Employment inputs and consumption outputs.

commodities. Second, it stresses that the growth in the number of service workers in the economy tells us nothing about the pattern of final production. More than half of those in service occupations contribute to final material production rather than services, and approximately half of those in the conventional tertiary industrial classification should be placed in the "producer services" category. There is therefore no solid ground for assuming that either consumption of services or employment in service industries and occupations will necessarily increase substantially in the future.

Time Budgets and the Choice between Goods and Services

The argument so far has in one respect been seriously oversimplified. It ignores completely the problem of the scarcity of human time.

Activities are to some extent constrained by natural cycles, days and weeks and years and generations. Some activities are tied biologically to time cycles; we must eat and sleep and possibly recreate with a minimum frequency every day or every few days. Some cycles of activity are imposed by economic and social systems. Adults are constrained to work in the formal economy for some period during the day or the week. There is of course no reason in principle that we should not, for instance, work intensely in the formal economic system for one year, and not at all throughout the next— but there are economic and social sanctions which prevent it. Low wages may make it impossible to save a sufficient surplus over the current expenses of existence. High levels of taxation—tied to a yearly cycle—make it difficult for high-wage earners to build up such a surplus. There is also a constrained sequence among activities throughout a life-cycle; we must be educated before we can get a job, and we must work in the formal economy before we are eligible for social security benefits. And finally, there is a social stigma attached to those who evade these cycles—particularly in relation to formal employment. For these reasons time has to be considered as a scarce commodity even within cycles which amount to only a tiny fraction of a human lifetime. Increasing time spent on one of the constrained daily or weekly activities means forgoing time spent on others.

In the previous section, the choice between the purchase of goods and of services, and thus between formal and informal systems of final provision, was described as being dependent on the relative prices and effectiveness of the two alternatives. We must clearly add to this a consideration of the opportunity cost of time spent in self-service activities. Increased work in the informal economy necessarily involves either less leisure time or less work in the formal economy. The inclusion of time in the calculation makes the picture slightly more complicated. The argument will initially be stated in words, but the formal model in the next section states the position with rather more clarity.

What underlies the choice between goods and services? We cannot expect to construct an adequate general explanation which includes all the motivations which underlie the choice, but we may gain some insight from a much more limited model that considers just the limiting constraints of economic rationality. We shall assume that the individaul is simply motivated to maximize his final consumption of services, and that he is absolutely indifferent between work in the formal and informal economies as a means to achieving that maximization. The rational individual may be expected to balance the time he spends working in the formal economy against the time he needs to use whatever goods he buys for the informal process of production of services.

If he works long hours in the formal economy, then he earns a lot of money, but he has only a little time left for informal production activities. Since he wants to maximize his total consumption of final services, he will therefore be likely to spend a large proportion of his earnings on services produced in the formal sector, and only a small proportion on goods to be used in the informal production of services: he will buy services rather than producing his own. If, however, he works relatively short hours in the formal economy, then he will have a lot of time left over for informal production activities, and he will be likely to spend a large proportion of his money income from the formal economy on goods, which he will use in the "direct production" of services for himself.

We can make this picture rather more determinate. Assume further that some informal activities are more productive than others. Our individual will clearly wish to spend his time in the more productive rather than the less productive activities. This suggests a criterion for choice between formal and informal production activities: where the price of a service purchased from the formal economy is less than the money earnings an individual forgoes in order to spend his time producing that service for himself, the individual's *rational* course of action—within our assumptions—is to purchase that service, and to work the extra period in the formal economy to pay for it. If the individual's wage rate is high relative to the cost of services (principally the wage level in the consumer services sector) then he will work long hours and *buy* services, whereas if his wage level is relatively low he will buy goods and produce his own services.

The wage rate is not the only variable, however: over time, as a result of technical change and investment in producer capital, the real price of consumer goods declines and their productive potential increases. So, holding relative wages constant, our individual can afford more productive capital as time passes, and hence the terms of trade between the formal and the informal economies change in favor of the informal economy. Time spent in informal production becomes more productive; for any given task, a given time spent in self-service activities would have to be matched by an increasing purchase of the equivalent service from the formal economy in order to justify its purchase. We would expect therefore that the decreasing price of goods relative to services would lead to a transfer from formal to informal production.[1]

We can put this in a more concrete form. A clerk in 1900 would, on the basis of a rational calculation, work all day at his profession and pay a servant to work all day at dusting and sweeping. The clerk's average wage was many times that of the domestic servant while his own production capacity for domestic services was presumably no higher than that of the servant; it therefore paid him to pay the servant. The technical innovation of the electric vacuum cleaner, however, increases the clerk's domestic productivity. (At the same time the wages of domestic servants have risen somewhat: to judge from advertisements in *The Times*, a personal servant in the U.K. can expect approximately the same yearly income as a Reader at Sussex University.) So in 1978 the rational clerk will, rather than employ even a part-time servant, work a few minutes less each day and clean his own house.

There are two different processes here. The first might be considered a *relative income* effect: at any point in time, or with given relative prices and productivity levels, the higher the wage the more services a rational individual might be expected to buy, and the longer the hours of work in the formal sector as against informal activities. The second is a *relative price* effect. As the price of goods declines against the price of services over time, rational individuals will tend to transfer gradually from the purchase of services, and hence employment in the formal economy, to the purchase of goods, and employment in the informal economy.

These two effects, though analytically distinct, cannot in practice be separated. As time passes, real income rises—or at least has in the past risen in developed economies. This must (at least under conditions of full employment—we will return to this proviso later) lead to a change in *relative* incomes within the economy. The formal provision of final services is necessarily labor-intensive and is not subject to manpower productivity improvements, whereas the production of goods is subject

---

[1] The difference between goods and service price changes is quite striking. Consider the U.K. data from 1954 and 74:

	1954	1974
All prices	100	268
Goods index	100	172
Services index	100	321

to such improvements. The effect of real economic growth therefore goes in one of two directions. Either the price of services (and hence the level of service wages) rises, less services are consumed, and total service employment declines; or service wages are forced down to compete with goods and service consumption is maintained or increased. The latter possibility is however unlikely in a buoyant economy; rather than accept lower wages, service workers would be likely to seek jobs in manufacturing industry. The former direction of change is therefore to be expected—and was indeed the case in the expanding economies of the 1950s and 1970s; where there was technology available to encourage the informal production of services—notably in transport and entertainment and domestic services, the formal provision of services declined.

This is the reason it is important to stress that the income effect is *relative*. Even though it is true that at any point in time rich people are more likely to consume services than are poor people, nevertheless as societies as a whole get richer over time it does not follow that the consumption of services increases. The difference between productivity growth rates in the formal production of goods and of services has the effect of increasing the relative price of services, and thus of making them less attractive to rational consumers, while the increasing sophistication of consumer capital goods makes the alternative to the purchase of services ever more attractive. We can therefore predict a shift away from time spent in formal productive activities towards informal ones. A preliminary comparison of two time-budget surveys carried out by the BBC (BBC, 1965; 1975) in 1961 and 1974/5 (Table 2) confirms this prediction.[1]

The proportion of time spent working for money appears to have declined over the period while the time devoted to housework (i.e., the informal production of services) has increased. Passive entertainment within the home—chiefly television watching—has also grown

Table 2. Allocation of Time, U.K., 1961 and 1974/5

| | | (Hours per day; weekly average per adult) | |
		1961	1974/5
Out of home:	Work	4.15	3.67
	Other	1.84	1.93
At home:	Domestic work	2.26	3.00
	Passive entertainment	2.39	2.41
	Other	13.36	12.99
		24.00	24.00

[1] See Addendum, p. 127.

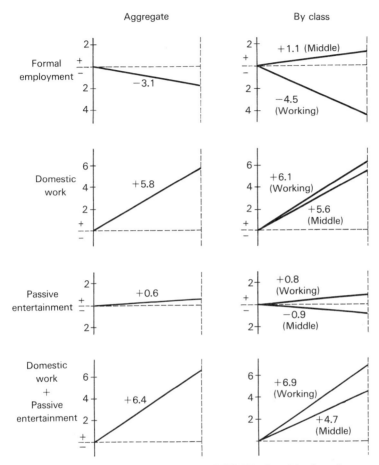

Figure 3. Change in activities, U.K., 1961–1974/75 (% of working hours).

somewhat at the expense of out-of-home entertainment, which again fits the self-service hypothesis and the data on expenditure on entertainment. Furthermore, the argument suggests that low wage groups will show a more decided shift towards self-service than will higher wage groups. The BBC surveys provides data on differences between middle- and working-class time use patterns which may be interpreted as supporting this prediction (Figure 3).

It should, however, be stressed that the time budget data presented here are subject to some inconsistencies; the author is at present engaged in a detailed reworking of the 1961 survey using the 1974/5 definitions, which should result in a more reliable comparison.

A Time Budget Model

Before examining the implications of this process for employment prospects, it will be helpful to restate the model in a rather more formal manner. The simple, timeless model of choice between goods and services entirely on the basis of their relative prices runs as follows. For a given weekly income I, the individual can choose among the various combinations of goods and services defined by Equation 1:

$$G = \frac{1}{g} I - \frac{s}{g} S \tag{1}$$

where G is the quantity of goods purchased, g is the price-index number for goods, s is a price-index number for services, and S is the quantity of services purchased.

Goods, we might remember, are not themselves consumed, but are a means to the informal production of services. We assume that the informal production of services is subject to diminishing returns: the first consumer capital good purchased—a vacuum cleaner, for example—is more productive of final services than is the last—an electric toothbrush, perhaps. We might express this loosely as Equation 2:

$$S' = f(G) \tag{2}$$

where f declines with increasing G and S' is the quantity of informal services produced.

This gives us a production frontier for formal and informal services with the shape of PB in Figure 4. If individuals are indifferent between

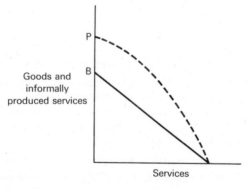

Figure 4. Choice betweeen goods and services: The timeless model (money budget curve).

the consumption of formally and informally produced services, their optimal combination is achieved where the slope of PB is equal to -1. Now PB is a function of BB; as the price of goods (g) falls relative to that of services (s), the slope of BB increases and the optimum point on PB moves leftwards in Figure 4—and the rational consumer's preferred proportion of goods to services rises.

We draw from this simple model an obvious conclusion: the optimal proportion of goods to services is in part determined by their relative prices. The simple model does not however tell the whole story; it leaves out the constraint of limited time. For an adequate picture we must consider the money budget together with the time budget. The time constraint is introduced by Equation 3:

$$I = w(M - T) \tag{3}$$

where w is the wage rate, M is the total time available for formal and informal production and T is the time devoted to informal production. For a given wage rate, the more time spent in formal production ($M - T$), the higher the income and the less time available for informal production. Combining Equations 1 and 3, we arrive at:

$$G = \frac{w(M - T)}{g} - \frac{s}{g} S. \tag{4}$$

This gives a similar picture of choice between goods and services, except for one feature. As income rises for a given wage rate, the amount of time available for informal production declines; the individual with a fixed hourly wage rate can buy an ever increasing quantity of goods, but at the expense of the time necessary for him to use them. We can model this in a simple fashion by assuming that a unit quantity of goods requires a fixed quantity of time p in order to produce a final service. That is, if the consumer capital goods that are purchased are actually to be used, then

$$T = pG \tag{5}$$

where p is the time required for the productive use of a unit of consumer goods.

Equation 5, when taken together with 4, implies that there exists for any individual at any point in time a saturation level, at which any further goods purchased could not be consumed. Consider Figure 5, which represents an individual whose whole income is devoted to the purchase of goods.

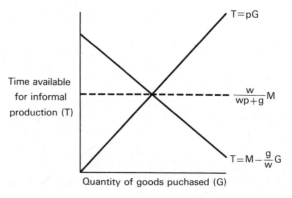

Figure 5. Time availability and the use of goods.

As the quantity of goods purchased rises, time *available* for informal production declines since the individual must work increasingly in the formal economy, while the time *required* for informal production using the goods rises. The two curves intersect at the point where

$$T = \frac{wM}{wp + g} \ ,$$

which establishes the saturation level for goods. If the individual were to work longer hours, he would have either to purchase further goods which he could not use, or else buy his final services.

This suggests that for any given wage rate and hours of work in the formal economy, there exists an optimum combination of purchase of goods and services. If the individual purchases less than the optimal quantity of goods for the number of hours he works in the formal economy he has spare time, time which is underutilized because he has established an insufficient quantity of consumer capital. If he buys more than this quantity of goods then he has laid up underutilized capital, instead of purchasing consumable final services. Different lengths of formal work define different optima; we find the locus of these optima by solving Equations 4 and 5:

$$G = \frac{w}{wp + g} M - \frac{s}{wp + g} S.$$

Figure 6 relates this locus, which we shall call the time budget line (TB in the figure), to the money budget lines used in the simple model. Obviously, the longer the hours of formal work, the lower the propor-

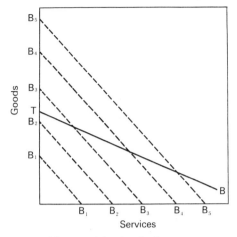

Figure 6. The time-budget curve.

tion of goods in the optimal basket of goods and services. Each point on TB represents a different combination of goods, services, time spent in formal production, and time spent in informal production.

The rational individual chooses one of the combinations of formal hours of work with its equivalent optimal basket of goods and services represented by the time budget curve. Our previous argument suggests which of these combinations will be chosen. We might postulate a production possibility curve related to the time budges curve by Equation 2. Just as in the simple case, we might argue that the distribution of production between the formal and the informal is determined by the slope of the time budget curve $s/wp + g$; the steeper the budget curve, the higher the proportion of goods to services.

This enables us to derive formally the two effects described in the previous section. We obtain the income effect when we consider that as w increases the value of $s/wp + g$ declines. So the higher the wage rate, the lower the proportion of informal to formal services consumed; high-wage earners will tend to work long hours for money, and spend a relatively high proportion of their money income on services. And similarly we get the price effect by considering that as s/g increases, the value of $s/wp + g$ increases. As services rise in price over time, as we have learned to expect them to do, we would expect the proportion of formal sector production of services to decline relative to informal production.

It needs hardly be stated that even in economic terms this is a very much simplified model. First, we have assumed indifference between what are in more conventional analyses considered to be leisure and work; though this is certainly no less reasonable than the usual assumption that people are motivated to work simply to *consume* leisure, it does leave out of the model the fact that some paid work is less intrinsically satisfying than many informal sector activities. (It should, however, be noticed that since low intrinsic job satisfaction is often correlated with low pay, the result of including this effect would be to accentuate the trends which are predicted by the model.) Second, in practice people are not free to decide on their own hours of weekly paid work; so the model should be considered as suggestive of long-term aspirations for consumption rather than of short-term individual decisions. Thirdly, we have ignored the plight of the very lowest-paid groups, who because of their low pay and the domestic circumstances (particularly overcrowding) which go with it, and because of the indivisibility of consumer capital items, simply cannot afford to buy goods. This group will tend to consume services, but services of inferior quality, involving a high proportion of direct labor. This phenomenon deserves more attention, but there is insufficient space to consider it here.

To sum up the discussion in this section, we have established that the proportion of services to goods purchased declines when:

g falls;

s rises;

p falls;

w falls.

The following section assumes that in the future s/g will continue to rise in such a way as to counteract any increase in w; we will assume that the trend towards the self-service economy will continue. But—to get a little ahead of the argument—this assumption is by no means necessarily true. As a result of exploring its implications, a rather different possibility emerges: the development of a low-wage service sector. We will return to this in the final section.

Employment Productivity and Consumption Growth Patterns

In this section we shall consider the effect of the self-service trend on future employment patterns. To get a perspective on how employment has changed over the last two decades, we consider a sample of seven OECD states (Canada, U.S.A., Japan, Germany, Sweden, France, and U.K.—see Figure 7). In all of these countries, the proportion of the work force employed in agriculture has fallen. From inspection, the

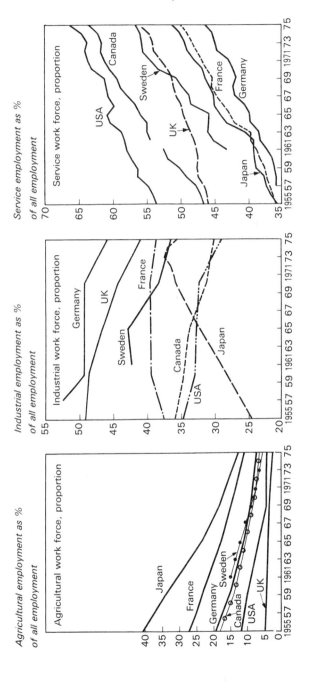

Figure 7. Sectoral employment in the seven OECD economies.

rate of decline seems to be proportional to the size of the sector, and the pattern of decline over time seems to be common to each of the countries. The pattern of change in manufacturing industry (including mining, utilities, and construction) is rather less consistent, with France and Japan having an initial growth in the manufacturing proportion of the work force. We might, however, note that in France and Japan initial agricultural proportions were considerably higher than in the other countries in the sample, and the growing manufacturing proportion was falling by the end of the period. The service proportion has grown in each of the economies; the rate of growth appears to be approximately constant over time, in each country, and not variant with the size of the sector. We must bear in mind that this sector includes both consumer and producer services; in the U.K. in 1975, for example, of the 45 percent of the working population in the service sector, consumer and producer services accounted for 22 percent and 23 percent, respectively.

In the seven states, industrial productivity grew continuously from 1955 until 1973 (Figure 8). Between 1973 and 1975 the trend was reversed; it appears however that this reversal was largely an artifact of

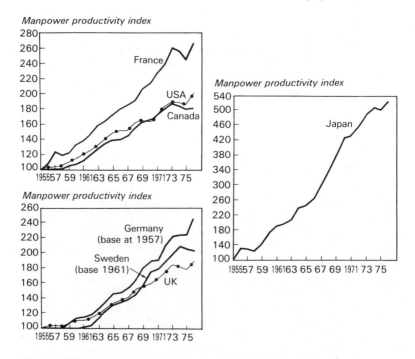

Figure 8. Industrial manpower activity in the seven OECD economies.

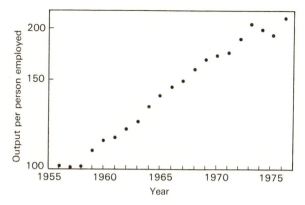

Figure 9. OECD industrial manpower productivity index (1955 = 100).

firms' reluctance to lose workers, legal requirements for redundancy payments, and government job-creation schemes, all of which contributed to a condition of "disguised unemployment" throughout the OECD. And it does seem that the manufacturing productivity growth trend has been resumed since 1975. Three groups emerge among the seven states. The North American economies, together with the U.K., had manufacturing manpower productivity growth rates averaging around 3 percent per year over the period. France and Germany both had rates of approximately 5 percent per year. Japan's productivity grew at about 8.5 percent per year. The figures for the OECD as a whole show very little variation from year to year (Figure 9).

There does seem to have been a very regular growth rate of a little more than 3.5 percent per year since 1958, deviating to a substantial degree only in 1974 and 1975, presumably for the reasons already described. We should however beware of projecting this steady exponential increase forward into the future, since a number of recent studies have suggested that the rate of manpower productivity increase may increase in the future, largely as a result of micro-electronics-based innovations in manufacturing production.

Comparative international data on manpower productivity changes over a longer period is difficult to amass. However, the U.K. does have a relatively reliable series stretching back to the first decade of this century; from this it does appear that the rate of growth of manufacturing manpower productivity has been not constant but *accelerating* (Figure 10).

It would surely be reasonable to speculate that the current generation

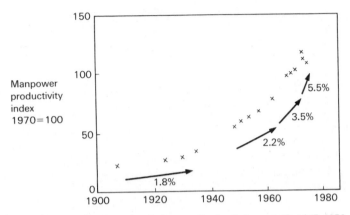

Figure 10. U.K. manufacturing industry: Productivity growth 1967–1975.
Source: *U.K. Census of Production.*

of advances in manufacturing technology might produce an increase in
the rate of productivity growth throughout the OECD, analogous to
those accelerations found in the U.K. However, the argument that
follows does not in fact postulate any such acceleration, but relies
simply on the continuation of past growth rates; if an acceleration is to
be expected, it will have the effect of amplifying the processes describeb
below.

Manpower productivity growth in the consumer service sector is
negligible; indeed, to the extent that most of the output of this sector
is calculated as the wages paid to service workers, real productivity
growth is defined out of existence. Producer services are however subject to a quite substantial growth in manpower productivity. Technical
and organizational change have already led to a considerable decline in
employment in retail and wholesale distribution, and current innovations in automatic sales check-out and computerized stock management
will tend to continue this decline. Banks and other financial institutions
are sizeable employers of clerical and routine professional workers
whose jobs are increasingly at risk from automation. Certainly some
technical and professional consultancy will be likely to gain "down-
stream" benefits from the increasing technical sophistication of the
production processes, but whether such growth could be sufficient to
compensate for jobs lost elsewhere in the producer services can only be
a matter for speculation.

One condition for maintenance of full employment in an economy
must be that the total product rises at the same rate as does the average
manpower productivity across the economy. Over the past two decades,

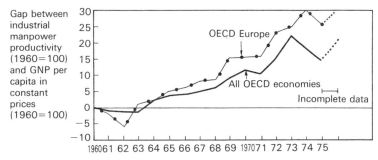

Figure 11. Gap between manufacturing productivity growth and GDP growth, 1960–1974.

throughout the OECD, manpower productivity in manufacturing industry has risen faster than GDP (Figure 11).

	A GNP growth	B Manufacturing productivity growth	C A − B
Canada	3.6	3.7	−0.1
U.S.A.	2.5	3.6	−1.1
France	4.4	4.8	−0.4
Germany	3.5	4.9	−1.4
Sweden	3.3	5.9	−2.6
U.K.	2.2	3.6	−1.4

Employment can only be maintained, under such conditions, by passing labor into the relatively low-productivity, low-productivity-growth service sector.

This then is the significance of the self-service trend for employment prospects: service employment is the means for balancing the widening gap between manufacturing productivity and total consumption. If we assume that this gap can only widen—and current OECD economic growth rates coupled with current advances in manufacturing technology suggest that this is likely—then anything that threatens the growth of service employment also reduces the possibility of a return to full employment.

Conclusion: Unemployment or... Low-wage Services?

In sum, we see two different ways in which technical advance reduces employment opportunities: first, conventionally, in automating the manufacturing process; second, less conventionally, in improving the performance and lowering the cost of consumer goods, so as to enable the production of an ever-wider range of services (and possibly goods) in an essentially extra-economic fashion. It seems reasonable to predict that in the future, today's bastions of service employment will, if not crumble, at least grow no higher. As yesterday the railways, so education, medicine, and social services tomorrow.

Certainly the social ills associated with future unemployment will be to some extent mitigated by the very forces which cause it. Social security payments mean that unemployed people need not actually starve. Unemployed people, at least to the extent that they have access to consumer capital goods, may still be involved in informal production processes. But no one would pretend that either of these conditions could make involuntary unemployment a desirable prospect.

To make matters worse, there is a further step that we must take in the argument. The self-service argument is based on the assumption of full employment, with service employment being increasingly restricted to highly paid professional workers. Under conditions of unemployment, however, the picture changes; we might now visualize unemployed workers being drawn into unskilled, low-pay, low-status service activities just for the sake of something to do. There is some evidence that this may already be happening in the U.K. The most recent statistics on the price of services show a slowing of the relative price rise of services; since 1974 service prices in the U.K. have risen no faster than those of goods. This may well be the first aggregate economic indication of a new growth of a low-wage service sector.

Sociological evidence on this process is accumulating fast. It is now widely accepted that a significant proportion of UK economic activity is to be found *between* what I have termed the formal and informal economies—in the extra-legal, unrecorded exchange of cash for predominantly low-skill services (see, for example, Henry, 1978; Outer Circle Policy Unit, 1978). The picture established by these authors is indeed that of a developing service economy—not the highly skill-intensive information economy of Bell or Fuchs, but rather more of an economy of skivvy- or navvy-services, always on the run from official accountancy and regulation.

References

Bell, Daniel. *The Coming of Post-Industrial Society*. London: Heineman, 1974.
British Broadcasting Corporation. *The People's Activities*. London: BBC, 1965.

British Broadcasting Corporation. "Daily Life in the 1970s" (mimeo). London: BBC, 1975.

Fuchs, V. *The Service Economy*. New York: National Bureau of Economic Research, 1968.

Gershuny, J. I. "The Myth of the Service Economy." *Futures*, April 1977.

Gershuny, J. I. "The Self-Service Economy." *New Universities Quarterly*, Winter 1977.

Gershuny, J. I. *After Industrial Society?* London: Macmillan, 1978.

Greenfield, H. I. *Manpower and the Growth of Consumer Services*. New York: Columbia University Press, 1966.

Henry, S. *The Hidden Economy*. London: Martin Robertson, 1978.

Marglin, S. A. "What Do Bosses Do?" *Review of Radical Political Economy*, Summer 1974.

Maslow, A. *Motivation and Personality*. New York: Harper & Row, 1954.

Outer Circle Policy Unit. *Policing the Hidden Economy*. London: Outer Circle Policy Unit, 1978.

Appendix: Data for the Self-service Economy Thesis

At any one point in time it is apparent that rich households do consume more services than poor ones (Figure A1). Nevertheless, over time the

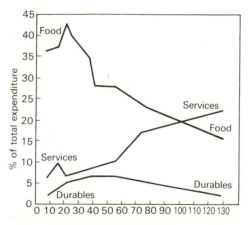

Figure A 1. Expenditure on services, U.K., 1954.

proportion of total expenditures on services does not (at least in the U.K.) appear to have increased, even though the economy has got much richer (Figure A2).

The explanation is that people's propensity to consume services has declined over the period (Figure A3). The data suggest that there has been a change in the social organization of final production of services, leading to a substitution of goods for services (Figure A4).

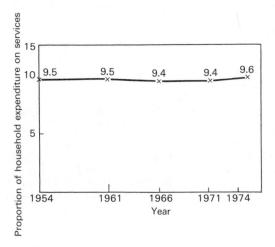

Figure A 2. Household service expenditure 1954–1974.
Source: *Family Expenditure Survey.*

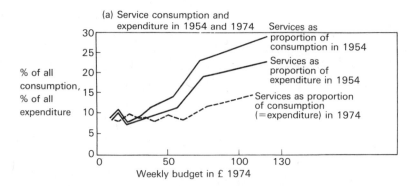

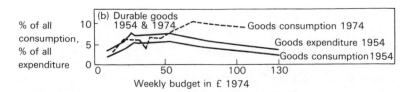

Figure A 3. Real consumption of durables and services, 1954 and 1974.
"Real consumption" is estimated by inflating 1954 expenditure by the price index for the individual commodity. "Expenditure proportion" is estimated by inflating 1954 expenditure with the overall consumer price index.

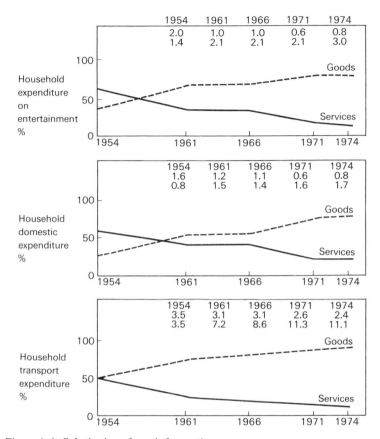

Figure A 4. Substitution of goods for services.

Addendum (July 1982)

This paper was written for Project INTERFUTURES in 1978. The time budget results, as a note in the text makes clear, come from preliminary analysis of survey material that was subsequently recoded, and the final results of this work are quite different from those cited in Tables 2 and 3; in particular, the reworked data suggest that domestic work time declined between 1961 and 1975. The original text of this paper is still in its 1978 form; for more reliable time budget results, see J. I. Gershuny, "Changement des Modeles de Loisir," *Temps Libres,* Vol. 1, No. 4, 1982.

NEW DEMANDS AND THE DEVELOPMENT
OF ADVANCED INDUSTRIAL SOCIETIES

YOSHIHIRO KOGANE

In considering the future possibilities for economic growth and employment in advanced industrial societies, people often refer to structural changes which are occurring today or are to occur tomorrow. They say, for example, that policies should be designed and implemented so as to respond to the structural changes occurring in advanced industrial societies, or that full employment under high economic growth will not be possible for the coming decades due to structural changes. In these discussions the notion of structural changes is the key concept.

Usually, the term "structural" change has been used to mean nonconjunctural and seemingly irreversible changes occurring in various areas of advanced industrial societies, e.g. people's attitude towards work and leisure, demographic trends in the labor market, the speed and direction of technological progress, relations between public sector and private sector, use of energy and raw materials, inter-industrial relations, international division of labor, etc. Policy discussions centered around structural changes will have to be based on analysis of these changes in various areas as well as conjecture about the influence which they could exert on the future development of advanced industrial societies.

However, it does not seem sufficient to collect piecemeal analyses of these changes to clarify the whole picture of the present and future problems of advanced industrial societies. Changes in these areas are interrelated. For example, a search for the cause of a certain change could end by imputing it to another change, and *vice versa*. In order to get out of this maze, it would be helpful to take a vertical approach which could connect the horizontal approaches to different layers of advanced industrial societies, i.e., from the top of the superstructure —e.g. changes in culture and moral—to the bottom—e.g. changes in electronics technology.

The same may be said with respect to the search for the solution to a policy problem which is supposed to be of a structural nature. Without the aid of vertical approaches, it would be difficult to explore the real source of structural diseases which are to be the objects treated by specific policy measures. The purpose of this study is to shed light on the relation between change in people's demands and techno-economic development as one of these vertical approaches.

Based on the examination of deficiencies of the implicit welfare assumptions presently used for the formulation of policies, a simple model can be constructed. It is different from ordinary models in the following ways.

First, the supply factors of welfare—i.e., responses to a person's demands (for becoming happy)—are the different types of use of his (her) and other people's time. Second, his(her) time is limited (e.g. 24 hours in a day). Third, there are two production sectors, one being the formal, consisting of the people with whom he(she) does not have personal contact and the other being the informal, consisting of him (her)self and other persons with personal contact; this formal/informal dichotomy may be contrasted to the private/public or market/state dichotomy of economics. Fourth, this person "exchanges" with others his(her) time, which is deposited to the formal sector. The terms of trade are assumed to be dependent on the size of the formal sector: that is, the larger (smaller) it is, the less (more) advantageous is the relation for the individual in question.

Then, the relation between change in welfare and in allocation of time is examined. The diagnosis of the contradictions of advanced industrial societies is as follows. First, there is an increasing tendency for intermediate or instrumental use of time as against the past where economic development reduced that related to transportation, housekeeping, etc., so that the opportunity for demand satisfaction is suppressed. Second, the productivity of the formal sector has declined, whereas its size has increased and is continuing to increase; meanwhile the efficiency of the use of time in the informal sector has increased so that the change of allocation of time which could have been effective in the past is no longer useful for improving welfare. Despite this, an adaptation of the social environment to such individual conditions has not yet taken place. The relation between the different use of time and the use of various material goods vigorously produced in advanced industrial societies is examined to verify the above diagnosis.

On the basis of the above analysis, three scenarios are proposed.

Scenario A may be called the "optimistic" trend scenario. The belief in the benefit of material goods for reducing the instrumental use of time continues to stimulate production and consumption of material goods responding to the demands of today: this maintains a rather high rate of growth of GDP—centering around the production of goods for information and communication. Unemployment tends to remain for rather a long time. But the increase of productivity in the informal sector (particularly due to informatization) changes people's attitudes, and hence the social environment, which gradually becomes adapted to new demands of individuals so that unemployment is directed toward a spontaneous dissolution. When this trend breaks down, it changes into the direction predicted by the "pessimistic" scenario described below.

Scenario B may be called the "discontinuity" scenario. The awareness of the condition of happiness suddenly changes to concern about its feasibility. Rate of GDP growth remains substantially low, but unemployment tends to decrease more easily than in the case of A since a change of attitude toward the use of time in the formal as well as informal sector takes place consistently. The problem of this scenario may be how and by whom such a sudden change will be made sustainable.

Scenario B′ may be called the "pessimistic" trend scenario. People suffer from a perception of a dilemma between shortage (of energy, etc.) and excess (of "needless" goods, etc.) of supply, and finally choose to escape from stagflation by a radical increase of employment absorption by the public sector. Workers become unhappy since they lose the time for "domestic" production which could be highly productive, while consumers become angry since their "imports" from the formal sector are so costly and of low quality. Consequently, authoritarian policies are introduced to make people live within the constraints of low productivity of the formal sector. The high potential for productivity of the informal sector accumulated in the past is thus neglected and finally disappears.

Change in Perceptions of Welfare

Reconsideration of the Ultimate Aim of Policy

Most of today's difficult problems within advanced industrial societies seem to stem from the failure of market (of goods, capital, and labor) and Welfare State, both of which seemed so promising, to promote happiness among the society members—or, in other words, to realize a welfare society. If so, the key to solving them may be, not the direct search for alternative institutions which exist or did exist (e.g. central planning organizations, medieval communities), but reconsideration of the objective itself; that is, what is the happiness of human beings, and what constraints is it subject to?

Despite the fact that these questions have been asked and answered thousands of times over thousands of years, it is still worthwhile asking them, for the following three reasons.

First, as they have no general solution it is always necessary to look for solutions which are feasible under the special conditions of each society, especially when the social environment and hence the conditions for people's happiness are rapidly changing.

Second, the basic assumptions of welfare economics which form the source of the legitimacy of institutions and practices in advanced industrial societies have mainly come from the empirical knowledge and social values of Northwest Europe and North America in the eighteenth and nineteenth centuries, and are considered by some people too obsolete and biased to treat the problems of today's industrial societies. A model-change will thus be required in the light of the empirical knowledge and social values of the industrialized countries in the twentieth and twenty-first centuries, which have been and are still becoming geographically and culturally far more diversified.

Third, such a model-change is needed also for reconsidering the basic conditions for the happiness of the people in the Third World. So far, the attempt to follow "advanced" countries does not necessarily seem to have made them happier than before.

Deficiencies of the Implicit Welfare Assumptions Used for the Formulation of Policies

In the formulation of policies in advanced industrial societies there seems to be an implicit assumption that an individual has a utility function of the following type:

$$U = U (y, u_1 u_2 \ldots\ldots\ldots) \tag{1}$$

where U is welfare (or output, satisfaction of needs, achievement, etc.); y is income (or consumption of goods and services as a fraction of income); and u_1, u_2, etc. are other welfare components (e.g. health, knowledge and skill, physical environment, security, etc.). This model seems to be deficient from the following points of view.

Wealth and Welfare. First, this function implies a direct relationship between welfare and income, which means that the richer a man is, the happier he will be.[1] For the other welfare components income also has a positive—even if small—effect (for example, with respect to physical environment the rich have a larger degree of freedom in choosing the site of their dwelling and/or work and leisure than the poor). Therefore everybody in advanced industrial societies today should be happier than their predecessors, inasmuch as the real income of the poorest member of the former exceeds that of the richest member of the latter. Many sample surveys carried out in advanced countries could prove that such an assumption is not feasible, so that the basic design of the model must be unrealistic.[2]

Equality and Efficiency. Second, this function is destined to bring forth serious contradictions between today's socio-cultural demands and techno-economic demands. According to the dominant values in advanced industrial societies, everyone is equally entitled to become happy in the everyday world. Thus, should income be the decisive determinant of happiness, it would be natural for the general public to claim an equal share (or strongly protest against the unequal distribution) of income or net national product distributed through either market or state. But the above welfare function—while justifying egalitarian distribution policies—does not ensure the equalization of productivity of individuals. Needless to say, egalitarian distribution of income (national product) would destroy the system of production which—being the source of welfare according to this function—is based on the cooperation of and the division of labor among individuals, whereas the capacity and willingness for production differ from person to person in quality and quantity. The victory of egalitarianism under the above conditions, therefore, would result in the decline of real income.[3]

---

[1] Although we could replace it by a logistic function, in that case we would have to fix the height of the ceiling (or saturation) according to an arbitrary judgment, affected by the special values held by the author.

[2] It may be argued that happiness is related to expectations, so that when it is sure that people will become richer they must be happier than otherwise. It may also be argued that when people become poorer, they will surely become less happy. But these arguments do not change the "fact" that many rich people were, are, and will be less happy than some poorer people.

[3] Theoretically speaking, there should be an optimal compromise between equality and efficiency—that is, a maximization of the average utility of all individuals who have different productivity or a maximization of the utility of individuals who have the lowest productivity through tax measures. But its practical application would involve enormous political difficulties arising from the behavior of individuals who want to maximize their utility by taking advantage of such an institution, and could finally result in economic disaster.

Variable and Invariable Restraints. Third, this function ignores or at least does not consider explicitly the invariable restraint imposed on the satisfaction of demands of human beings—that is, available time. It assumes implicitly that this person would satisfy his(her) increasing demands in the course of time since variables such as income, knowledge and skill, etc. are supposed to be able to increase in the future in general.

Therefore, his(her) expectation tends to expand almost unlimitedly (especially during the period of prosperity) without awareness of the physical limit of demand satisfaction: one cannot drive a car and a boat simultaneously; one cannot play chess and bridge simultaneously, nor expand a day to 48 hours to do these successively. However rich or intellectual, people cannot have more than 24 hours a day to utilize their potential command of goods and services or of knowledge. People who are not aware of this fact cannot avoid being dissatisfied with their achievements at any time. If even the richest or cleverest people suffer from such a feeling, average people would pursue their objective in life only to become disappointed.

Moreover, the policy makers who are supposed to help people to satisfy such unlimited demands are only capable and responsible within the given fraction of time in which they are entrusted with power. Whatever future satisfaction is promised or whatever past misery is stressed by them, people will never excuse incapability on the part of public officials.

This does not justify policies aimed at only temporary treatment of policy problems, and it is true that people in advanced industrial societies have a longer time horizon when looking at their lives than others (who may have more expectations of an afterlife). However, it cannot be denied that the implicit assumption mentioned above could have been one of the sources of the aggressive attitude of people of advanced industrial societies (toward nature, other nations, their countrymen, etc.) and their everlasting irritations in spite of unprecedented affluence. Moreover, dissatisfaction under such assumptions tends to be directed toward Malthusian type suppression of people's demands in taking into account the limits to progress or "growth" of human beings which need not be really "invariable."

Demand for and Supply of Welfare in a Given Period of Time

Should welfare be a product of human beings, rather than a gift from

Heaven, it should be possible to distinguish the demand side and the supply side as in the case of production of market goods. Moreover, we could assume that, in a given fraction of time, a person's demand for welfare should be more or less balanced with its supply, since otherwise he(she) would become bankrupt.

With respect to the time horizon within which the analysis should be carried out, we shall refer only to one time unit, the year, since it covers most of the aspects of human life: work-leisure, health-illness, routines-ceremonies, seasons, and so on.[4]

Demand for Welfare

We shall assume the following demand function for welfare of a person with regard to a given year, in the form of a linear equation as the first approximation:

$$U = a_1 u_1 + a_2 u_2 + a_3 u_3 + a_4 u_4 \qquad (2)$$

where U is total demand for welfare; u_1 is good functioning of the body (including brain, nerves, etc.); u_2 is friendly relations with other people; u_3 is friendly relations with non-human objects (e.g. pets, clothes, tools, houses, neighborhoods, etc.); u_4 is removal of frustrations[5]; and a_1, a_2, a_3, a_4 are weights of demand components; these could differ from person to person, year to year, etc., but their sum should be 1.

Equation (2) differs from Equation (1) in that all variables on the right-hand side have their maximum values within a given fraction of time, namely:

—u_1 cannot exceed $\bar{u}_1$, which shows perfect physiological functioning throughout the given year;

—u_2 cannot exceed $\bar{u}_2$, which shows perfect friendly relations with the maximum number of people with whom an individual can be in

---

[4] Analyses with respect to days, weeks, or months are of course possible.

[5] Everyone would admit that it is impossible to maximize the values of u_1, u_2, and u_3 but nevertheless would make an effort to fill the gap in order to mitigate the pain coming from such dissatisfaction. This is the reason why the variable u_4 is necessary. What is demanded under this item may vary: a memory of the good old days in the case of an old man; the dream of marrying a prince in the case of a poor girl; the promise of going to Heaven in the case of a Christian, etc. No material input may be needed for satisfying this demand, but usually something is required, e.g. an album, a bed, a book, a movie theatre, etc. Alcohol or drugs could be an efficient input but could have perverse effects on health, i.e., u_1. The u_4 should not be mixed up with "expectations" which do not make sense unless realized and which, when realized, no longer mitigate the holder's frustration since they have shifted to the realm of u_1, u_2, or u_3.

contact during the given year, e.g. 730 persons, assuming that, on average, the necessary contacting time is one half-day per person (including multilateral contact and communications through telephone, letter, etc.);

—u_3 cannot exceed $\bar{u}_3$, which shows perfect friendly relations with the surrounding objects with which the individual can be in contact during the given year (the number and kind of objects are limited since a substantial amount of time is necessary to have a friendly relation with one's surroundings as in the case of human beings);

—u_4 cannot exceed $\bar{u}_4$, which shows perfect removal of the tensions accompanying life in the given year.

Therefore, u_1, u_2, u_3, and u_4 could be measured as fractions of their maximum values, setting the values of $\bar{u}_1$, $\bar{u}_2$, $\bar{u}_3$, and $\bar{u}_4$ at 1. Then we could have the value of $\bar{U}$, i.e., the maximum overall welfare, as 1. This means that this utility function has—despite its linear type—a maximum value based on the assumptions concerning the "facts" (i.e., not those concerning mathematical formulation).

Supply (Production) of Welfare

We shall assume the following supply (or production) function of welfare of a person in regard to a given year in the form of a linear equation as the first approximation:

$$V = b_1 t_1 + b_2 t_2 + \tau_1 T_1 + \tau_2 T_2 \qquad (3)$$

where V is total supply of welfare; t_1 is time consumed for immediate satisfaction of demands without effort (e.g. sleeping for u_1 and u_4, having a chat with family for u_2); t_2 is time consumed for immediate satisfaction of demands with effort (e.g. playing sports for u_1, u_2, and u_4, cooking for family for u_2); T_1 is time transferred from other people with personal contact (e.g. a family member who cleans one's living space for u_1 and u_3, someone who drives one in a car for u_2); T_2 is time transferred from other people without personal contact (e.g. workers in a restaurant for u_2 and u_4, doctors and nurses of a hospital for u_1); and b_1, b_2, τ_1, τ_2 are contributions of a unit of time to the production of welfare.

Different from demand factors, production factors of welfare (e.g. time) are subject to an invariable constraint among themselves which assures the "closed" nature of the model.

Everybody has the same fixed amount of time rationed by Nature and allocates it in the following way:

$$t_1 + t_2 + t_3 + t_4 = \bar{t}, \tag{4}$$

where t_1 and t_2 are defined as for Equation (3); t_3 is time consumed for intermediate (or instrumental) use; t_4 is time consumed (both directly and indirectly) for satisfying the demands of others without personal contact; and $\bar{t}$ is constant (e.g. 365×24 hours).

The sum of t_1 and t_2 represents the total input of time for satisfying own demands—or producing own welfare—in the "informal" sector (e.g. oneself, family members, club members); t_3 represents the time necessitated for making a direct input of time for producing welfare, e.g. time consumed in walking to a cinema (in this case, inputs for production are t_1—time for sitting and seeing the screen—and T_2—transfer of time from employees in the cinema, directors, actors, cameramen, etc.); t_4 represents the input of time for producing welfare in the "formal" sector (e.g. factory, shop, government agency, school, hospital) in responding to the demands of those with whom there is no personal contact—in other words, time transferred to the formal sector.

In order to import, one has to export, i.e., input t_4 into the formal sector. In the case of a family with one worker, the imports exchanged for his exports are redistributed among family members. Inasmuch as exportable time is limited, one cannot import time unlimitedly. A case such as a large amount of inherited property may be the exception, but even in this instance most of it will be taken away by the formal sector—i.e., by taxation—in advanced industrial societies.

Import-export relation is, thus, approximately

$$wt_4 = pT_2, \tag{5}$$

where w is wage per hour (or, more broadly, including benefits such as social security and public services from state) and p is price of imported time per hour (or more broadly, including taxes and contributions to the state).

When a gap between the two sides—i.e., a surplus or deficit in balance of payments—exists, this person will accumulate assets or liabilities. When there is an equilibrium, Equation (5) can be expressed as

$$T_2 = \frac{w}{p} t_4. \tag{5'}$$

The coefficient w/p shows the terms of trade between imports and exports.

From the national point of view, the following relation (ignoring the

international exchange of time) should hold between the sums of transferred time:

$$(1 - \theta) \Sigma t_{4i} = \Sigma T_{2i} (i = 1 \ldots \ldots n), \tag{6}$$

where n is working population and θ is the fraction of nation's time
used for running and/or expanding the formal sector.

With respect to the average exporter (and importer) of time, there
will be the following relation with national figures:

$$t_4 = \frac{1}{n} \Sigma t_{4i}, \quad T_2 = \frac{1}{n} \Sigma T_{2i} = \frac{1}{n} (1 - \theta) \Sigma t_{4i} .$$

Therefore, we get $w/p = 1 - \theta$. Then, generally,

$$T_2 = (1 - \theta)t_4 . \tag{7}$$

Effects of Value (Cultural) Changes and Income (Economic) Changes on People's Behavior

As mentioned at first, these functions only refer to the case of an
(average) individual, and therefore their parameters are subject to
change year by year according to his(her) "personal" situation. But as
the life of an individual is affected by other people, the personal situation of an "average" person cannot be free from the effects of changes
in others, i.e., from the "social" environment. In other words, the
"individual attitude" is affected by the "aggregate attitude," and then
brings forth feedback to the latter. We may distinguish changes in the
social environment affecting people's demands for happiness by
relying on the preceding way of thinking.

The first type of "new" demand appears when there is a change in
values which may be expressed by a change in parameters a_1, a_2, a_3,
and a_4 in Equation (2). For example, in the emergence of new ascetic
values such as Puritanism or militaristic nationalism, the coefficient
a_1—the weight attached to the satisfaction of physiological demands
or u_1—will decline, whereas the coefficient a_4 or the weight of demand
u_4 will increase to mitigate the pain accompanying the sacrifice of physiological demands; or the coefficient a_2 will decrease and a_3 as well as a_4
will increase in the emergence of consumption competition as described
by Veblen. These changes cannot occur independently since their
sum must always be 1. Such value changes could also change the
maximum of demand components $\bar{u}_1$, $\bar{u}_2$, $\bar{u}_3$, and $\bar{u}_4$. They must cause

a fundamental change in people's behavior since they change the existential "meaning" of human life. Moreover, there must be interrelations between various demand factors insofar as it is possible to substitute some welfare elements for others.

The second type of "new" demand appears when there is a change in living environment which affects the efficiency of different types of use of time and may be expressed by change in parameters b_1, b_2, τ_1, τ_2, w, and p in Equations (3) and (5). This could be caused by a change in average quantity and quality of physical (including environmental) goods and the pattern of their distribution, independent of the metaphysical conditions or culture or—according to Daniel Bell's definition—expressive symbolism of the people. They try to change or maintain the use of their time according to, or resisting against, these parametric changes in order to increase (or prevent the decrease of) the value of V which should be equal to U, i.e., happiness.

The analysis of the first case could be called "above-the-line" analysis, and that of the second case "below-the-line" analysis. It might be possible and indispensable to carry out both in order to elucidate the "mystery" of human welfare since these two are the different faces of the same coin which comprise the invisible foundation of human society and hence cannot be independent of each other. But to mix up these two realms is dangerous since it could confuse the analysis by treating heterogeneous factors without awareness that they could evolve, to some extent, autonomously. This study from now on will focus on "below-the-line" analysis since this seems to be the shorter way to confront the presently dominant method of analysis of human welfare, i.e. economics.

Analysis of Productivity of Welfare in Advanced Industrial Societies

The Model

Let us analyze the conditions for increasing or supporting the welfare of an average worker in advanced industrial societies by employing the above set of hypotheses about demand for and supply of welfare. They are:

$$U = a_1u_1 + a_2u_2 + a_3u_3 + a_4u_4 \qquad (2)$$

$$V = b_1t_1 + b_2t_2 + \tau_1T_1 + \tau_2T_2 \qquad (3)$$

$$t_1 + t_2 + t_3 + t_4 = \bar{t} \tag{4}$$

$$T_2 = (1 - \theta)t_4 . \tag{7}$$

We shall assume $U = V$, and reduce the number of equations to the following:

$$U = b_1 t_1 + b_2 t_2 + \tau_1 T_1 + \tau_2 (1 - \theta)t_4 \tag{8}$$

$$t_1 + t_2 + t_3 + t_4 = \bar{t}. \tag{4}$$

This model cannot be workable since it has six variables and only two equations. In order to make it an operational tool, we shall need some "behavioral" equations which explain the mechanism of substitution among the variables involved in this model.

For example, we may assume:

$$t_1/t_2 = f\left(\bar{t}_1, \frac{p_1}{p_2}\right),$$

where $\bar{t}_1 =$ minimum necessary t_1 for physiological reasons; $p_1 =$ the degree of physical and psychological pain accompanying the use of time t_1 (i.e. the boredom of doing nothing "stimulative"); and $p_2 =$ the same accompanying the use of time t_2 (the discomfort, tiredness or danger of doing something which needs "effort"). Choices should be made: for example, whether to stay at home reading (t_1) or play golf (t_2) on a vacation day.

We may also assume:

$$t_2/t_4 = \phi\,(\bar{t}_4,\, p_2/p_4),$$

where $\bar{t}_4 =$ minimum necessary t_4 for sociological reasons; $p_2 =$ the degree of physical and psychological pain accompanying the use of time t_2; and $p_4 =$ the degree of physical and psychological pain accompanying the use of time t_4. Choices should be made: for example, whether to do additional work for one's employer or to help with the housework.

We may also assume

$$T_1 = (t_1,\, t_2,\, t_4,) .$$

This means that the degree of getting help from those with direct contact depends upon the time spent with or without them, e.g. time for dining, chatting, helping, working, etc.

People's actual behavior when pursuing an increase in or maintenance of their welfare could be explained by the help of these equations. However, their formulations and the numerical values of parameters should differ greatly according to individual's physiological and social conditions, e.g. age, sex, physical strength, value, class, profession, nationality, etc. As they are so personal and cultural in nature, we shall avoid going into detail unless supported by empirical data such as sample surveys or parameters obtained by statistical analysis.

Relations between Change in Welfare and Allocation of Time

But even so we could demonstrate how an individual would behave in order to increase welfare (resulting in either satisfaction or dissatis-faction) by utilizing a simplified version of the above model; in other words, we could make a more realistic forecast than that which depends on the assumption that the agent has perfect information about equilibrium or optimum.

Let us denote the sum of t_1 and t_2 by $\hat{\imath}$, and its coefficient by b. Then,

$$U = b\,\hat{\imath} + \tau_1 T_1 + \tau_2(1 - \theta)t_4 \qquad (8')$$

$$\hat{\imath} + t_3 + t_4 = \bar{\imath}. \qquad (4')$$

Assume that, under the same allocation of time as, e.g., in the previous year, this person has found that his(her) welfare is not satisfactory. This may happen either when his(her) aspiration level has increased—because of cultural change "above the line"—so as to increase the target value of U, or when his (her) production of welfare is declining—because of the decline of parameters b, τ_1, τ_2 $(1-\theta)$ "below the line"—so as to decrease the forecast value of U for this year.

Then he(she) will try to increase the quantity of either $\hat{\imath}$ or t_4 to the extent that they are controllable variables which can contribute to increased welfare. What is important in this case is that *ceteris paribus* clauses cannot be applied due to the existence of explicit inter-relation-ships between $\hat{\imath}$, t_3, t_4, and T_1.

If he(she) is going to increase $\hat{\imath}$, i.e., time spent for domestic produc-tion of welfare or for production in the informal sector, or—utilizing the more popular expression—time for leisure, the incremental increase of U responding to that of $\hat{\imath}$ could be derived from (8') and (4') as:

$$\frac{\partial U}{\partial \hat{\imath}} = b - \tau_2(1 - \theta) - \tau_2\,(1 - \theta)\frac{\partial t_3}{\partial \hat{\imath}} + \tau_1 \frac{\partial T_1}{\partial \hat{\imath}}.$$

The constant term on the right-hand side comprises the basic part of marginal productivity of leisure time of this person this year; that is, if $b > \tau_2 (1 - \theta)$ and *ceteris paribus*—or if $\partial t_3/\partial \hat{t} = \partial T_1/\partial \hat{t} = 0$, this change in allocation of time will result in an increase of welfare, whereas if $b < \tau_2(1 - \theta)$, there will be a reverse situation.

If he(she) is going to increase t_4, i.e., time transferred to those without personal contact—or working time in the formal sector—the incremental increase in U responding to that in t_4 could be derived from (8′) and (4′) as

$$\frac{\partial U}{\partial t_4} = \tau_2(1 - \theta) - b - b\frac{\partial t_3}{\partial t_4} + \tau_1 \frac{\partial T_1}{\partial t_4}.$$

Then, if $\tau_2(1 - \theta) > b$ and *ceteris paribus*—or if $\partial t_3/\partial t_4 = \partial T_1/\partial t_4 = 0$—increase in working time will result in an increase in welfare, whereas if $\tau_2(1 - \theta) < b$, there will be a reverse situation.

Thus we would arrive at the work/leisure zero-sum game; that is, if the variable parts of these partial differentials are to be ignored, when $b > \tau_2(1 - \theta)$, an increase in leisure promises an increase in welfare whereas an increase in work will inevitably decrease welfare by the same amount; when $b < \tau_2(1 - \theta)$, the situation is completely reversed. But such an assumption is obviously unreasonable. Generally speaking, the following relationships seem to be plausible:

$$\frac{\partial t_3}{\partial \hat{t}} \geq 0, \quad \frac{\partial T_1}{\partial \hat{t}} \gtreqless 0, \quad \frac{\partial t_3}{\partial t_4} \geq 0, \quad \frac{\partial T_1}{\partial t_4} \gtreqless 0.$$

If leisure (working) time increases, instrumental use of time, i.e., t_3, will also increase so as to reduce the increase of welfare. The increase in leisure time could either increase the transfer of time from those with personal contact, T_1 (e.g. when it accompanies the longer stay with family or friends), or decrease it (e.g. when it accompanies longer absence from them). The increase of working time could either have a beneficial effect (e.g. in the case of working with family or improving friendly relations with colleagues through the increase of time spent together) or a detrimental effect (e.g. in the case of staying longer away from home or community when working in a big organization, or increasing hostility against colleagues through intensified competition for professional success with respect to the transfer of time from those with personal contact).

The situation described above could often lead either to the "failure" of market and/or state or to the "regret" of individuals. An example of the former may be the case in which the offer of seemingly attractive opportunities for leisure (or work) could not attract sufficient consumers (or workers) because they were wise enough to foresee the possible decline of welfare accompanying a change in use of time. In this case, either the state or the enterprise will suffer from a financial deficit which will be fed back to taxpayers, consumers, investors, etc. An example of the latter may be the case in which the decision (of spending or taking the job) could not bring about the satisfaction expected since the consumer or worker was unwise enough to overlook the possible reduction of welfare accompanying the change in his use of time. In this case, the injured person is the individual. However, a cumulative effect might be resentment of the general public against the state or the enterprise or "capitalism" itself.

Contradictions of Advanced Industrial Societies

The contradictions of advanced industrial societies seem to be explained to some extent by utilizing the method previously mentioned.

First, there seems to be an increasing tendency toward intermediate use of time. Although many people, including leaders, tend to consider that this is "necessary" for happiness, such an instrumentalism could not be dominant if most people were to recognize that their available time is limited so that the more they use it directly to satisfy their demands the more satisfied they will be (or, the happier they will be).

It may be true that many people increased their welfare in the process of development of advanced industrial societies, but this could be explained better by the fact that the increased supply and use of material goods reduced their intermediate input of time (for, e.g., transportation, housekeeping) than by the fact that they increased such an instrumental input of time for working life and/or leisure life. The latter explanation, which is preferred by instrumentalists, ignores the fact that human beings have only 24 hours a day and that the use of time for immediate and perfect satisfaction of demands, such as eating, sleeping, or loving, is the foundation of human welfare. Utilizing Equations (8′) and (4′) in the previous section, this may be interpreted in such a way that the quantity of t_3 tends to increase so as to suppress the quantity of U through the reduction of either $\hat{t}$ or t_4.

The revival of consummatorism today is not that of Puritanism— by which anything related to work or saving was the immediate and perfect satisfaction of demand arising from a religious belief—but must be a reflection of the above awareness which could evolve into a new rationalism in the twentieth and twenty-first centuries. More precisely, the distinction between consummatory and instrumental is itself inseparably connected with the world-view or values held by the people. Today, much of the use of time which was formerly assumed to directly serve demand satisfaction is becoming perceived as simply instrumental. This is partly due to the past achievement of industrial societies, examples of which may be easily found in the cases of doing or having various things which were previously regarded as "prestigious," "honorable," "courageous," "skilled," etc. But this does not justify decision-makers in continuing simply to endorse what were thought formerly to be consummatory uses of time. It may be difficult to distinguish and encourage new consummatory uses of time, but it would be easier to recognize the failure of instrumental uses of time and help people to economize on them as much as possible. This does not seem, however, to have been done so far.

Second, there seems an increasing tendency toward "frictional resistance" against the trial of defending or increasing welfare by a change in use of time. It seems that, until recently, there was a substantial gap between the efficiency of time imported from (and hence exported to) the formal sector and that of time spent in the informal sector. In other words, $\tau_2(1 - \theta) - b$ could have been so large that a small amount of increased working time (especially e.g. in the case of housewives in Western countries, or of dependent workers in Japan) could be expected to increase welfare substantially. Moreover, the intensification of human relations with colleagues in workplaces (i.e., the positive value of $\partial T_1/\partial t_4$) could also have been expected, particularly in the above cases.

The disadvantage for the increase of leisure time as the reverse side of the advantage for that of working time could have been mitigated by the fact that the increase of input of time for leisure was made possible without increasing instrumental use of time because of the rapid reduction of time necessitated for carrying out leisure activities, which could be expressed as a parametric change of the relation between t_3 and $\hat{t}$.

Nowadays, however, the advantage of the increase of working time is rapidly decreasing due to the narrowing discrepancy between b and $\tau_2(1 - \theta)$. The comparative advantage of increasing leisure time has been substantially increased but not well recognized; moreover, the social environment—or, more precisely, the institutions and practices—which should legitimize the shift from formal production to informal production has not yet been prepared. The relation with instrumental use of time is becoming unfavorable.

At the same time, many people still look for increasing working time which accompanies little increase of instrumental use of time and could intensify friendly relations with their colleagues; but, if such conditions were not satisfied, they would prefer to be unemployed since that is the way to preserve their welfare. This does not mean lessened demand for employment opportunities in the formal sector; therefore, the job vacancy/unemployment ratio tends to increase insofar as the quantity of job offers regardless of their quality is to increase and/or insofar as the "quantitative efficiency" of work is to be continuously pursued.

Role of Material Goods in the Use of Time for Responding to Demands

The above conjectures will have to be verified by empirical analysis of the relation between the use of time and that of material goods, since any kind of input of time needs to be accompanied by material goods in order to produce real welfare (as opposed to "expected" welfare or simple illusion) for ordinary people. For example, a hungry man needs bread in order to spend time in eating; a poor girl needs a bed in order to spend time in dreaming of becoming a princess; a Christian needs a cross for prayer; etc.

Looking at Table 1, which demonstrates the relation between the input of time and the use of material goods in industrial societies, we find that most "traditional" goods are for consummatory use. That is, their existence itself is sufficient for perfect satisfaction of demands, in either the formal or the informal sector.

The demands for consummatory goods are subject to limitation according to the biological, technological, or cultural characteristics of the use of time (e.g. raw meat, raw material), so that an increase in their supply does not—once it exceeds a certain line—increase or even decrease the contribution of a unit of used time for satisfying the demands (e.g. excess supply of dishes, excess supply of medals for soldiers, etc.).

Meanwhile, most goods for which demand is increasing in industrial societies have been of an instrumental nature, i.e., oriented towards an increase in productivity of time or decrease in instrumental use of time, and often combined with a network of services in order to be advantageous for their objectives. This could, at the early stage of industrialization, have only increased the contribution of a unit of time "imported" from the formal sector, but its spillover effects must have spread to that of time for "domestic" production. For example, the increase of supply of hardware for producing movies increased the productivity of time spent by producers, directors, and Hollywood stars at first, but now increases that of producers of home-made movies.

In connection with this, the first problem may be that the efficiency of instrumental goods—for reducing instrumental use of time—is levelling off partly because of the limit on technological improvement of the

Table 1. Relation between the Use of Time and Material Goods

Nature of material goods / Use of time	Consummatory (directly serving for the purpose of time spent)	Instrumental (increasing the productivity of time spent or reducing instrumental use of time)	
		Without software	With software
Consummatory use without effort (t_1)	Drinking water Milk Medicine	Instant food Restaurant dish Tailored suit Camera Refrigerator Park Air conditionner	Supermarket TV set (amusement) Book (amusement) Hospital Movie theater
Consummatory use with effort (t_2)	Cloth (sewing) Meat (cooking) House (maintenance) Ball (football)	Football grounds Swimming pool Sportscar	TV set (learning) Book (learning) School Health center
Intermediate use (t_3)	Electricity and gas (using housing equipment) Gasoline (driving a car)	Washer Vacuum cleaner Passenger car Highway	Railways Telephones Airways
Export to the formal sector or "work" (t_4)	Energy Raw materials Intermediate goods (steel, chemicals, etc.)	Commercial car Business equip. (machine, ship, computer) Highway Armaments	Railways Telephones Airways Data banks

Note: Human services directly related to the use of "hardware" are not regarded as "with software": e.g. work of tailor on a tailored suit, work on maintenance of park, work of a driver of a bus.

goods in view of the purposes to be served, e.g. transportation, house-keeping, etc., and partly because of socio-political developments (e.g. overpopulation of large cities, over-grown administrations, excess complication of regulations, etc.). It cannot be overlooked also that, as instrumental goods become increasingly available, their use tends to lose its implications and become perceived as simply instrumental (consider the case of driving one's own car, which in the beginning of motorization could have been a direct satisfaction of a demand for demonstrating car-ownership).

The second problem may be that the contribution to demand satisfaction of a unit of time imported from the formal sector tends to decrease because the workers are more and more alienated from the face-to-face or skin-to-skin relation with the "importers" of their time (e.g. in the case of shopping, school, hospital, etc.). This is because the mass production system has been diffusing from material production to the field of service production and is wrongly perceived so that it is contributing to the increase of welfare. The decline of "real" (in the sense of responding to the demands of importers of time) productivity could also stem from internal alienation or the fact that the relations between teammates tend to be less and less intimate because of the pursuit of more "efficient" or "rationalized" organization.

Scenarios and Policies

The following alternative scenarios for the future of advanced industrial societies could be drawn from the foregoing analysis.

Scenario A. The awareness about welfare remains traditional. Recovery to high growth of material production is attempted. The growth of production is centered around instrumental goods for information and communication since this is the realm in which substantial reduction of instrumental input of time can be expected. Consequently, the productivity of the formal sector remains rather high. This continues to increase the productivity of the informal sector, especially concerning people's learning activities, so that a gradual change of social environment responding to the new demands of individuals appears. People gradually begin to find themselves at ease in the informal sector, resulting in the spontaneous dissolution of today's structural unemployment. The chance of a crisis in the early stage, since structural unemployment will generate social trouble, depends on the speed with which the social environment changes as described above. A resource crisis is avoided since rapid transformation to an informatized and less resource-consuming economy takes place due to the effort of the private sector and the policy of the public sector. Change in the social environment generated by growth has been assumed to be so rapid that this may be called the most optimistic scenario; it assumes that a continuous attitude supported by a belief in the "good" of materials for improving the use of people's time will, after all, lead to a happy ending.

Scenario B. Awareness about the conditions for happiness suddenly changes. This is the most difficult—though some people may consider it the most desirable from a normative point of view—process to forecast since the behavior of people who change their world-view is very difficult to predict. So this may be called the "discontinuity" scenario. The rate of growth of material production remains substantially low. But as the attitude toward work in the formal sector also changes rapidly, structural unemployment disappears much earlier than in Scenario A. As people do not find the necessity of increasing productivity of the formal sector (since they shift to the informal sector and enjoy the high productivity there), the shift of production to instrumental goods for information and communication is delayed, assuming it is still to happen. The problem of this scenario may be how and by whom such a sudden change in people's attitudes could be made sustainable. In viewing this, the probability of this scenario may be said to be restricted (or, in other words, subject) to the special conditions of the society concerned.

Scenario B'. Awareness about the conditions for happiness changes only superficially. People are sensitive to the constraints of available natural resources, and at the same time perceive the disappearance of the utility of material goods; i.e., they continue to stay in the contradiction between shortage and excess. Despite such an uncertainty, unemployment is the greatest concern of the people since to produce something in the formal sector is still the essential value. Consequently—and due also to the recognition that there are already too many "needless" material goods—rapid increase of productivity is rejected, and the absorption of employment by the public sector—which has low productivity—is accelerated. People's frustration advances since the welfare of neither the employed nor the recipients of their services is increased. That is, workers lose their time for production in the informal sector (which could be highly productive) in exchange for their "export" of time, whereas consumers (and taxpayers) become angry because of the low quality and high prices of the services offered by the formal sector; in other words, the continuation of stagflation reaches breaking point.

Consequently, authoritarian policies are introduced in order that this scenario continue to be valid. People are forced to live under the constraints of a low productivity level in the formal sector. This is the scenario in which the achievement-oriented people try to change their achievement from work to leisure, and lose both. The high potential productivity of the informal sector is meanwhile abandoned and finally disappears. This may be the most undersirable but is seemingly the most plausible scenario, assuming that the foregoing analysis is correct and that the fundamental attitude of people does not change so long as doomsday does not arrive.

Actual development of the economy and society in advanced industrial societies will fall somewhere inside the triangle with the above three poles. In line with differences in traditional values and attitudes, there may be a differentiation among industrial countries. But the key problem for policy-makers in general may be how to avoid the occurrence of an evolution resembling Scenario B'.

THE CONCEPTUAL FRAMEWORK OF
INFORMATION ECONOMICS*

YONEJI MASUDA

Information economics is an entirely new economics overriding the past classical and neoclassical schools of economics. It is also marked by its character as a futurist type of economics.

Viewed historically, all new economic theories have always made their appearance as radical economics. Take, for instance, Marx, Walras, Schumpeter, or Keynes: they all appeared as rebels against the existing economic theories and established new economic theories by breaking the frameworks of classical economics. We should note in this respect that there were always historical socioeconomic conditions for the birth of these new economic theories, and it is particularly important in this connection for us to realize that a new economic theory was constructed on the basis of a new development in productivity.

For instance, Smith's *Wealth of Nations* was published in the early days of the Industrial Revolution, and his system of economics, expounded in the *Wealth of Nations*, was based on the development of productivity centered on "division of labor" against the background of his time.

Similarly, various other theories of economics such as mercantilism and physiocratism correspond to the development of productivity in their respective periods of time and were designed to serve the new economic developments. Schumpeter's theory of "innovation" and Rostow's concept of "take-off" in his *Stages of Economic Growth* may be cited as instances explaining the relations between the development of productivity and different economic theories.

It is especially necessary to point out here that the development of productivity in the past, which lies at the basis of each new theory of

* This paper appeared in *IEEE Transactions on Communications*, Vol. COM-23, No. 10 (New York: Institute of Electrical and Electronics Engineers, Inc.), October 1975.

economics, centered mainly on material and industrial productivity. Particularly in the later period of capitalist society, innovation provided a major background to the development of economic theories.

In view of the above, information economics arises in historical conditions which make it a dually new theory of economics. First, today we stand at the threshold of a new development of productivity. Second, this productivity is information productivity, which is entirely different in nature from material, industrial productivity. Concretely speaking, it represents the development of information productivity due to a combination of computer and communications technologies—a development of a new type of productivity of intangible information. If we accept the supposition that there are close relationships between the development of productivity and the birth of new theories of economics, this supposition may analogically apply to the formulation of information economics as a new theory of economics.

In addition, information economics is strongly marked by its character as a futurist economics. Among the existing theories of economics, Marxist economics is marked more than the other theories by its nature as a futurist economics. Our era is very like the time when Karl Marx wrote his *Capital,* when the Industrial Revolution was entering the stage of rapid growth. Similarly, the information revolution based on computer and communications technologies has just begun and is expected to develop fully in the twenty-first century.

The Triple Concept of Information Economics

Three basic concepts of economics constitute the conceptual framework of information economics. The first of these is globalism as the spirit of the time; the second is time-value as a new concept of human value; and the third is information productivity as a core of the new economics.

Globalism as the Spirit of the Time

The first of the frameworks that constitute information economics is *globalism.* Each new economics has its own spirit of the time corresponding to it. Smith's economics is based on the justice of bourgeois society, and Ricardo's on the economic thought of capitalism. Thus their economic theories incorporate the thoughts of the time as their ideological backgrounds.

However, in building up the framework of information economics, it is necessary to base them not on a spirit of a relatively short period of time, as in the case of existing economic theories, but on a spirit or thought of a longer period of time, for it is an entirely new economics, overriding all of the classical and neoclassical economic theories.

If we examine the spirit of the time (*Zeitgeist*) common to all of the classical economic theories from this standpoint, we may say that the spirit of the Renaissance is the ideological pillar of the economic theories corresponding to industrial society.

The Renaissance, which arose in Western Europe in the fifteenth and sixteenth centuries, represents the emergence of a new society to replace the old medieval social system, and it brought with it an expansion of the cultural and social environments. The spirit of the Renaissance was based on a change in values from belief in a future existence to the pursuit of earthly pleasures, from medieval doctrines and stoicism to the liberation of man, and the thought of the time was that of humanism, calling for human dignity and the independence and freedom of individuals.

It was on the basis of this spirit of the times as its ideological support, on the one hand, and on the basis of the remarkable development of material production through the Industrial Revolution, notably through the invention of the steam engine and machinery as its technological basis, on the other, that the classical school of economics was formed.

Then what is the spirit or thought of the time that provides the ideological support for information economics, when viewed from a similar standpoint? The spirit of the time, which should be the ideological backbone of information economics, I consider, is *globalism*, and the thought of the time is *coexistentialism*.

The spirit of globalism is the spirit of a neo-Renaissance in that it appears in the process of transition from the old industrial social system to an information-oriented social system and that it aims at the further liberation of man. However, as the historical background to information economics differs entirely from that to the classical school of economics, the neo-Renaissance is basically different from the Renaissance in character and content.

The first characteristic feature of globalism is the space-ship idea. If we think of the Renaissance as an era of explosion, the neo-Renaissance is an era of implosion. There are no longer territorial frontiers for mankind. This is graphically illustrated by the shortage of natural resources. Particularly noteworthy is the shortage of fossil fuels and metals, beginning with petroleum, copper, and lead. This makes us recognize as a realistic problem the appearance of an entirely new situation after the Industrial Revolution—a situation in which even if industrial productivity is increased and if man's material expectations are raised in the future, industrial production will sooner or later level off because of the shortages of raw materials.

Mankind succeeded in soft-landing on the moon. However, it is impossible to settle tens of thousands of people on the moon, though it was possible to do so on the North American continent when it was discovered. There is no alternative for the 3,500 million people of the earth but to find their destiny on this closed planet called the earth. Here is the historical background to the formation of the "spaceship earth" idea.

The second characteristic is coexistentialism. This is the idea of peaceful coexistence of mankind and nature, a new thought of the time, overriding liberalism and individualism. The historical bcckground to this is the development of ultimate sciences and the appearance of pollution problems. The first appearance of an ultimate science was the harnessing of the power of the atom. The development of atomic energy, which threatened to extirpate mankind in a thermonuclear war, led to the realization of a peaceful coexistence system between the United States and the Soviet Union, overriding ideological differences, through a curb on nuclear weapons. The subsequent development of ultimate biological sciences, including the conversion of chromosomes and artificial impregnation, make it urgently necessary for us to establish a new view of ethics, particularly with respect to the ultimate problem of life.

The essence of pollution problems lies in the enormous industrial productivity based on the utilization of science and technology with mass production and mass consumption based on the emergence of a society of high mass consumption. The consequent discharge of large quantities of industrial and consumption wastes are causing damage to nature and environmental disruption, so that a serious danger is now posed to the normal life and health of human beings. The appearance of pollution and damage to nature have created the new science of ecology and have given rise to the idea of coexistence of nature and man.

The third point is the quality of life, which represents a change from material value to human value. The spirit of the Renaissance gave rise to values based on materialism and the pursuit of earthly pleasures; and the industrial society produced large quantities of consumer goods, resulting in the so-called society of high mass consumption. Today, however, because of aggravating pollution, shortages of resources, the tendency of the marginal utility of material values to decline, and the appearance of an administered sector in the private enterprise system, values are tending to change in the direction of attaching more weight to human values than to material values. Thus, the desire for a new human emancipation, expanded social welfare, the search for a life worth living—or, in other words, improved quality of life—will form the center of the new values.

In this way, modern thought, originating in the Renaissance and based on the material view of values, liberalism and individualism, is losing its historical significance, and is being replaced by globalism as a new spirit of the time, based on the ideas of quality of life and coexistentialism.

Information Productivity as the Core of Information Economics

The second of the frameworks that constitute information economics is *information productivity*. The greatest characteristic feature of information economics is that it is based not on material productivity, as are the conventional theories of economics, but on information productivity.

It is true that various information media such as newspapers, radio, TV, books, etc., have economic value and are functioning in the national economy, but these kinds of information carry far less weight in economic value than material products. However, the information revolution through computer and communications technologies will heighten information productivity by leaps and bounds so that there is a possibility that the production of information values will exceed that of material values.

The first historical significance to economics of the development of computer and communications technologies lies in the mass production of original information by an electronic device. We may cite the language, writing, printing, and communications revolutions as the four information revolutions in the past. In each of these revolutions, information itself was created by the human brain. However, the appearance of computers has made it possible for man to create original information by an electronic device.

The computer is an electronic device which can mass-produce original information electronically if it is fed with data and programs. The computer is thousands or hundreds of thousands of times superior to man's brain in information productivity. The increase in material productivity made possible through the invention of steam engines and machinery in the Industrial Revolution was on the order of hundreds of multiplications at most. As compared with this, the increase in the scale of information productivity by means of computers is incomparably large.

The second economic significance of the development of computer communications technologies lies in automatic control and feedback. Computer communications technologies are capable of automation functions incomparably more versatile than conventional mechanical automation.

First, they are capable of automatic production and services. Industrial production is precisely the process by which natural resources are worked upon to be turned into useful goods through the application of the natural sciences, while the computer is capable of performing the function of quickly feeding back to production changes arising in production processes. Computer automation began with numerical control and is now being applied to control of groups of systems and even to the whole of an entire production process. In the near future, a fully automated factory will become a reality. Further, in the area of services to human beings, various kinds of automatic service equipment such as automatic vending machines and cash dispensers are taking the place of human service labor.

Second, the computer replaces man's intellectual labor. Where human intellectual labor is performed according to certain logic procedures, the computer can replace it by programming such logic procedures. Thus, automation is already being introduced into fairly broad areas of human intellectual labor such as design automation, accounting, and the diagnosis of patients suffering from cardiovascular ailments. If human decision-making processes become more scientific and logical in the future, fairly sophisticated intellectual human labor may be automated or semi-automated.

Third, the computer is capable of automatic control of systems. This does not mean control of and feedback for individual functions, but automation of systems through an organic combination of subautomation functions. Such systems-oriented automatic control overrides restrictions due to spatial distances. (Note, for instance, passenger-seat booking systems for airline companies.)

In this way, the development of automation centered on computer communications technologies will have a tremendous social impact, liberating people from their places of production and enabling them to enjoy much more free time. Whether automation will cause unemployment or increase free time is a major problem for the future information-oriented society to solve. However, just as, in past history, development of productivity ultimately led to an increase not in unemployment but in income and free time, automation due to development of information productivity in the future will benefit mankind not only in the form of increased income but also in the form of increased free time such as shorter working hours and a three-day week.

This is due to restrictions imposed by limited natural resources and also to a limit to the quantitative expansion of material production.

The third significance to economics of computer and communication technologies is the production of qualitatively higher knowledge-oriented information. The application of computer and communication technologies not only has made it possible to mass-produce knowledge-oriented information by an electronic device but also has made it possible to largely exceed man's limits in the qualitative productivity of information.

First, it is custom-made information meeting individual needs. The printing and communications revolutions made it possible to mass-produce information. But these revolutions were based on the production of copies of the same information. The computer permits the production of information meeting the diverse requirements of different persons and organizations.

Second, the computer permits the production of compound information. It can produce higher-quality organic and compound information by processing hundreds and thousands of data different in nature but mutually related. Further, the information thus provided can be fed back to achieve a purpose according to changes in the situation.

Third, the computer makes it possible to produce normative information, that is, information which will enable us to get a conceptual picture or vision of something desirable and feasible in the future.

Meanwhile, production of highly systems-oriented, knowledge-oriented information called compound information has made possible the solution of complex socio-economic problems, which was impossible in the past.

Any of such difficult problems as inflation, environmental damage, or shortage of natural resources confronting all countries of the world is beyond the limits of man's intellectual capacity in its scale and complexity. But if man's thinking and intuitive capacity were well combined with computer communications technologies, it would be possible to delve into the very nature of such a problem and get a clear picture of it in its entirely and its future trends, and also to go a step further and create a compound system as a foundation for its possible solution.

Here, development of a new social system must be attributed to the social transformational impacts of a marked expansion of man's knowledge-creation capacity. Particularly, the two areas of medical care and education will be radically transformed. The system of medical care will be based on broad area health-maintenance systems, emergency medical-care systems, and medical-care systems for isolated islands and areas, while the education system will be radically changed from "teaching" to "self-learning," from "collective education" to a "personal type of education," from "cramming" to a "problem-solving type of education."

The second impact will be an increase in lifetime value. People's general pattern of behavior will be to engage in more purposeful acts because of the amplification of their objective-attaining ability. By so doing it will be possible for people to make their lifetimes more worthwhile.

The fourth significance to economics of computer and communication technologies is the public utilization of information. The public utilization of information will be made possible through a combination of computers and communications networks. Such information networks—which are to be formed through a combination of superlarge capacity, real-time, on-line computers and time-sharing systems and highly advanced communications technologies such as broad-band communication lines and communication satellites—are marked by qualitatively high functions such as (1) real-time centralized information processing, (2) real-time diffusion of information, (3) both-ways feedback, (4) real-time response. Particularly, the appearance of communication satellites has made possible the formation of a global information network.

The formation of such an information network will promote public utilization of information and will make it possible for any person to utilize necessary information anytime, anywhere, at low cost.

The production cost of information is characterized by the fact that its initial cost is relatively high and that its marginal costs are substantially reduced as the volume of production increases. In the case of material production, when a product is manufactured additionally, certain amounts of raw materials corresponding to the product are needed. However, in the case of the production of information, it is possible to produce it at its processing costs plus something, because of the unconsumable and nontransformable characteristics of information value. Particularly in the case of the production of knowledge-oriented information for public purposes, this tendency becomes more marked. This lowered production cost through accumulative production is a decisive factor for promoting the effective utilization of information.

The first effect of public utilization of information is the expansion of education opportunities. It will make it possible for any person to utilize intellectual information freely any time, anywhere, and for education to be liberated from restrictions imposed by income, place, and time. As a result, educational opportunities will be greatly expanded.

The second effect is the improvement of participatory activity. Future public information utilities will be a tool not only for mass sharing of information but also for reflecting citizens' will in politics and administration, for information utilities make it possible to realize both-ways feedback of information, to and from large numbers of people.

The third effect is enlarged options in career selection and use of time. People will be able to obtain far more ample information quickly on the possibilities of their own occupations and new opportunities through information utilities. This naturally enlarges their options in the selection of their future directions in social life and also in the selection of their occupations, and will enable them to utilize their lifetimes all the more effectively.

In this way, the public utilization of information will have a tremendous impact on industrial society. One such impact will be the emergence of participatory democracy. Present-day parliamentary democracy based on indirect participation has already been reduced to something like a shell, and citizens' participation in politics and administration in the form of citizens' movements and autonomous management of local affairs is already being realized. This tendency will be further promoted through a system by which citizens' wishes may be reflected in politics and administration through information networks.

The second impact will be the establishment of a knowledge industry. The more the public utilization of information is expanded, the lower will be the cost of information, and the demand for information will increase all the more. In this process, a knowledge industry will make its appearance as a tertiary industry. The knowledge industry will consist of knowledge services in the narrow sense (education, intellectual services, research and development, etc.) and information services (information equipment, software, information-processing services, etc.), and will be a leading industry in the future.

The third impact is the flourishing of individuals' futualization. The word "futualization" is a portmanteau word from "future" and "actualization." This word means the self-actualization of people in the future through purposeful utilization of their lifetimes. Individuals' futualization is made possible only through the combined mutual effect of increased free time through automation, increased lifetime value through knowledge creation, and enlarged options in career selection and use of time through information utilization.

Time-Value as a New Concept of Human Value

The third of the frameworks that constitute information economics as a new economics is *time-value*. The theoretical system of information economics is established with a new concept of value—time-value—as its basic starting point, and this time-value is amplified only by the development of information productivity through computer and communications technologies. By time-value is meant the value that is created by man when he spends his free time in a purposeful way. To begin with, time is an intangible, abstract concept, and it in itself means the passage of time. However, we regard it as man's lifetime, and if man uses his time for the satisfaction of his wants, time produces use-value.

The development of information productivity through computer and communications technologies has given rise to a new basic concept of economics—time-value, to take the place of material value. In the following, we will explain the relations between information productivity and time-value—on how the development of information productivity produces time-value.

The first point is the increased effectiveness of purposeful action. Computer and communications technologies make it possible to mass-produce objective-oriented, logical and action-selective information. As a result, the effectiveness of our purposeful action is remarkably increased. This change in our pattern of action necessarily tends to make us attach more importance to time-value, or effective utilization of time.

The second point is the importance attached to time as a necessary ingredient of a compound process. Knowledge-oriented information created by computer and communications technologies is characterized by the fact that it is compound and normative information. Such information largely removes limitations on the scale and time of our purposeful action, and in this way the process becomes an important factor for producing time-value. By "process" is meant here the occurrence in time of the interaction of a purposeful subject on the field or compound space on which the subject acts.

The third point is the increase in free time. Computer and communications technologies greatly increase automation functions in material production. Replacement of human feedback functions in material production promotes automation, liberates people from time restraints for material production, and further increases free time.

For these three reasons, a substantial improvement of information productivity through computer and communications technologies makes it possible to create new time-value to replace the conventional material value as a basic concept of economics.

Time-value, as seen from the standpoint of economics, consists of the three frameworks of the subject of action, field, and process. We introduce these troublesome concepts here because the nature of time-value becomes clear only when they are introduced.

Since time-value means the value created in the process of time expanded by purposeful action, the subject of purposeful action is needed so that time-value may be created. Further, in order that the subject of action may act in an objective-oriented way, the field on which the subject of action acts is needed. Further, relations between the subject of action and the field on which it acts change dynamically with the passage of time, and this is precisely the process.

As for the subject of action, that is, the subject which works on the field with objective-consciousness, it may be any individual, group of individuals, or organization engaging in social action with some objective: an individual, enterprise, nonprofit organization, local autonomous entity, government, state, consumer movement, or group of people engaged in a citizens' movement.

As for the concept of field, it is the space, with concrete content, on which the subject of action acts, conscious of its objective. However, the field in this case is not an objectively preexisting field, but is necessarily related to the working of the subject of action and also to reality.

Another new concept of field is the field of information space. This is the field provided in the new space which has never existed before and which is connected with networks of information. This field of information space is characterized by the following two features: (1) the field does not have boundaries like those of a territorial field, and (2) in this field, elements related by objective-oriented action are related to each other through information networks. The concept of field in information-oriented society will be represented more and more by this concept of information space.

As for the third concept of process, it is the development in time of a situation created artificially by the interaction between the purposeful action on the field of the subject of action and the reaction of the field to it, and it is regarded as the dynamic process of a system comprising both the subject of action and the field. By the artificially created situation is meant a situation purposively created by the objective-oriented action of the subject of action so that the objective may be attained.

Further, this process changes and develops dynamically with the passage of time, and it is characterized by the fact that it is finally completed. This is because the subject of action puts an end to its action when it attains its purpose or when it gives up attempting to attain its purpose.

The result of achievement produced from the frameworks—the subject of action, field, and process—is precisely time-value. Time-value is measured according to the degree and quality of the results achieved. Further, time-value may be the situation itself in which the process is terminated, or it may be the sum total of the value produced during the process, depending on the value judgment of the subject of action.

This time-value is on a higher plane in human life as compared with material value, the conventional basic value of economics. This is because time-value corresponds to the satisfaction of human and intellectual wants, in contrast to the fact that material value corresponds to the satisfaction of physiological and material wants. If we define physiological and instructive wants as primary wants, the desire to satisfy oneself through purposeful action may be called a secondary want.

In conclusion, it may be said that the increase in productivity of knowledge-oriented information is the only propelling force that can directly heighten time-value. Herein lies the reason why information economics has time-value—a new concept of economics—as its basic starting point.

The Law of Feed-forward as a New Principle of Economics

In order that the future information economy may maintain its organic harmony as a national economy or as a global economy, there is need for a regulating framework in which order may be established in the economy as a whole according to its own law or by external law. As is well known, the motive of private enterprises to seek profits and the principle of free competition are regarded as the *prima mobile* of economic development in classical economics, and economic anarchy and confusion are considered to be automatically avoided by what Smith calls the unseen hand or by the operation of the law of prices, as a natural or divine law.

Then what is the regulating framework in information economics which is to replace the above law in classical economics? It is my view that individuals' selfish futualization motives and the law of "feed-forward" as the unseen hand will be a new framework for autonomous regulation.

As we have seen, by futualization is meant the creation and realization of people's own time-value through their objective-oriented acts, and we call the behavioral consciousness of such people "futualization motive." In a future information society, not the satisfaction of material wants but the realization of their lifetime value will be the basic desire of people, and in a mature system of information economy people will spend only a small part of their time for the sake of subsistence (or labor for acquiring goods necessary for their living) and set aside a larger part of the remaining free time for the satisfaction of their desire for futualization.

The big-leap development of information productivity 1) promotes automation of production and services, and 2) this in turn results in shortening working hours and increasing free time, and at the same time, 3) mass production of normative and compound information and its public utilization will become general, 4) which will help raise the probability of people's objective-oriented acts being accomplished.

However, free social acts and economic operations based on individuals' futualization motives may be reasonable in their own individual ways, but, viewed as a whole, these countless selfish futualization acts may produce socially harmful results. Therefore, there is a need for regulation of some kind to maintain social and economic order. And the first principle of information economics that makes this possible is the law of feed-forward.

By *feed-forward* is meant the control by the subject of action of the direction and method of its action toward the objective to be attained. In short, the law of feed-forward is the law of objective-oriented control.

It is possible to grasp the general idea of "feed-forward" if you remember an urban traffic control system. Just as a driver drives his car to his destination, guided by red and green signals at the intersections, a person may be able constantly to control his object-oriented acts according to a variety of signals provided by various kinds of public information networks, promoting his own futualization and avoiding a clash with others' futualization acts in this way.

So that this low of feed-forward may be carried through, at least the following five conditions must to be met:

1) Formation of nationwide information networks;

2) Proper operation of forecasting and forewarning systems to communicate to citizens all the information necessary for the general maintenance of social and economic order;

3) Establishment of a system which will enable all the citizens concerned to participate in the management of such information systems or networks;

4) Accessibility to all citizens as utilities of these information systems or networks; and

5) Constant attention of all citizens to signals and information

from these forecasting and forewarning systems and autonomous control over acts against this through self-regulation.

The most difficult conditions to meet among these five are 2) and 5). First, is it possible to develop a forecasting and forewarning system for the maintenance of general social and economic order? Further, even if such a system is developed and operated, will all the individual citizens autonomously control their objective-oriented acts according to information provided by such a system? Whether or not citizens can carry out their autonomous control completely is relevant to the question of whether or not the law of feed-forward can be carried through. It is because of this that the third condition—participation of all citizens in the management of forecasting and forewarning systems—is of special significance.

In case social regulation of some kind or another is considered necessary, all the persons concerned are required to continue serious discussion and debate until they reach a general agreement. In case all the people concerned reach an agreement and make a decision, they are required to observe the decision as their rule. This is the most important and basic condition for the establishment of the law of feed-forward, and at the same time the basis of participatory democracy as a new democracy for the information society.

Further, the need for the improvement and development of citizens' behavioral consciousness should be emphasized here. The expansion of consciousness from individuals' futualization motives to collective futualization motives should be emphasized here as another important condition necessary for the establishment of the law of feed-forward.

As is clear from the words, individuals' futualization motives are the motives of futualization based on individuals' personal motives. We can speak of individuals' futualization motives when futualization is based on personal motives, and these motives are the starting point of the realization of time-value.

However, individuals' futualization is self-assertive and externally disturbing. Thus, the more a person, as the subject of action, ignores the conditions under which he is required to work, the greater is the probability of his success in his attempts at futualization. If he adjusts his futualization motives according to the conditions under which he works, the results he obtains will not be satisfactory to him, even if he succeeds in attaining his objective. Therefore, so that he may attain futualization by changing conditions in a way desirable to him, it is necessary for him to confine his futualization motives to a small area where he is less related to society. In short, he is compelled to engage in independent labor like Robinson Crusoe, who had to lead a completely self-sufficient life.

The only way to break and overcome this antinomical self-assertion is to endeavor to unify individuals' futualization and collective futualization—the setting of an objective common to a large number of people and the attainment of the objective through their participation and synergy. Collective futualization can be unified with individuals' futualization when the following three conditions are met:

1) The general direction of collective futualization coincides with individuals' futualization desires.

2) Individuals participate in collective futualization through their free will.

3) Individuals participate autonomously in the social labor allotted to them in the process of collective futualization.

The prototype of this kind of collective futualization will present itself in two different patterns. One is participation in enterprise activities in the form of autonomous labor. For instance, people with one and the same enterprise objective will gather to establish a venture business, with each person functioning and engaging in his respective field in enterprise activities according to his ability and conditions and sharing enterprise risks with others. The management policy of the enterprise and the distribution of profits and losses are decided through the general consent of all the participants.

The other pattern of collective futualization is participation in autonomous public social labor. Probably, people will participate in this kind of social labor by spending part of their free time on it, and their labor will be offered without compensation. The major social change that will take place in this connection is one in the relationship between autonomous administration and citizens' life. This will take the form not only of citizens' participation in the planning of the public enterprises of local autonomous entities but also of citizens taking upon themselves the partial or complete execution or management of such enterprises. In this way, autonomous control by citizens of roads, parks, schools, hospitals, and other institutions will become general.

When this collective futualization reaches a certain stage of development, voluntary communities will be developed sooner or later. By voluntary communities is meant a community in which citizens will participate voluntarily under a common objective and which will be created by such citizens' synergy. This shows, so to speak, one of the peaks of social futualization. Collective futualization will at first take the form of accomplishment of a common objective by a number of people and will be carried out independently by individual persons. But this will gradually develop into a concept of voluntary community, and this differs essentially from autonomous control by citizens of local autonomous entities in that it is not autonomous management within the framework of existing administrative organizations; rather people seeking to attain the same objective gather to form their own community, unhindered by existing organizations or frameworks.

Probably the future information society will be constituted as an assemblage of a large number of such voluntary communities. This anticipates the emergence of an autonomous, decentralized state as opposed to the centralized modern state in present-day industrial society. Further, the formation of communities of such relatively small social groups will facilitate the accomplishment of the law of feed-forward, for it is desirable that social order will be maintained in respective communities autonomously.

When individuals' futualization is developed into collective futualization and further into social futualization in the above-mentioned way, it will become possible for the law of feed-forward to avoid social and economic disorder and confusion that may be caused by individuals' selfish futualization motives in the information economy and to maintain society as a whole without disrupting orderly, organic inter-relations.

What we must emphasize here is the fact that the law of feed-forward is an autonomous regulation based on individuals' consent and autonomous participation and is entirely different in nature from external compulsion by law or power.

A Global Futualization Society as a Vision of Information Economics

The above is a general outline of the conceptual frameworks that constitute my information economics. Further, I must add some explanations of the vision of information economics. Since a new theory of economics is based on a new spirit of the time and a new development of productivity, it is natural to think that a new vision is born with it.

I am particularly interested in Smith's vision as a vision of economics. In his draft copy of *The Wealth of Nations*, he introduces a vision of a "universal opulence society." His universal opulence society is the society in which almost all people are provided with economic conditions which enable them not merely to enrich their material living standards but also to liberate themselves from dependence and subordination and to gain independence for autonomous action.

Adam Smith's vision of universal opulence is based on the thought of his time, "justice in the bourgeois society," and on "labor productivity with division of labor as its technical basis" as a basic concept of economics. Then, what is the vision of information economics? In this case, I would like to present a "Global Futualization Society" as its vision.

We may define the Global Futualization Society as the society where a large variety of voluntary communities will flourish on a global scale, and where these semi-independent autonomous communities are maintained harmoniously as a whole while individual citizens, of whom each community is constituted, will satisfy their own futualization desires.

This global futualization society is a far-reaching utopian vision of man's destiny. The global futualization society is the farthest end to which mankind will attain, as the global futualization society, starting originally as individuals' futualization—individuals' completely autonomous futualization—develops into collective and social futualization.

Let me here draw a bold vision of a Global Futualization Society.

(1) The ideas of globalism, time-value, and objective-oriented behavior will be our common, universal social concepts.

(2) A large variety of voluntary communities such as regional voluntary communities, voluntary enterprise communities, and voluntary information space communities will be the core social organizations, while states, provinces, and other territorial administrative organizations will be reduced to shells or become virtually extinct.

(3) Each person, while seeking to fulfill his futualization desire through his objective-oriented action, participates socially in one or more voluntary communities and works together with other people, and participates voluntarily in the attainment of objectives common to mankind as a member of the global society.

(4) A global information center is established, which functions as a forecasting and forewarning system for the maintenance of a global socioeconomic order, including the questions of securing basic natural resources, adjusting population, and conserving the natural environment.

(5) There will be a global education system, which will make 90 percent of the total population of the world literate. This will make a measurable contribution toward eliminating the cultural and economic gaps between people in the North and those in the South. When a

global education system is realized people will be speaking some kind of international language, distinct from Esperanto.

(6) There will be realized a global medical-care system, which will eliminate leprosy, smallpox, and indigenous diseases, and serve to lengthen man's average life span to more than 80 years.

The realization of this Global Futualization Society is the greatest vision for the 3.5 billion members of the human race on this crowded spaceship in the remaining quarter of this century through the twenty-first century.

Appendix A: Information Economics Compared with Classical Economics

Differences between the classical school of economics and information economics are compared below in an itemized way, as it will be in this way that the entire system of information economics will be grasped more clearly.

(1) The classical school of economics had the spirit of the Renaissance and the ideas of humanism as its ideological support, and its technical basis was the development of material productivity through the Industrial Revolution.

(2) Its basic concept of economy lay in the realization of material values, which was made possible through the production, sale, and consumption of useful goods as commodities.

(3) The production of useful goods is a process by which natural resources are turned into useful goods through the application of scientific rules to natural resources. Industrial productivity was greatly raised as this process took the form of industrial production utilizing the steam engine and machines.

(4) Further, production of useful goods as commodities was carried out in the economic system characterized by the free competition of private enterprises and the principle of profit-making.

(5) Later, industrial production entered the stage of mass production of manufactured goods, which attained the stage of mass consumption, supported by democratic ideas and trade unionism. This process led to the realization of high mass consumption societies in industrially advanced countries.

(6) However, mass production and mass consumption produced large quantities of industrial and consumption wastes, causing pollution and environmental disruption.

(7) Further, mass production and mass consumption have caused

shortages of natural resources, making it clear to all eyes that petroleum, copper, lead, and other natural resources are limited. This situation signifies a fatal limit of the classical school of economics based on the development of material productivity.

The above is a historical survey of the classical school of economics from its appearance up to the present day. In contrast to this, the expected future development of information economics will be marked by the following features.

(1) Information economics has the spirit of globalism and the idea of coexistentialism as its ideological supports, and its technical basis is the development of information productivity through the information revolution.

(2) Its basic concept of economy lies in the realization of time-value, which is made possible through the production, distribution, and utilization of information as an economic value.

(3) In the past, production of information was carried out by brainwork, that is, through man's intellectual thinking, but the appearance of computer and communications technologies has made electronic production of information possible and has resulted in remarkably raising information productivity.

(4) Later, electronic production of information will enter the stage of mass production, wider spread, and expansion through the establishment of time-sharing systems and formation of communication networks. This stage will sooner or later pass on to the stage of mass sharing of information through the development of computer utilities (or public utilization of computers).

(5) Further, computer and communications technologies will contribute to the development of pollution-free and resources-saving technologies and systems by being combined with systems sciences, and, in the future, will promote the development of ecological and recycling-oriented technologies and systems.

(6) In this way, mankind will enter an era of coexistence of man and nature on the globe as a spaceship, and will realize high futualization.

Appendix B: Development of Computerization

Information economics is future economics. It is necessary in this connection to ask historically at what stage we have arrived in the development of information productivity centered on computer and communications technologies and what direction information productivity will follow in the future. The first stage is that of megalo-science, in which computers were utilized on a large scale for state projects, such as national defense and space development projects. The second stage is that of enterprise-basis utilization of computers, in which private enterprises and government agencies utilize computers such as MIS's actively for the purpose of increasing management efficiency. The third stage is that of social-basis utilization of computers, in which computers will be extensively utilized for the improvement of medical care, education, and other social welfare activities. And the last, fourth, stage is that of individual-basis utilization of computers, in which individuals will engage in knowledge creation, utilizing computer utilities by means of man-to-machine systems. Viewed internationally, it may be said, we are, in the 1970s, in a transitional stage from the second stage of enterprise-basis utilization to the third stage of social-basis computerization.

Appendix C: Tempo Comparison of the Power and Information Revolutions

Now let us examine the tempo of development of power technology, which provided the basis for the power revolution. It was in 1708 that the first Newcomen steam engine was developed, which kicked off the power revolution. This was followed by the invention of a more efficient steam engine by James Watt in 1775. The first railway came into existence in 1829, the first motor car in 1909, and the first jet plane in 1937. There is a passage of time of about 230 years from the Newcomen engine to the jet plane.

Now let us see how rapidly information technology, centered on computers, has developed. The first-generation computer made its debut in 1942, and the first on-line system was developed in 1957. The first information network came into existence in 1970, and it is estimated that the first information utility will be formed in 1990 or thereabout. Thus, it will take only 48 years for computer technology to mature. In this way, the tempo of development of information technology will be about four times higher than that of power technology.

Now let us examine these two kinds of technology with respect to the formation of transportation networks and communication networks.

The work on the construction of a transcontinental railway line in the United States was started in 1828 and completed in 1869; it took about 40 years. In comparison the start of a time-sharing system in the United States was around 1965, and it was about 1972 that the whole of the United States was covered with information networks. Thus it took only about seven years for the information networks to be completed in the United States. In this way, the passage of time required for the completion of the information networks was about one-sixth of that required for the completion of the transcontinental railway line.

Further, we can compare the manufacturing and information industries and estimate the time required for the formation of these industries. In the case of manufacturing industries, about two centuries passed from the development of the Newcomen engine in 1708 to the establishment of the motor industry in 1910 through the manufacture of the Model T Ford.

Let us compare this to the formation of the information or knowledge industry. It was in 1942 that the first ENIAC computer model made its debut, and it is estimated to be about 1985 or 1990 at the latest that the information industry will reach its stage of considerable development in the United States. The lapse of time between these is about 50 years, at most. Thus, the tempo of development is also four times faster here.

In this way, it may be estimated that the tempo of the information revolution is about four times higher than that of the power revolution.

The passage of time from the invention of the Newcomen steam engine to the start of the era of motorization in the United States, or what Professor Rostow calls the high mass consumption stage, is about 220 years. In contrast, if we suppose that it will take about one century, or about half of the above-mentioned passage of time, for the high mass knowledge creation stage to be reached, the information society will reach its period of maturity in about 2040, counting from the year 1942 when the first ENIAC model made its appearance.

THE INFORMATION SOCIETY: AN APPLICATION OF THE PATTERN MODEL TO INDUSTRIAL SOCIETY

YONEJI MASUDA

This paper deals with a method which utilizes model application of societal formation pattern by attempting to establish the conceptual framework of an information society beyond the industrial society.

Concretely, the model is the common and basic pattern which was witnessed in the formation process of the past agricultural society and the industrial society. In this manner, the framework of future society is constructed.

The Computer as the Motive Power for Future Society

This decisive starting point in forming a new societal system after clearing the old societal system is epochal technical innovation and rapid development of accompanying productive power. The revolutionary transformation from nomadic society to agricultural society resulted from development of agricultural technology which led to swift development of agricultural productive power. At the same time, the transformation to industrial society from the agricultural society was based on the development of the steam engine which led to rapid development of industrial production power.

What is the epochal technical innovation which will become the driving force in the transformation from the industrial society to the next stage? The answer is development of information processing technology centering on computers. A rapid growth of information production power is anticipated through this process.

Agricultural technology was based on productive power of land in ancient times. Added to this was the help of weather and other natural forces to raise the productivity of agricultural crops. In essence this was nothing more than reproduction of plants through effective use of natural phenomena. On the other hand, the emergence of industrial technology was based on the change in motive power from muscle and natural power to machine power. In addition, man succeeded in transforming natural resources into useful products through the development of natural science and application of natural laws.

Therefore, the basic difference between industrial technology and agricultural technology is that, while agriculture stopped at effective reproduction through application of natural phenomena, industrial technology made it possible to transform natural pehenomena. In other words, man was able to produce on a mass scale various types of useful industrial products which did not exist as natural objects before.

Independent and Systems-oriented Information for Rapid Growth of Knowledge Productivity

The basic function of the computer is data processing or production of information. This is combined with communications technology and systems science which is expected to lead to rapid development of information processing technology in the future. As a result, the production of information value is expected to greatly exceed production of industrial products in future society. A new society will be formed centering on information production. This is the information society.

The term "information" used here refers to target-oriented information, which is defined as "symbol pattern which has been evaluated toward a specified objective in human and social organization."[1]

There are two essential differences in the mass-produced information of the future society when compared to existing information. The first difference of character is independent selection. A typical example can be seen in newspaper reports. Mass communication information is passive and one-way traffic. It is uniform information and used only once.

In contrast, information produced by the computer is two-way: it makes possible question and answer exchange between the information supplier and user. Moreover, feedback is possible, and the information is tailor-made to respond to the specific needs of the user. The most conspicuous feature is that the information user becomes the constituent in information selection.

The second special character is the systems-oriented information of this process. "Systems mean to combine numerous useful elements which possess independent functions and to maintain interdependency

---

[1] "Introduction to Information Society Theory" by Kenichi Kohyama (Separate edition of 1968 Winter *Chuo Koron*).

among them. In general it points to something which is composed to demonstrate high-level functions along certain objectives."[2]

Therefore, systems information is a "useful information complex to serve in achieving a certain objective of human and social organization as a whole combining different individual information." This type of systems-oriented information will become the center of new productive power in the development and formation of the future society.

The productive power of information is concretely demonstrated by substitution and amplification of human brain work. Substitution for brain work is to use the computer to carry out human office management, calculation, labor supervision, judgment, business management, and other brain work.

In a manner similar to the motive power revolution, which saw human labor substituted by machines, the "brainy" robot is expected to take over in the information revolution. The computer will use freely the superior memory, calculation, and feedback functions of the computer and operate machines and handle office work. This will result in knowledge production power on a large scale and lead to rapid expansion.

At the same time, the unification of man and computer will lead to a new system which will deal in a rational way with such complex social phenomena as pollution and the commodity price problem as well as the anticipated development and growth of multi-functional industries such as the housing industry and space and ocean development. A remarkable development is expected in the qualitative improvement and expansion aspects of knowledge productivity.

In this manner the basic character of information production power lies in rapidly improving the qualitative and quantitative production of human knowledge. From this standpoint, there is a basic difference of direction, as agricultural production power and industrial production power were aimed at improvement of material productivity.

Multi-functional Society Leads to Release from Time Restrictions and Place of Production

One of the greatest impacts of the rapid development of information production power on society is that people will be released from limitations on place of production and from time restrictions.

In the case of the old agricultural system, production power depended decisively on land and weather conditions. As a result people

[2] "Introduction to Information Society Theory" (see note 1).

were restricted to the land and completely unable to escape from the conditions of seasonal time flow. Under the structure of this production power, farming centered on compulsory labor and a village-centered society was formed. This led to the establishment of permanent and traditional society. On this basis, the paternalistic status society was developed.

Industrial society, on the other hand, depended on motive power and science for industrial production power. This released people from the shackles of land and weather conditions. But the change restricted them to the establishment (enterprise, factory, hospital, and other facilities), and labor form changed from compulsory labor to employment labor.

The development of industrial production power resulted in concentration of capital and mass production under the principle of free competition. There was increasing expansion of establishment scale, and at the same time urbanization caused population concentration. During this process, there was an improvement in mankind's living standard and culture.

However, the establishment of mammoth enterprises and mass production of industrial products simplified human labor and furthered subordination to machinery. At the same time, overcrowding of cities led to housing difficulties and pollution problems which caused deterioration of the social environment. The result was human alienation in the controlled society.

In the case of the future information society, manual labor as well as brain work will be substituted by the computer. Furthermore, the functions of information media possessed by man will be replaced by information network systems which will free man from place of production and time restrictions.

The effects and changes on society brought about by the information system is epoch-making. First of all, the result will bring an end to the urbanization phenomenon. Most likely, there will be no concentration of business offices in the heart of the city in the future society. The rush hour crowding experienced by workers every morning in the commuter trains is expected to disappear in the future.

A major change will also take place in the educational system. There will be no school facilities for mass education and no uniform grade system as education will switch to individual learning by means of the computer dialogue method.

In this manner, people will be freed from the establishments which now serve as places of production. But these will be replaced by very close functional ties with affiliated management bodies. This is because people connected with such management bodies as specified enterprises, governments, and schools as well as facilities and resources will be functionally linked together far more than ever by means of systems-oriented information. The relation between the individual and the management body will be centered on projects and will change to contract labor. The working period will be in the form of project units which means that the ties between the individual and the management body will be fluid and temporary and change from project to project.

Since the information society is functionally linked together through systems-oriented information, it could be called functional society. This functional society is not merely a matter of systematic joining of fixed-order relations between managment bodies and industries. This is because even in each management body, the subfunction levels which compose management functions can directly join together systematically on a mutual basis.

In the case of business, for example, there will be a mutual tieup of various departments such as sales, production, accounting, and personnel through development of MIS (Management Information Systems). This horizontal management will be carried out not only in the top class, but at the various strata of the middle managment and operational levels as well.

As a result, the past vertical management system and the new horizontal management system will be combined into a multiple management system which is expected to become the general form of future business management. In this way, the functional society of the future will become a multifunctional society which resembles macromolecular structure.

Establishment of Society in which Man Himself Will Select and Design the Future

The second big impact produced by the rapid increase of information production power is the shift of economic activity from the production of useful goods to the production of function and systems.

For example, construction businesses which built warehouses in the past were merely building and selling the warehouses, which are useful facilities. However, in the information society, the warehouse business will be producing and selling an unattended warehouse system which is a complex functional system including an information system.

In the information society, production will center on information, but this does not mean that industrial production will be replaced with information production. The increase of information production power will result in further increase of industrial production power. Moreover, the weight of production of value on this basis will shift to production of systems from production of goods. This is the desired form of the information society.

If we view this change from the industrial structure side, two new epochal changes will be seen. The first is the emergence of the information and knowledge industry as the fourth industrial sector. Through the first industrial revolution of the past, manufacturing industry developed rapidly as the new secondary sector. In a similar manner, the result of the present second industrial revolution is predicted to lead to the development of the information and knowledge industry as the fourth sector.

It is anticipated that in the future the information industry will surpass manufacturing industry. The information industry can be broadly separated into the following three categories:

1) Information processing (calculation center, joint calculation center, etc.);
2) Information service (data bank, information service center, etc.);
3) Software (development of computer utilization technique such as programming).

At the same time, the knowledge industry will become a new industry which is formed by combining the past intellectual service industry with the information industy. The knowledge industry can be broadly divided into the following three categories:

1) Intellectual service (combining the information industry with newspaper, publication, and broadcasting activities);
2) Education (combining the information industry with education and consulting activities);
3) Research and development (combining the information industry with the research and development industry).

The second epochal change is the formation of a matrix industry structure through the development of systems industry. Systems industry is formed by combining the various existing industries on a multiple basis with the information industry forming the nucleus. This can be broadly divided into a functional industry and a complex systems industry.

Functional industry is established by joining the information industry with specialized manufacturing industries. The unattended warehouse system mentioned earlier is an example. In addition virtually all of the manufacturing industries, including machining centers and traffic control systems, etc., are expected to become part of functional industry in the future.

Complex systems industries will be formed by joining the information industry with several existing industries. The representative industries are ocean development, space development, housing, integrated transportation, the health industry, leisure industry, etc. These industries will eventually form mammoth industries on an independent basis.

Functional industry and complex systems industries are qualitatively different industries when compared to manufacturing industries according to products. The new matrix industrial structure is formed at this stage by combining functional industry with the complex systems industry. As a result a matrix industrial structure is formed, with the past industrial classification according to products serving as the ordinate axis and the systems industry forming the cross axis.

In this manner, the development process will lead to information industry, knowledge industry, functional industry, and complex systems industry in that order. This will result in rapid increase in the production of information, function, and systems and cause their production value to exceed the value of goods production.

The number of employees in these new industries is expected to eventually exceed the number of workers engaged in the goods and service industries. This type of society will form the future information society.

When the development of information production power, which makes possible functional and systems production, reaches a fixed stage, it will result in qualitative changes in information production power. At this stage man will have the potential to design and compose not only economic systems, but the human system and the social system as well.

This development will have great significance. The development of agricultural production power made possible effective reproduction possible through natural phenomenon while the development of industrial production power made it possible to transform natural phenomenon.

With the development of information production power today, it has become possible in part to transform natural phenomena on a large scale (e.g. development of canals through application of atomic energy). Moreover, it will become possible to transform even on a partial basis natural order and the system itself, and there are indications that it will become possible to freely design new human systems in the future.

The following are some of the concrete signs that have already started to appear:

1) The development of biological engineering, biochemistry, and other fields will make it possible to freely change human biological and physiological systems. This will enable parents to obtain male or female offspring as desired, and in the future it will become possible to control and change human heredity and the mechanisms of sense and feeling.

2) The development of environmental engineering and meteorological engineering will enable man to change the system of natural phenomena and create an artificial environment which will completely shut out weather and seasonal effects.

3) Since man will be able to utilize massive production and systems-oriented information, he will be able to destroy slums and building areas and design and build a completely new regional society.

Questioning Value Outlook and Strict Ethical Standards

The third major impact resulting from the rapid development of information production power is the change in human values and the ethical outlook. Concretely, there will be a change from material-oriented value standards to knowledge-creation-oriented value standards as well as a switch from negative ethical standards to strict ethical standards representing self-control and a sense of mission.

There have been historical changes in human value outlook and ethical view together with the development of production power. In the case of agricultural society centering on agricultural production power, it was difficult for people to exist without depending on natural power such as land and weather. Therefore, the natural system was the value of human standard itself. This resulted in the establishment of religion centering on Aristotelian universe views and the thinking standards of the medieval and ecclesiastical principle. Those who opposed and violated the law of the gods were classed as immoral and heathens.

On the other hand, man possessed the capacity to change natural phenomenon by applying natural science as a weapon in the industrial society. As a result the value standards changed from nature-centered to human-centered values. Accompanying this was the switch in value standards from spiritualism centering on future life to a life of pleasure centering on materialism.

In this manner, man no longer existed merely to maintain life; the human behavior principle centered more on satisfaction of sensual and emotional desires. Ethical standards then changed from abiding by the law of the gods to respect for human freedom and rights and protection of ownership rights.

With the establishment of the information society, man will be able to mass-produce useful goods on an unprecedented scale and make it possible to produce new social functions and systems through the rapid development of information production. Therefore, a natural result will be the historical necessity to adopt values and ethical standards which can cope with the new information society.

The old value outlook and ethical standards of the industrial society which is based on material satisfaction are being questioned today. Because of technological progress, people have virtually satisfied their physiological and material desires. In this sense the reason for existence of the value outlook centering on materialism has already been lost.

Democracy has based its principles on protection of individual freedom and rights as well as ownership rights. But the ethical standard of democracy is being confronted with a crisis from the logic of free democracy itself. Abundant consumer goods have satisfied individual desires, but such problems as traffic accidents caused by overcrowding of cities and housing shortages have created new social problems.

Furthermore, the increasing numbers of such decadent people as drug addicts are signs that mankind itself is declining. It has become impossible to prevent decadence through ethical standards such as guaranteeing individual freedom and rights. The destruction of ethical standards is attributed to the change in human relationships from attacker versus victim to attacker and victim at the same time.

What type of new value standards and ethical standards will be desired in the future information society?

In referring to value standards first of all, knowledge-creation is expected to replace past materialistic value standards. The knowledge-creation referred to here is not merely satisfying the biological desires of man. It is aimed at creation of a more human method of living as well as a social life which satisfies higher human desires.

In other words, it is the pursuit of a "purposeful life." A "purposeful life" means a deep emotion felt by man when he wholly and completely burns the various functions possessed by man to a point of sublimation. Moreover, "purposeful life" is achieved at a higher dimension when it exceeds the individual framework and possesses a social meaning. By pursuing this high-level "purposeful life" and producing knowledge-creation to realize this, people will be able to achieve new value standards in the future information society.

Naturally, there is need to cope with this new ethical standard which is based on the new value standard of knowledge-creation. In this case, man will be faced with the problem of accepting a strict ethical standard never before experienced by man. There are two reasons for this. The first is that man will have to be prepared for revenge from god when he shakes himself free from the natural system and attempts to design his own system. The second is that mankind has already developed extreme scientific powers which has enabled mankind to burn "the fire of heaven" (atomic energy) and fly to the moon.

These developments have a very serious meaning: in the event a new human society is designed through the use of information production power, there is the possibility of inviting a terrible result which could affect mankind's fate in case of error in choosing and designing a new human society. This is because the value outlook of knowledge-creation itself will be questioned.

As the first new ethical standard in the information society, strict self-control will replace respect for individual freedom and rights. The self-control mentioned here rejects freedom in no way. Instead, it means positive emphasis on freedom.

There are two sides to future freedom. Liberation from restraints is a negative side of freedom. The positive side of freedom is nothing more than choosing the future through a completely free intention. In carrying out this choice, man must sacrifice the possibility of other choices and impose self-restraint.

In case future choice exceeds the individual framework and is fixed on a social target, the partial share of the complex function must be borne in order to achieve the target. In this case the restraint from functional participation means that a double restraint must be borne. Furthermore, a more severe self-control is sought when man himself attempts to design the system of future society.

Mankind must adopt a modest attitude toward the natural system. The huge materialistic production power already developed has destroyed the natural environment, and people should bear in mind that this has led to retaliation in the form of pollution. The idea of harmony with the natural system and coexistence is nothing more than carrying out the ethical standard which means self-control.

The second ethical standard of the new information society is the sense of mission. When burning desire unites with the sense of responsibility, the result is a sense of mission.

Only through the support of strict ethical standards will it be possible for man to realize, for the first time, development of a new dynamic society centering on knowledge-creation.

At various stages of history, people have made various choices whenever a prosperous society was formed. The ancient Greeks built a magnificent shrine to honor Apollo and carved a beautiful statue of Venus. The Egyptians build huge pyramids for their Pharaohs while the Romans built the Coliseum to watch slaughters. The Chinese constructed the Great Wall to keep out invaders. What type of knowledge-creation society will the culture which developed the atomic energy and reached the moon build in the twenty-first century?

Fortunately, while man is standing at the dawn of the change from the industrial society to the information society, there are many big projects of worth which will be based on new values and ethical standards.

People will have information production power at their command to tackle such problems as death-dealing cancer, urban pollution and overcrowding, and poverty and endemic diseases in nations which are isolated from technological innovation. With this power, man himself will able to design new systems as mankind marches toward the twenty-first century, which could be called the historic age of choice.

The question asked of mankind today is not for "what purpose man is living" from the standpoint of philosophical proposition, but "how should man live" from the standpoint of human wisdom.

VALUES, DEMANDS, AND SCENARIOS

YASUSUKE MURAKAMI

Value change has been a key factor in each turn of history. Probably we are now in one of those turns. Through the unprecedented economic prosperity after World War II, the modern industrial world has now achieved freedom from the toils and pains of living—the freedom which mankind has always been looking for throughout its history. Now in advanced industrial societies (AIS) almost no one is worried about tomorrow's bread and housing. This experience, entirely new to mankind, is very likely to result in some basic changes in values and behavior patterns.

Hannah Arendt once warned that "such a [consumers' or laborers'] society, dazzled by its growing affluence and caught in the smooth functioning of a never-ending process, would no longer be able to recognize its own futility" (Arendt, 1958, p. 135). Yet what we have observed in the last decade is a growing anxiety that industrialization might be futile after all, and its very success might undermine its foundation. In order to give expression to what is emerging in people's value orientations, many terms have been invented such as "postindustrial," "post-bourgeois," "post-material," "expressive," "consummatory," "non-exploitative," "non-acquisitive," "quantity-to-quality," "communal," etc. Each of these concepts attempts to express a change in each component of the system of industrialism. These terms are indeed correlated, but they are not identical nor even consistent. In what follows, we attempt to present an exposition which is to fit various value components into one consistent scheme.

As distinct from *value change*, we might also highlight the problem of *demand change*. Demand may be defined as man's actual attempt to specify necessary physcial and human means in order to attain his own goal under such situational impacts as income change, price change, etc., whereas value may be defined as man's commitment to certain norms or criteria which he thinks of as universal. Value refers to a potential or latent framework behind man's actual efforts to realize his own demand. Value and demand are not always consistent, but they cannot continue to be inconsistent for very long. In what follows, we shall see what kind of demand change is occurring and how it is about to interact with value change.

Thus, if the value system of the advanced industrial society is to show a basic change and its demand pattern is also subject to major changes, some restructuring of the social system may well be necessary. A society is a "self-organizing system" so that its future is open to choice and uncertain. Hence, necessary restructuring can be shown only as alternative scenarios. Towards the end of this essay, I try to present some such scenarios.

Three Components of a Value System

Components and Strata

In order to study the problem of value and its change, let us here present a conceptual scheme of three axes: (1) activism *versus* passivism; (b) individualism *versus* collectivism; and (c) instrumentalism *versus* "consummatorism."

The first two axes, (a) and (b), represent man's basic attitude toward circumstances around him. The *active-passive* axis describes man's attitude toward the external world or "nature," namely, the non-human circumstances. The *individual-collective* axis portrays the individual's attitude toward other persons, namely, the human circumstances. The *instrumental "consummatory"* axis attempts to describe people's choices of mode of action.

(a) *What is activism?* By *activism* we mean here a desire and belief in man's ever-increasing control over the external world or "nature." Man is confronted with nature, yet he is deemed basically superior to nature or the world's master. This idea seems embedded in the Judeo-Christian religious tradition. In contrast, we may choose a world *passivism* to mean the idea that man is an integral part of nature just like other modes of existence such as animals, plants, or even inanimate materials. In the Hindu and Buddhist cultures, man is in one phase of transmigration from some mode of existence to another.

It might be stated that originally man has both of these two orientations, activism and passivism. However, relative emphasis between these two ideas has been shifting from time to time or from society to society. The most important determinant throughout this shift of emphasis is probably the types of religion—particularly, a contrast between the Western-type religions such as the Judaic and the Christian (and probably the Islamic), and the Eastern-type religions such as the Hindu, the Buddhist, and the Confucian. The Western-type religions are based on the idea of a "personified creator-god," while the Eastern-type religions start from the idea of a "cosmological principle" such as *Brahman* in India or "Universe" in China. In the West, man is created as an image of the God (so that the God is psychologically an image of man), while man in the East shall merge in the cosmological order which is embodied in nature and society. These two main currents of historical religions seem to give rise to two contrasting attitudes toward nature.

(b) *What is collectivism?* Collectivism in the present context has no particular implication of socialist planning or similar practices. By *collectivism* we mean here that man's final identity is with some group or, as Talcott Parsons calls it, collectivity (Parsons, 1951, p. 41). If man is collectivist in this sense, he will sacrifice—for his collectivity—his own pleasure, his opinions, and, as a final test, possibly his life. Evidently, "sacrifice" is already an individualism-biased expression, because what he feels is not so much a sacrifice as a devotion to what will outlive him eternally. Such everlasting existence of collectivity is associated with such "natural" principles as kinship, co-territoriality, or cultural identity. Hence collectivism here is a sense of belonging to what the sociologists used to call a community or *Gemeinshaft.*

In this context also, man has two potential orientations, namely, that of self-actualization and that of belonging. Our individual-collective axis describes a spectrum of various mixtures of these two potential motives. Individualism in modern Europe is a polarization out of this mixture. A main source of this European individualism is, in my interpretation, again in the Judeo-Christian religious belief, in which each individual is directly faced with God in a voluntaristic (non-intellectualized) way. In contrast, the Eastern historical religions tend to emphasize an intellectualistic grasp of harmony between society and individual.

As a matter of historical fact, all cultures other than the modern European ones are more collectivist, although to different degrees. Every great civilization in the "agricultural stage" of the history of mankind was a society based on a combination of collectivism and individualism. In Greece and Rome, society was a two-level system of the *oikos* as a basic collectivity and the *polis* where each man—a head of *oikos*—actualized himself. In China, an enormous number in the lower-level subsystem called the *tsu* (a kind of patrilineal clan) were loosely controlled by the upper-level subsystems of the famous literate bureaucracy and the merchants' associations, where the principle of individual-based competition had primacy. Individualism in modern Europe is not a mere atavism from classical antiquity, but a product of crossbreeding of the Christian and the Greco-Roman (and probably the Germanic).

(c) *What is instrumentalism?* Mode of action may be classified as follows. Man's action may be called *instrumental* if it is a means or instrument to some end. On the other hand, an action is called "*consummatory*" or expressive if the action itself is an end and provides an immediate gratification to the actor. Hence delayed gratification characterizes the instrumental action. In the instrumental action, the actor distinguishes the means from the end, and he has to be aware of a causal relation from the means to the end. The category of *means and end* is essential.

An evident merit of instrumental action is that it may achieve outcomes which are far greater than those obtained by taking advantage of this causal relation. On the other hand, its demerit is a two-fold burden on the actor. First, it is costly for him to discover and confirm a necessary causal chain. Second, as causality is always uncertain, the actor has to bear the risk of failure. Therefore, as the knowledge of necessary causal relations is accumulated and becomes more certain, greater benefits can be expected from the instrumentalization of actions. Hence, what distinguishes man from other animals is an unceasing widening and deepening of instrumental actions, because man is the only animal that can accumulate and systematize his knowledge in terms of symbolic media. Another more popular way of saying this is that man is an animal with tools, because tool-making is one big step in man's process of instrumentalization. Instrumentality in action is an inherent characteristic of human beings.

However, instrumental action is not considered man's ultimate aim. As Aristotle said, "What is worthwhile pursuing for its own sake is more ultimate than what is worthwhile for the sake of other things" (*Ethica Nicomachea*, Book 1, Ch. 7). An instrumental action can be applied only to the world where the means-end category can be defined, and most typically to the world of fabrication or of *homo faber*. There are other spheres of human activities where instrumental actions are not so vital. On the one hand, within man's life processes such as consumption, procreation, and so on, his actions are mainly "consummatory" rather than instrumental. On the other hand, in his exchange of ideas and emotions—of understanding and sympathy—instrumental actions are hardly useful, because those human interactions are not subject to any definite causality. A concept of instrumentality has an unquestionable relevance to man as a builder or fabricator (namely, *homo faber*), but not to man as a biological being (*animal laborans*), nor to man as a mutual interactor (*homo symbolicus*).

We may give the term *instrumentalism* to an attitude which causes the range of instrumental actions to be widened and deep-ended, probably beyond the domain of *homo faber*. Conversely, the term *consummatorism* may be given to the opposite attiude which causes the range of applications to be narrowed; "consummatorism" is defined as anti-instrumentalism.

Instrumentalism or "consummatorism" is, in fact, a kind of norm or value, since it actually regulates man's pattern of actions. However, instrumentalism can hardly be an ultimate value, because any instrumental action needs a specification of an end which only some deeper value can offer. For historical examples, it may be said that a declared ultimate aim of modern instrumentalism was, at the outset, the God in the Protestant conception; later it was the greatest happiness; then the survival of mankind; and so forth. In this sense, we may say that the instrumental-"consummatory" axis belongs to the superficial or less deep stratum of the value system as a whole, while the active-passive axis and the individual-collective axis belong to the deeper strata.

(d) *How do value systems change?* In answering this big question, we have to start by pointing out and examining preliminarily some related issues. One of these issues is Abraham Maslow's (1954) approach or its recent extension by Ronald Inglehart (1977). Maslow argued that people pursue a number of different "needs" in a hierarchical order, according to their urgency for survival. Most urgent is, as he calls it, "the sustenance need," and "the safety need" comes second. Inglehart groups these two kinds of needs as the *materialist* or physiological needs. Then, as the third priority, "the need for love, belonging and esteem" is pursued, and finally "the aesthetic and intellectual need" comes to the fore. The third and fourth kinds of needs are grouped by Inglehart as the *post-materialist* needs. Maslow's priority hierarchy is primarily a scheme to explain changes in "needs" (demands in our present terms), yet Inglehart tries to use Maslow's scheme for value changes.

It seems important to distinguish between *values* and *demands* (Maslow's needs may be identified with demands in our terms). Each person's system of values is a broad potential frame of reference. On the other hand, his demands are the responses to various situational impacts within the framework of values and institutions. For example, one's demands or "needs" can change only due to situational impacts such as an income rise to the level of affluence, even if one's value system remains unchanged. In other words, if a person's income were again to be lowered, an old pattern of demands would reappear provided that the underlying value system had not undergone any change. Change in demand (or "need" in Maslow's term) does not always imply change in values.

We can agree with Maslow or Inglehart that, if the urgency for survival is relaxed, say, by a substantial rise in income, then the demands will become post-materialist rather than materialist or physiological. It may be held that a change from materialist to post-materialist is, as I will argue, a shift from *basic* demands to *selective* demands; recent value changes, if at all, cannot be summarized as a shift from materialistic concern to an idealistic one. More specifically, the priorities among post-materialist demands are not so definitive as Maslow supposed. The priorities depend on the type of value system or basic culture. Maslow viewed "the self-actualization need (the aesthetic and intellectual need)" as the ultimate demand, yet his view probably reflected an individualism of European origin. We shall later attempt to show that the priorities among "post-materialist needs" or selective demands in our terms depend on the kind of underlying values, i.e., whether instrumentalism or "consummatorism" dominates.

How do value systems change? In trying again to answer this, let us here suppose two tentative hypotheses of value dynamics in terms of three value axes. The first hypothesis concerns a distinction between a radical change and a gradual change. If an impact on the value system is acute, strong, and articulate, then it will penetrate into the core of people's way of thinking and change the deeper strata of the value system so that the whole value system may be subverted. On the other hand, if the impact is moderate, chronic, and blurred, then the value change is likely to start—probably *via* demand changes—at the surface and then spread to the deeper strata. As we will see later, many changes in the coming stage of industrial society seem to be chronic rather than acute so that the emerging value changes will follow the pattern of gradual change. Thus our first hypothesis of value dynamics is that value changes will be first observed on the instrumental-"consummatory" axis, but there will be a lagged response for the more profound change of value on the active-passive axis and the individual-collective axis.

Our second tentative hypothesis concerns a coherence inside the value system. In our first hypothesis, we supposed that the value change will start on the instrumental-"consummatory" axis. The second hypothesis then supposes that some adjusting changes will occur on the other two axes; more specifically, activism and individualism will adjust themselves to the decline of instrumentalism. A piling up of such adjustments may ultimately lead to a total subversion of the value system of industrialism. Yet, in the foreseeable future, we shall probably observe a process of zigzag adjustment to recover mutal coherence among the three value axes.

The Value System of Industrial Society

According to the scheme presented above, the nucleus of the industrialistic value system may be shown to be a complex of *activism* and *instrumentalism*, or, more simply, *instrumental activism*. Prior to the formation of this value complex, however, there had been a history of crosscurrents of ideas and beliefs. One important point at stake is whether *individualism* is essential to the value system of industrialism.

One main source of the industrialistic value system is probably the Judeo-Christian religion, although the relationship between Christianity and industrialism is not straightforward, but intricate and even paradoxical. As we noted, Christianity is a religion of the "personified" creator-God. Thence follow two important potential orientations. One is anthropocentrism (man-centered-ness) or potential activism, in the sense that man as an image of God is qualified as a master of this external world. The other is egalitarian individualism in the sense that each man is directly faced by and communicates with God: *omnes namque homines natura aequales sumus* (Gregory the Great).

Indeed, it has been repeatedly debated which was more essential to the formation of the Modern Age: medieval Christianity or classical antiquity. From the eighteenth century's enlightenment movement throughout the secularizing nineteenth century, more emphasis seems to have been placed on the Greco-Roman influence. In many recent excellent works on medieval history, however, this tendency toward the classical culture has been somewhat reversed. Anyway, it is of vital importance to recognize that these two sources of modern Europe are distinctly different.

First, with respect to their attitudes toward nature, classical antiquity and medieval Christianity make a remarkable contrast. In Greek mythology, man is often transfigured into a plant, an animal, and so on, and even the gods transform themselves into various kinds of animal; for example, Zeus changes himself into a swan. A half-man animal such as a centaur, satyr, or nymph is a legitimate being like a man in Greek mythology. In medieval Europe, however, any transfiguration of man into other modes of existence was viewed as against God's will, and considered to be the devil's deed. It is true that the Greeks were natural philosophers, while the Indians were metaphysicians and the Chinese moralists. But the Greeks' interest in nature was that of harmony and sympathy. It was Christianity that divided man and nature so as to introduce a potential confrontation between the two.

Second, with respect to attitudes toward society, it has been generally believed that medieval society was a world of orders, estates, and hierarchies, whereas the Greek *polis* or the Roman *civitas* was a sphere of freedom and equality. To modern admirers of Greece and Rome, the quintessence of the Modern Age lies in a renaissance of the classical ideal of individual freedom, whereas the Middle Ages was only a dark intermission in the development of individualism. This is in a sense a misunderstanding. As is well known, the state of freedom was given in Greece or Rome only to the head of the household, who ruled over the family and its slaves; the household was the center of the strictest inequality. It was the Christian belief that brought about an idea of universal equality of all men. (Another secondary factor was probably the fact that the Germanic tribes at the advent of the Middle Ages were not very far from the state of acephalous or egalitarian clans.) It is true that medieval men faced many kinds of inequalities in their secular activities. But "to the men of the Middle Ages the notion of equality meant the approaching equality of death. . . . The thought of equality in the Middle Ages is closely akin to a *memento mori*" (Huizinga, 1955, p. 62). As far as this world was denied as meaningless, this egalitarian individualism remained potential. However, if activities in this world came to have any significance, it would no longer be latent, as in the case of Calvinist Protestantism. So it may be held that the European value paradigm of activism and individualism would not have been formed without Christianity in the Middle Ages. The Greco-Roman influence does not suffice to give birth to these important undercurrents, activism and individualism.

In the sixteenth century, there occurred three great events which gave rise to an explosion of those undercurrents: the great navigational exploits, especially the discovery of America; the Reformation; and the beginning of modern science symbolized by Copernicus, Galileo, and the invention of the telescope. European provincialism was suddenly exposed to new experiences such as unheard-of continents and oceans and the undreamt-of split in Western Christianity. The telescope presented new evidence which betrayed the theologico-contemplative approach to truth and faith. These three events irrevocably undermined medieval confidence in the world and God. In particular, the creed holding that truth reveals itself and human capabilities are adequate to receive it was lost.

The point at stake is whether this loss led to resignation or to renewed activity. As a matter of fact, as we know, the seventeenth and eighteenth centuries were an age of vehemence for truth and faith that was exemplified by the works of Descartes, Spinoza, Newton, Leibnitz, Locke, Kant, and so forth. What was then lost was not the will for truth and faith, but the certainty that formerly accompanied it. "Just as the immediate consequence of this loss of certainty was a new zeal for making good in this life, so the loss of certainty of truth ended in a new, unprecedented zeal for truthfulness" (Arendt, 1958, pp. 277-78). In order to compensate for lost certainty, man had somehow to prove himself worthy and capable of pursuing truth and faith. Now it was not by contemplation or *theoria* but only by actions—namely, by building a man-made world inside or outside himself—that man could win truth. Thus, the world of medieval contemplation was turned into the world of modern activism where the concept of *homo faber*, of man as builder and fabricator, provides an ideal.

As Max Weber pointed out, "modern man" tried to compensate for the certainty of salvation by "innerworldly asceticism," which resulted in erecting, outside himself, a human artifice called the capitalist or industrial economy. As Descartes initiated, modern man tried to build, inside himself, a world of the self by means of introspection. By beginning with "doubt" about everything—about thought and experience— Descartes expected finally to arrive at the certainty of the I am: "Nobody can doubt of his doubt and remain uncertain whether he doubts or does not doubt. . . . I doubt, hence I am." To be sure, as Hannah Arendt said, "Introspection must yield certainty, because here nothing is involved except what the mind has produced itself" (1958, p. 280). Modern philosophy since Descartes has been exclusively concerned with the self and how certain the self is. From the Weberian viewpoint it is this worry and care about the self that motivated the enormous mundane activity called industrialization or capitalism. Individualism in its modern sense is an urge to overcome this anxiety about the self and its certainty. The self in this modern sense is, after all, a human artifice.

By thus building the man-made world inside or outside himself, namely, by being *homo faber*, modern man attempted to obtain self-assurance. What is most essential to *homo faber* is the category of means and end which is a generalization of the fabrication experience. Hence, the leading motive of the modern age is "the typical attitudes of *homo faber*: his instrumentalization of the world, his confidence in tools and in the productivity of the maker of artificial objects, his trust in the all-comprehensive range of the means-end category . . . " (Arendt, 1958, p. 305). Especially for a while after the so-called industrial revolution, the activity of man as *homo faber* reached a peak in the building of an enormous artificial world of factories, machines, and steam engines beyond the imitation of natural processes. It was in this rise of industrialization that activism, individualism, and instrumentalism were fused—the value complex of industrialism was formed.

However, such victory was self-defeating for *homo faber*. For his activity starts only when an end is given, and an end ceases to be an end when it is attained. *Homo faber* might fabricate almost everything, but an end is the thing he cannot fabricate. In other words, he is capable of applying the means-end category to the whole world so as to instrumentalize it, but he is not capable of supplying an end to the world nor of understanding the meaning of an end. Anthropocentrism in Europe being given, the only way out of this meaninglessness is to make man himself an end. One example is the famous Kantian formula that every man must be an end in himself. But this formula begs a further question: what ultimate end does man have?

One answer was given by Bentham, when he stated that "nature has placed mankind under the governance of two sovereign masters, pain and pleasure." The celebrated principle of "the greatest happiness of the greatest number" was a corollary of this calculus of pain and pleasure. It then seemed that the industrial society as a whole—and each person in it—was provided with the ultimate end called "happiness"; it is to be noted that happiness is a sense which entirely relied on introspection. However, the Benthamite concept of happiness (pleasure minus pain) was highly questionable—for example, compared to the more scrupulous interpretation by Epicurians and Stoics of late antiquity. In spite of the efforts by Bentham himself and later by J.S. Mill, the utilitarian principle based on introspection could not define the concept of pleasure as distinctly different from self-indulgent egotism, because the only inner sense that withstands the test of introspection is pain, not pleasure. Thus pain is definable, and it is related, among other things, to the "pain and toil" of living—hunger, cold, illness, and so on. Bentham's concept of pain probably reflected his concern and worry about these hardships of the people—especially the industrial workers—at that time. This Benthamite radicalism has been inherited—*via* J.S. Mill, Alfred Marshall, and A.C. Pigou—by contemporary welfare economics, which is, therefore, a modern variation of the attempt to complement and retain the *homo faber* value complex.

Pleasure can be defined as a distinctive positive vlaue only when it is related to something beyond man as such. In contrast, pain can be related to the toil and pain of living as such. Therefore, the "happiness" principle tends to be subject to the principle of *animal laborans,* as Arendt put it—that is, man as a biological being—rather than the *homo faber* principle. Thus, "we find another point of reference which indeed forms a much more potent principle than any pain-pleasure calculus could ever offer, and that is the principle of life itself. What pain and pleasure . . . are actually supposed to achieve is not happiness at all but the promotion of individual life or a guaranty of the survival of mankind. If modern egoism were the ruthless search for pleasure (called happiness) that it pretends to be, it would not lack what in all truly hedonistic systems is an indispensable element of argumentation —a radical justification of suicide. This lack alone indicates that in fact we deal here with life philosophy in its most vulgar and least critical form. In the last resort, it is always life itself which is the supreme standard to which everything else is referred . . . " (Arendt, 1958, p. 311).

Nevertheless, this gradual defeat of *homo faber* remained long unknown. The reformist camp of economists believed—and many walfare economists still believe—that utilitarian rationality is correct as a principle, but only its practice is inadequate due to the egoism and interest pursuit of the rich and powerful. On the other hand, Marxists flatly denied utilitarianism (Marx himself called Bentham "a genius of bourgeois stupidity") and, without knowing it, undermined the ideal of *homo faber* by consecrating man as an *animal laborans*. However that may be, since the end of the 1950s people in advanced industrial countries have begun to experience an unprecedented, pervasive material abundance, in which most of the population becomes finally free from the "pain and toil" of living. It seems that this experience will force everyone, sooner or later, to be aware of the dethronement of utilitarian calculus and the *homo faber* principle. This probably implies that as a reality to mankind nothing is left but the principle of life. The value complex of industrialism seems to undergo a serious restructuring.

We have so far argued that, in the history of Western thought, activism, individualism, and instrumentalism form an inseparable trinity. To be sure, activism and individualism were important, if latent, factors in the fabric of medieval Christian society. However, it was not by the spontaneous development of those latent trends but by a kind of reversal of such developments that activism and individualism became an explicit driving force of modernity. For example, it was not Duns Scotus, William of Occam, or Gabriel Biel, who emphasized the freedom of will in salvation, but Luther and Calvin, who denied such freedom, who gave birth to modern individualism. It was in order to compensate the loss of certainty and to overcome the unbearable doubt that modern man became *homo faber* by building the world of inner self, on the one hand, and the world of industrialization, on the other. In the historical context of the European world, industrialization is an outcome of the whole value dynamics whose primary origin was in Christianity.

However, for the whole of mankind industrialization is about to have a meaning beyond an outcome of the value dynamics in one of its subcultures called Europe. As "the fertile crescent" started the *agricultural stage* of the history of mankind ten thousand years ago, Europe made a creative breakthrough to start the *industrial stage*. Just as agriculture has diffused to the entire earth and produced so rich a variety of societies, industrialization will yield various types of societies different from the European prototype. With respect to the dynamics of value, non-European societies are likely to follow different courses from the historical experience of Europe. All elements of the European value complex—activism, individualism, and instrumentalism—may not be essential to the non-European attempts at industrialization that we observe today.

It may be agreed that activism and instrumentalism are both necessary for successful industrialization. Industrialization is an outgrowth of the human activity called fabrication, and "an element of violation and violence [against nature] is present in all fabrication, and *homo faber*, the creator of human artifice, has always been a destroyer of nature" (Arendt, 1958, p. 139). Without the activistic belief that man is the lord and master of nature, humans cannot dare to bring about a violation or violence against nature in the name of industrialization.

Furthermore, industrialism is not a mere outgrown fabrication, but an ever-increasing differentiation and expansion which is institutionalized as *specialization* and *investment*. Specialization (division of labor) materializes the idea that each man becomes an instrument to other men and so to the society as a whole in order to expand the productive capacity of society. A laborer's work on an assembly line is only instrumental and hardly "consummatory." Investment (or saving) implies that each man's *present* action is made instrumental to his (or his descendants') *future* satisfaction. Thus, industry and frugality are basic virtues in the industrial society. The activity of fabrication always includes such instrumental actions as design, tool-making, working, and reworking. Yet a particular constellation of activities called industrialism necessitates an extension of instrumentalism to the sphere of human interactions (specialization) as well as to the intertemporal coordination of human activities (investment). Without a pervasion of instrumental virtues such as industry and frugality, industrialization cannot be maintained.

On the other hand, it is doubtful that industrialization necessitates individualism, because there are several viable examples of collectivist industrialization. One example is, of course, socialist countries. Another type of example is the cases based on non-Western cultures, the first of which is probably the case of Japan. Considering these examples, we might present the following hypotheses:

(1) Individualism is not a necessary condition for industrialization. Only in order to initiate industrialization for the first time in history, as in the West, is individualism necessary for creative breakthrough.

(2) Collectivism can sometimes be congruent to industrialization, if the underlying collectivity satisfies the following conditions: (a) such collectivity has a group ideology of instrumental activism, and (b) such collectivity is large enough to be a basic agent (firm) of the market system. If a preindustrial society is based on the collectivity satisfying the above conditions, it can be industrialized in a decentralized (capitalist) way.

(3) If a preindustrialized society is not based on such collectivity and is forced to industrialize, then it can be industrialized only in a centralized (socialist) way.

As we can all admit, the basic unit component of any industrial society is not an individual but a collectivity or an organization called a factory or a firm: an individual plays only an indirect role through a factory or a firm to which he belongs. Therefore, the issue at stake is not whether an industrial society is based on a collectivity or an individual, but rather whether an instrumentally activist collectivity necessitates an instrumentally activist individual or not. This issue is an empirical problem, and the case of Japanese industrialization offers, I presume, affirmative evidence. Each of two types of industrialization—individualist and collectivist—has its own list of strong points and weak points. For example, the individualistic type is likely to be innovative, because an innovation is essentially an exceptional individual's adventure, while in the collectivistic type each factory or firm is likely to be firmly integrated, because each individual has a sense of belonging to a firm or a factory. Which type is more likely to succeed as an industrial society seems to depend on the case.

However, a firm or a factory in industrial society cannot be a community in its total sense, because an industrial firm is an organization primarily for production, but not a place of total belonging. Each worker's sense of belonging is primarily due to a money income which the firm pays to him. Therefore, as the level of income rises and the income motive is weakened, the sense of belonging will decline. Thus we may add a fourth hypothesis:

(4) Individualistic behaviors will finally appear in any type of

industrialization—whether the basic culture is individualist or collectivist—if the society reaches the state of affluence. This kind of behavioral individualism should be distinguished from individualism as belief, and may be called *pseudo-individualism.*

Characteristics of Industrialization

Syndromes

As agricultural society started with "the Food-Production Revolution" (V.G. Childe) around the eighth millenium B.C. and developed with agriculture, industrial society began with "the Industrial Revolution" (A. Toynbee) in the eighteenth century and developed with industrial activities. Industrial activity is distinctively different from agriculture. In agriculture the production process is almost entirely subject to a rhythm inherent in the growth of plants, whereas in industry the process of production is designed by man and its progress is under human control.

Such a difference between agriculture and industry gives rise to a difference in degree of specialization. In agriculture, the growth rhythm of plants demands work—such as ploughing, sowing, weeding, harvesting, and so on—each at one point of time. In industry, on the other hand, man can control the production process in such a way that many production processes of the same kind go on in parallel with phase differences, and so many kinds of work have to be done at each point of time. Herein comes specialization of work. Thus, specialization of work is most effectively introduced in the process of fabrication (industry), but not so in the biological process (agriculture), nor in the process of human interaction (services).

However, simple specialization of work brings forth only a limited productivity rise. Yet if workers can be artificially allocated among jobs, work itself can be reallocated within the process and motion can be reallocated within work. "The Industrial Revolution" means radical reallocation of work and motion with the help of machines and nonanimal energy, and its consequence is a spectacular rise in manufacturing productivity. The first syndrome of industrialization is a union of specialization, machine and non-animal energy, which we may call *mechanized specialization.*

Mechanized specialization yields constant demand for machines. As the value of activism promotes an ever-expanding scale of production, the demand for machines surpasses the level of depreciation, which means constant net investment. However, a mere increase of machine input (labor input being given) results in decreasing marginal productivity of machine-capital, a phenomenon Marx termed "the decline of average rate of profit." Therefore, a constant level of net investment can be maintained only if technological innovation breaks a trend of decreasing marginal productivity. Thus the second syndrome of industrialization is investment coupled with technological innovation, which we may call *innovative investment*.

These two primary syndromes almost logically give rise to the following secondary syndromes: (1) large-scale allocation system; (2) bureaucratization; (3) intermediate organization for production; (4) institutionalized education; and (5) split of production and consumption. For the sake of the following argument, let us explain here some of the secondary syndromes. In concluding the list of these syndromes, we have, of course, to emphasize the importance of the value syndrome, namely, (6) diffusion of instrumental activism.

Allocation System

Mechanized specialization divides producers and users—suppliers and demanders of products. Hence, in order to connect demanders and suppliers, some form of allocation system becomes indispensable. As the specialization becomes more and more differentiated, the allocation system has to be more and more complicated. Moreover, constant innovative investment brings about waves of unceasing transformation. The allocation system has to be flexible enough to adapt to these transformations. The *market system* is one type of attempt to respond to this demand. The *planned economy* is another type of attempt, and a mixture of these two types is conceivable.

It is held that the market system is efficient in allocation, because all possible exchanges are mediated by money so that finally a unique exchange rate dominates and a rule of "one price to one good" holds. However, in order for this rule to hold, every good has, first of all, to be *identified* and *quantified*. In other words, all potential buyers and sellers must be confident that what they buy or sell is one and the same thing. Moreover, this "same thing" must be measured in some physical unit, because otherwise its exchange rate to money, namely its price, could not be defined. As we argue later, people have various demands, which are not always identifiable or quantifiable. Indeed, manufactured goods are generally easy to identify and quantify, because they can often be standardized in manufacturing processes and their quality can be controlled. But, even among manufactured goods, consumer goods are already difficult to standardize. Consumer goods in the *deluxe* category are often "differentiated products," which simply means that remodelling outspeeds identification.

It is often believed that the market system should be self-regulating. However, as Karl Polanyi (1957) pointed out, a self-regulating market is only one side of the market system. In order to be self-regulating, the market has to commercialize or distribute three primary factors: labor, land, and money. These are, in fact, most difficult to identify or quantify. For example, a supply of labor cannot be separated from a supplier himself. Hence, unless the supplier himself is standardized and quality-controlled, unless he is "manufactured" in some sense or other, labor cannot be sufficiently identified or quantified. Unskilled laborers in miserable living conditions might behave as if they were mere standardized suppliers of labor, but industrial society in general shows, contrary to predictions prevalent in the last century, no tendency toward a pervasion of unskilled labor and impoverishment. Thus labor is now generally bought or sold on the basis of agreements (labor contracts) about how to identify and quantify the labor supplied. The smooth functioning of the "labor market" depends on the stability of labor agreements, and disputes over labor agreements are a political phenomenon beyond the market rather than an economic phenomenon within the market.

Another example is that land cannot be separated from a community in which the site is located. Except in religious or spiritual communities, the fact of living together is an essential element of community, so that one of the main concerns in a community is "who lives where." In economic jargon, land use is characterized by remarkable "external effects." An element of community politics often enters into the "land market."

Labor and land are thus fictitious goods, and so is money. Money has no inherent value of its own, as symbolized by paper money. The value of money depends on peoples' confidence in the market system as a whole. Hence, money cannot be separated from the performance of the social system as a whole. Except for the regime of the gold standard system, it was always a political power that determined money supply. The formation of a self-regulating market, namely the separation of economy from policy, was necessary in eighteenth-century England to free the potential industrial revolution from traditional political bondage or mercantilism. Generally speaking, however, the conventional modern ideal of a self-regulating market is only one of the possible alternative forms of the allocation system.

All in all, the market system can deal only with those demands which are somehow identifiable and quantifiable. The less identifiable or quantifiable a demand is, the less allocative efficiency is attained by the market system. Yet it is to be noted that a planned economy faces a similar problem, because a central planning bureau can plan efficiently only with regard to well-identified and well-quantified commodities, and, moreover, a variety of such standardized commodities has to be restricted due to computational limitations. Therefore, the problem is whether a particular demand should be met by the economy or the polity, rather than whether it should be met by a market system or by a planning system.

Intermediate Organization

Industrial society consists of intermediate organizations, but not of individuals. Except in family businesses such as those in agriculture or the retail trade, an individual can join the activity of industrialization only *via* intermediate organizations like firms or factories. For, within a framework of mechanized specialization, each individual does specialized work, and only the cooperation of many men can produce meaningful achievements.

Nevertheless, the view that industrial society is a system based on individuals still seems prevalent. There are several reasons for this preoccupation. First, at the start of industrialization, many architects of modern society from Locke to Saint-Simon thought that a firm or a factory could be organized on the basis of a family, and that society as a whole should be a republic of family heads who were propertied and educated. This classical modern ideal has not yet died.

Second, though an industrial firm is, to be sure, an organization of many people, the only indispensable member may be an individual who plays the role of entrepreneur. In this sense, each firm is, in its very essence, individual-based; it is symbolized by one person. In this interpretation, industrial society is, in fact, a system of creative individual leaders.

The third, more popular, interpretation is that an industrial firm is a voluntary association of individual members. Not only capitalists or managers but also laborers join the firm by voluntary contracts. Thus each firm is individualistic in the sense that every member leaves and joins the firm only of his own will; even unemployment is the result of a voluntary refusal of too low a wage.

However, this myth of individualism cannot be supported by historical evidence. As more machines are installed in each factory and machines themselves become more complicated, as in the twentieth century, each firm can no longer be a voluntary human organization which can be dissolved at any moment, but is an organization bound to capital invested in machines. Moreover, against many previous predictions, the introduction of machines meant not so much increased demand for unskilled labor as increased demand for specific skilled labor; machines and laborers became more closely linked. Laborers have to be employed as long as machines endure. Training of laborers in machine techniques on the job now becomes another major investment. Now, as machines are one type of capital, employees become another type of capital—"human capital," as Gary Becker put it. At least since the 1930s, most firms have been turned into everlasting organizations which transcend the will of any member—a laborer, a manager, an executive, or even a large shareholder. Thus an element of collectivism has crept in, as foreseen by David Riesman's "other-directed-ness" or W.H. White's "organization man." Business organization—intermediate between the nuclear family and nation-state—is a basic component of today's industrial society.

Split of Activities and of Values

The industrial firm is an organization primarily for production. Efficient preduction is its main target, so its level of production is endlessly adjusted in response to market demands, and its plan of production tends to be ever-expanding due to investment and innovation. Bankruptcy and unemployment are by no means rare. Such unpredictable man-made patterns of change cannot be harmonized with a constant rhythm of nature which includes, as a part of it, man as a biological being—as a father (or a mother or a child), as a consumer, or as a laborer. Hence, since the industrial revolution, production has become entirely alien to consumption. (Consumption here includes not only consumption in its narrow sense but also every household or communal activity such as child care, care of the aged, medical care, mutual care, education, etc.) It is for this reason that the "factory" was invented as a workplace where all consumptive activity was strictly excluded. A modern factory is in sharp contrast with a craftsman's workplace, which was always incorporated into the master's household. "Alienation" of production from consumption is symbolized by this spatial segregation between workplace and family.

This split was unprecedented in the history of mankind. In all past examples such as *oikos* in Greece or Rome, *tsu* in China, "das ganze Haus" (Otto Brunner) in feudal Europe, or *ie* in preindustrial Japan, man produced and consumed on the same basis of collectivity. In such agricultural societies, production and consumption were fused in the life of each farm. The life of a farmer is, as admirers of physiocracy or pastoralism used to say, an ideal way of living—at least insofar as man is understood as a biological being or as an *animal laborans*. In industrial society, however, man is a laborer only in the factory and a consumer only within his family. His personality thus tends to be dissociated between that of laborer and that of consumer so that he is likely to lose integrity as an *animal laborans*. (Incidentally, most people in industrial society cannot retain their integrity as *homo faber* either, for each worker is engaged only in minor specialized work and plays, as he feels, no major role in production activity.)

The alienation of production from other human activities, or, more visually, the segregation of the workplace from the household or community, has had a definite influence on value orientations in industrial society. As we already pointed out, human action has two kinds of mode, instrumental action and "consummatory" action. Throughout history, man's instrumental action was mainly seen in productive activities, while his "consummatory" action was centered literally around his activity of *consumption*. Yet, in preindustrial societies, as production and consumption were not divided, instrumental value and consummatory value were mixed and balanced. In a farmer's or craftsman's household, two kinds of value were integrated in designing his total way of living. Every housewife had instrumental value as a co-worker and co-manager with her husband. Children learnt the link between instrumentality and consummation by closely watching their parents work together.

In the industrial era, however, the place for production and the place for consumption have been distinctively separated so that the sphere of instrumental action and the sphere of "consummatory" action tend to be polarized. There has been no place or institution (except perhaps parliament as the last resort) to integrate these two values. Hence it becomes a sheer personal problem, mainly for each family head who commutes between his workplace and his family, to overcome this potential value split. Where they are emancipated from the toil and pain of production, housewives and children tend to become an end in themselves. Thus, separation of production from consumption is a strong potential factor to bring forth a polarization of values, the instrumental and the "consummatory." In the early phase of industrialization, this separation might promote a relative overgrowth of instrumentalism in the minds of laborers. From now on, however, this seems to stimulate an overgrowth of "consummatorism" in the minds of the population as a whole.

Affluence and Its Value Implications

Postwar Economic Prosperity

The postwar world in the capitalistic West was reconstructed generally on the basis of the classical modern system of parliament and market, which was, however, revised by learning the lessons of the eventful interwar period. These lessons gave Western postwar industrial society the following characteristics:

(a) *Keynesian demand management policies* aimed at full employment; the myth of the self-regulating market, particularly for labor and money, was exposed by the lessons of the Great Depression.

(b) *Welfare-state* policies to remove inequalities; these policies had a big income redistribution effect, and enabled the Labor Party of each country to participate in parliamentary politics—a cautionary moral of the failure of "mass democracy" in the 1930s.

(c) *The IMF-GATT system* based on the principle of free trade and rule of fixed exchange rates; the malfunction of the gold standard system and failure of bloc economies were another bitter lesson of the interwar period.

Besides these three, we should particularly emphasize the following fourth factor:

(d) *Unprecedented surge of science and technology* due to the systematic joining of science to invention, e.g. nylon, semiconductors, and many technological advances stemming from military activities in World War II.

Due to these four factors, there was a quarter century's boom in the world economy which was greater than that of any previous period in economic history. Up to the middle of the "golden '60s," the classical Western system of market and parliament seemed revitalized so that the "conventional modern" value system of industrialism also seemed reconfirmed.

In particular, the coupling of science and technology made an unprecedented impact on human society and transformed it basically. Up to World War II, science as the foremost symbol of *activism* was only linked with technology as the essence of *homo faber* or his *instrumentalism*. None of the past great inventors such as Watt, Edison, Marconi, Ford, and others were professional scientists. However, during World War II and after, science and technology became one combined activity. Combined efforts created an impressive list of innovations: semiconductors, polymers and plastics, electronics and computers chemicals and synthetics, optics and lasers, aerospace and nuclear technologies. It seemed that instrumental activism was heightened to a new peak.

However, during the late 1960s many adverse effects began to pile up in the advanced industrial societies. Under the shadow of the Vietnam War, the IMF system failed; stagflation prevailed in most advanced industrial countries; student revolts became a worldwide phenomenon; the work ethic seemed to decline as shown by absenteeism; pornography was permitted in many countries; unconventional life styles became popular among the youth of many countries. Anxiety about energy resources, food supplies, and the environment was expressed by a growing number of people; a celebrated manifestation was the Club of Rome's *The Limits to Growth*. These dysfunctional phenomena seemed due to the very economic success mentioned above rather than any economic failure. In this context, three main issues may be examined:

(1) The problem of outer limits; direct effect of intensified and extensified industrialization.

(2) The problem of inner limits; indirect effect *via* high mass consumption and high mass education, namely, so-called "affluence."

(3) The problem of international order; effect of changes in the distribution of economic power among nations.

It may be conjectured that these problems are the outcome of the unprecedented postwar economic prosperity. The following argument attempts to examine this conjecture. (In this essay, however, we do not deal with the third problem of international order.)

Direct Effects of Industrialization

(i) *Over-extension?* "Extension" is a catchword of modernity. Man in the industrial era has been repeatedly challenging the limits to his effort to extend, and he has succeeded by and large. At the present moment, however, many people seem to be starting to wonder if man's active effort has finally reached its outer limits. There is good reason for this pessimism. For the first time in history, man's physical macro-activity—his challenge of the outer limits—might surpass the limits of this planet Earth. What man has so far conceived as "nature" is, in fact, no other than this planet. However, the following events might foretell the coming of a new epoch:

(a) Space ships can travel to other celestial bodies.

(b) Nuclear bombs can destroy this planet or at least everything on its surface.

(c) Pollution can upset the climatological balance of the entire earth.

The possibility of these events exposes the earth as the old niche of mankind. Many industrial activities also tend to strengthen this impression. For example, any two points on the surface of the earth can now be connected by telecommunication on a "real-time" basis or by jet-plane travel in a few hours. All of these imply that the earth is too small for today's mankind. It seems that industrialization faces its outer limits.

People's growing awareness of pollution should be understood mainly in this context. Through the almost ten thousand years of the agricultural age, mankind often experienced more acute pollution than we have now, but only at a local level. People could find relief in a limitless expanse of untouched nature beyond a particular polluted locality. In contrast, people today are frightened because there seems to remain no uncontaminated nature which can absorb the wastes of industrial activities. Man's ability to pollute has attained the same magnitude as the capacity of the earth.

Is the earth an absolute limit to mankind or his activism? In other words, can activism become trans-global? It seems that no one can answer this question at the moment. But we may point out that trans-global activism is at least conceivable. The example of exploration or immigration to other planets may be too fantastic, yet man's control of nuclear fusion or global climate may be viewed as a step to trans-global activism. However, right at this moment no one is confident even of those incipient trans-global attempts. Mankind is now hesitating to leave this planet.

All in all, mankind is afraid of the outcome of his own activities such as industrialization or scientific pursuit. Therefore, it is natural for some people to argue that man should build a stable and harmonized world within the limits of this planet, and restrain and confine himself to this harmonious order. At some points of history, it becomes difficult to conserve the old value system. However, it is often harder to create a basically new value system by eradicating the old. In the present context, the very idea that man should bring harmony to nature on earth is still *activist* and anthropocentric. At least to a genuine Buddhist or Hindu, such man-made harmony is no more natural than another man-made order called industrial society. To put it differently, any such endeavor to design harmony will sooner or later face certain questions: What part of fauna or of flora is to be conserved? How is eugenics to be applied? However, after a two-hundred-year secularizing process, man today has no transcendental principle to answer these questions.

What man can invoke is perhaps, as Hannah Arendt termed it, "the principle of the survival of mankind and of the promotion of individual life." For example, many environmentalists are still man-centered in this sense, when they argue that environmental pollution is fatal to the survival of mankind.

In the advanced industrial societies (AIS) man cannot get away from activism. He is only sidetracking the most basic issue. As man's *macro-activity* seems to reach its limit, his *micro-activity*—that is, the study and reworking of his own biological body—seems accelerated. Medical science is, it seems, immune from many current criticisms which other scientific disciplines have to face, because it definitely contributes to the survival of mankind and the extension of the lifespan. As medical science makes progress, however, it will finally face questions similar to those raised above. Can we allow euthanasia? How far can we use artificial organs? On the day that molecular biology is sufficiently developed, how shall we distinguish between the natural and the artificial? Thus man's micro-activity is destined to face the same kind of impasse as his macroactivity. For the time being, it will remain one of those activities on which all men can agree. Yet it is only another form of activism.

To be sure, in today's advanced industrial societies man's belief in activism can no longer be as firm and naive as it used to be. However, there is no new belief or religion ready to take the place of activism in its widest sense. Mankind has come a long way from the naive state where man and nature are "happily" fused. As man is, in essence, *homo symbolicus*, enormous knowledge has been accumulated so that mankind cannot return to the state of naiveté. Should any new philosophy or belief appear, it will have to incorporate modern knowledge of science and technology. Historically, activism has been transforming itself; at the outset, it was based on the deistic concept as in seventeenth- or eighteenth-century thought; then it was allied with mundane intellectualism as in the enlightenment movement or nine-teenth-century positivism, and the utilitarian principle of happiness gave another justification for activism. As Arendt pointed out, however, the final ally of activism is now "the principle of the survival of mankind and of the promotion of individual life." Hence activism may be dethroned only if the value of individual life is judged in relation to other types of values—as a symbolic example, the value of death dedicated to some ultimate end. Indeed, the Eastern historical religions—Hinduism or Buddhism—postulated a kind of affinity between man and his death. It can be understood that some people in the advanced industrial societies show interest in Hinduism or Buddhism. Nevertheless, those

Eastern religions will not be able to give them ready-made relief, because none of those religions incorporates—and then transcends—the
accumulated knowledge of the Modern Age as symbolized by science
and technology.

We may tentatively conclude as follows. As a result of accelerated
industrialization in the last quarter-century, modern activism is now
facing a kind of limit. However, no new belief or philosophy is likely to
take its place in the near future. Mankind today is probably in the phase
of trying several variations of activism which include not only trans-
global activism or exploration into a biological micro-cosmos, but also
an attempt at anthropocentric reconstruction of the harmony between
nature and man. A total subversion of activism is not so imminent as
many people tend to imagine. There are obstacles to the emergence of
epochally new ways of thinking, to be sure, in the inertia of ideas,
experiences, and vested interest in the past. But these are not all—not
even a major part—of the reasons for the viability of activism. For we
cannot yet deny that man's activism—with his extraordinary ability as
homo symbolicus—is an integral part of the vast cosmic meta-harmony
which infinitely transcends such a confrontation between nature and
man, as we can readily observe today.

Indirect Effect Via Affluence

By *affluence*, we mean here the state in which the *basic demands* of man
as a biological or physiological being are saturated—that is, the state
which is free from the necessity of sustenance. It may be debatable whether we can define and measure the saturation level of basic demands—
food, clothing, and housing. However, it is difficult but not impossible to
portray a healthy living standard for an average man by counting necessary calories and grams of protein per day, listing various items of
seasonal clothing per year, and designing a standard house which has
enough room per head and is well insulated. When an income is far
greater than the total of the cost of these basic demands, such a living
standard may be called "affluent."

One of the crucial points in this definition is that this level of income
has to be maintained stable. In other words, not only must the income
be high enough in terms of expected value, but also its variance must
be small enough. A social security system—such as unemployment insurance, medical insurance, damage insurance, a variety of social pensions, and the like—stabilizes the incomes of mass consumer-laborers
by removing uncertainties. Therefore, economic vicissitudes being

given, so-called welfare policy is, to a certain extent, a necessary element of the affluent society.

It is to be emphasized that affluence in our sense does not always mean financial abundance. Under certain conditions, some non-basic demands or *selective demands* might become very strong. For example, such consumer durables as television, automobiles, or central heating are not truly basic. Yet it so happened that in many countries demands for these items exploded, gaining in priority over some basic demands. Some economists tried to explain this as demonstration effect or conspicuous consumption. Nonetheless it does not follow that the demonstration effect is the sole reason for strong selective demands; the demonstration effect might well be a pre-affluence phenomenon, when the instrumental virtue of success was still esteemed. For another example, in certain social groups in certain cultures, the demand for education is given a high priority for some cultural reason other than for demonstration effect. Thus, for many reasons, selective demands might be so strong that even people in the affluent societies can feel financially disadvantaged. In this sense, the term "affluence" may be too eulogistic to apply generally.

However, it is necessary as well as important to distinguish basic demands from selective demands categorically. Basic demands are imperative, while selective demands are subject to choice. Selective demands may differ from person to person or from society to society, whereas basic demands show variety only within certain climatic or ethnic differences among societies. The concept of affluence is thus here defined physically rather than psychologically, objectively rather than ideologically.

This state of affluence was first attained in the U.S.A. around 1960. In the 1960s, many West European countries became affluent one by one. Canada, Australia, and New Zealand belong on this list. By the 1970s, Japan could be viewed as affluent, too. In these affluent societies, almost every mass consumer-laborer becomes freed from the necessity of worry about sustenance. Throughout the history of mankind, an average man's activity has always been devoted to or *instrumental* to the end of sustenance. In preaffluent industrial society, he was a servant to this end under the reins of material reward and penalty. In affluent societies, however, each consumer-laborer is liberated from the merciless rule of the market mechanism and the imperative of income motives. His activity now need not be instrumental in this fundamental sense.

At least to an average consumer-laborer, however, all this implies an anarchy of motivations and values rather than genuine freedom or progress in the Maslowian priority order. As we have already pointed out, the industrial value system has long been stripped of its religious meaning, and was divorced from its later ally of the idea of historial progress in the nineteenth century. It value hierarchy in the twentieth century has been reshaped in secular and non-historical terms, in which the aim of sustenance and individual life has a paramount place and any sublimer aims are not in sight. The "instrumental" virtues such as industry, frugality, or marital fidelity played crucial roles in this conventional hierarchy of values. However, now even this secularized paramount aim is being lost, so that the "conventional modern" hierarchy of values is disintegrating. Such counter-virtues as leisure, prodigality, and free sex are not yet seen as new virtues, but they are now at least meaningful "consummatory" actions. There is no rule of priority among the disintegrated sub-values or sub-aims. Therefore, man has to pursue each sub-goal almost for its own sake, which means a trend toward, in our terms, "consummatorism."

From a different angle, we may observe that "consummatorization" tends to give rise to "privatization" or "pseudo-individualism." As we already noted, man in industrial society confronts a dissociation between production and consumption, workplace and family, or instrumentalism and "consummatorism." Each consumer-laborer has to hold himself in balance between two types of values. However, if he becomes less interested in a workplace as his source of income, as he is likely to be under affluence, then the balance will lean toward consumption, family, and "consummatorism." He behaves as if he were no longer dependent on production or workplace—as if he were free from instrumental interdependencies outside his private sphere. His primary concern is centered on consumption activity (in its wide sense, as mentioned before) based on his family, but not on activities of production, allocation, or politics outside his personal sphere. This is more clearly the case with those who do not directly work for wages, such as housewives, children, welfare recipients, etc.; it should be noted that they form a majority of the population. Such a tendency is what is often called "privatization."

In contemporary industrial societies where production and consumption are dissociated, affluence tends to bring forth "privatized consummatorism." This is often misunderstood as a deepening of individualism. As I have argued, however, this post-affluence phenomenon does not mean that people gain confidence in their own "selves" and in the integrity of their values, but that they lose the overall integrity of their value system and recede into their own limited personal domain. This is not to be referred to as individualism but, more exactly, as "pseudo-individualism." Under affluence, such pseudo-individualism is likely to spread, irrespective of whether the basic culture is individualistic or collectivistic.

In other words, we have so far paraphrased our first hypothesis of value dynamics, that *instrumentalism* as a less basic value is more responsive to gradual changes due to affluence than more basic values such as *activism* and *individualism*. We may now proceed to examine our second hypothesis, that activism or individualism as a deeper value will try to adjust itself to a decline of instrumentalism—that is to say, an emergence of "consummatorism." Various interactions might occur among three value axes.

First, can individualism be adjusted to "consummatorism"? A casual observation might conclude that "consummatorism" in its privatized version is congruent to individualism; privatized "consummatorism" is, if pseudo, individualistic after all. However, it is to be noted that two kinds of values can be consistent only in certain domains of human actions. Each individual's attempt at self-actualization includes—particularly under conditions of affluence—aesthetic and intellectual pursuits, which are likely to be "consummatory" actions confined to the private, personal, subjective, or sensual domain of human actions. Recent "sensualistic" trends in arts, leisure activities, and sexual relationships symbolize an alliance of individualism and "consummatorism" in a privatized way.

However, in other non-private spheres of human action such as production, allocation, coordination (of individual interests), etc., a large-scale complex system has to form a network of instrumental interdependencies. In particular, while to "the collectivists" a society can be an end in itself, to "the individualists" a society is a means or instrument to individual self-realization. To organize a society of individualists, an idea of mutual instrumentality is essential as shown in the classical theories of social contract. Therefore, all-pervasive "consummatorism" might be a potential danger to a viable individualistic society. As a symptom of a schism between "consummatorism" and individualism, people even in Western societies attempt, it seems, to find "a true commune"—a collectivity which is not a means or instrument but which satisfies the individual's desire to belong, i.e., to have roots. To summarize: in the early stage of affluence, "consummatorism" and individualism are likely to ally successfully, even to reinforce mutually, but in the long run the two value orientations may well be contradictory if the "consummatoristic" trend is too pervasive. "Consummatorism" may lead to "communalism," attempt at collectivism in the contemporary context.

Similar types of discrepancy may be predicted between activism and "consummatorism." Industrialism as a materialization of activism is contingent on such instrumental activities as specialization, investment, science and technology, organizational duty, tax responsibility, and so forth. Therefore, if "consummatorism" should diffuse into every stratum of the society so that no one would carry out instrumentalism such as specialized work, saving (or investment), scrupulous administration, etc., industrial society would not maintain its activist vigor. If anti-instrumentalism spreads beyond a certain extent, it may be a chronic but fatal disease to any industrial society (to any individualistic society, too, as we mentioned before).

Hence, if industrial society is to continue to exist, we may have three possible choices to resume a link between instrumental actions and "consummatory" actions: Instrumental value and "consummatory" value should be linked and balanced, either (a) in every individual "citizen" (this case may be called the *quasi-classical* prescription), or (b) in a certain type of basic collectivity (this case may be called the *quasi-syndicalist* formula). Instrumental value and "consummatory" value should be borne by different social strata the case of the *quasi-elitist* formula.

All these three ideas have been recurrent in the history of modern society. In the Lockeian *classical* scheme, a society is a parliamentary democracy based on open debate and reasoned persuasion among classical citizens, who are educated and propertied heads of the households in which production and consumption are both carried out, and instrumental value and "consummatory" value live together. On the other hand, if the contemporary *quasi-classical* formula is to be put into practice, then all members of the society—whether male or feamle, head of household or not, propertied or unpropertied—must be just like Lockeian classical citizens. Every member of the society must be reasonable and wise enough to consider instrumental rationality in the social context, especially in his voting behavior. A fundamental problem in this formula is whether every member of the society can reach agreement with all the other members and achieve a social decision. The Marxist idea of class struggle is a typical example of the negative view of this problem.

In the intellectual tradition of French socialism from Saint-Simon and Fourier to latter-day anarcho-syndicalism, a central role is played by the idea of a self-sufficient productive community—such as Fourier's "phalanx"—where every aspect of human action is expected to be carried out. Most socialist leaders under Marxist influence have been critical of this "imaginary" idea. On the other hand, however, since the 1930s firms and factories have been becoming more like communities than they were in the nineteenth century. The idea of a community-like productive organization may be taking on an actual meaning. In Japan, for example, firm or a factory is more community-like—more phalanx-like—than in other industrial countries. In other industrial countries, also, labor mobility, especially that of blue-collar workers, seems lower than it used to be. Communitization of a factory is not purely imaginary. However, a fundamental problem in this *quasi-syndicalist* formula, as we may call it, is what kind of policy can integrate such a collectivity-based society. It seems that the policy in this case cannot be a mere extension of parliamentary democracy based on individuals.

A tradition of *elitism* or aristocratic supremacy is as old as history itself. However, what elitism means today is almost opposite to the elitism of the past. In Greece or Rome, the citizens were to perform "consummatory" actions such as polemics, arts, sports, and so on, whereas instrumental activities like production, commerce, manufacturing, and so on were borne by sub-citizens or slaves. In the present-day industrial society, however, a limited number of people called "technocrats" are responsible for instrumental decision-making and its implementation, whereas the rest of the population are to enjoy "consummatory" actions of their own. By way of bold historical analogy, the technocrats are the "slaves," while the mass consumers are the "nobility." In spite of the conventional modern ideal of society, this type of *quasi-elitism* is actually creeping in. However, a basic problem remains, because the technocrats' actual power is likely to be too strong, whereas their legitimacy will remain poor insofar as they are viewed as "public servants." We may ask if elitism is possible at all without legitimacy and nobility.

Recent Change in Demand

An Overview

Orthodox economics has defined the concept of "demand" too narrowly—at least for our present purpose. Let us here define the demands as those wishes which are somehow—vaguely or definitely—specified *ex ante* with reference to necessary physical means and/or necessary relations to other persons. When necessary physical means or necessary interpersonal relations are not referred to at all, the wish is purely sub-jective. In the following, such a subjective wish is simply called a *want*. At the other extreme, if the physical or human means are uniquely deter-mined, such a demand will be called a *need*. In other words, "demand" is the name for the whole spectrum between two poles, the purely sub-jective "want" and the purely objective "need."

Generally, the basic demands such as food, clothing, and housing can be almost physiologically specified. Hence they require, in a definitive way, certain physical means. The basic demands are very close to what we called needs. However, when affluence arrives so that the selective demands relatively increase, man can choose among an increasingly wide variety of combinations of physical and human means necessary to materialize those selective demands. A process of increasing affluence is the process in which the demands lose their need-like character. Or-thodox economics has been, in fact, studyimg needs but not demands in our sense.

The crucial problem is whether or not demands in this broad sense can be economic demands—or, more exactly, market demands. In the case of basic demands, a combination of necessary physical and/or human means is uniquely determined, and those means can be supplied by the market, so that the basic demands are marketable. However, as we later saw, many selective demands are unlikely to be marketable. In order to study this problem more closely, let us here distinguish three kinds of effects: (a) income effect: shift effect from basic to selective demands due to income rise to the level of affluence; (b) value effect: acceleration and differentiation of shift *via* "consummatorization"; and (c) external effect: external effect inherent in many new selective demands. Recent changes in demand due to affluence are a composite of these three effects.

Income Effect

A shift from basic demand to selective demand brings forth a number of new structural characteristics. As many economists have pointed out, these new characteristics may be summed up as a transition to "service" demand. However, service in the present context must be understood in its widest sense. We must have in mind all kinds of services, implicit or explicit. They include not only the usual services obtained through the market, but also various non-routine efforts to organize many means and activities in order to satisfy amorphous selective demands.

Kelvin Lancaster has said that "consumers possess preferences for collections of characteristics, and preferences for goods are in-direct or derived in the sense that goods are required only in order to produce characteristics" (Lancaster, 1971, p. 12). His observation seems to hold with selective demands rather than with basic demands. For, in the case of basic goods, consumers prefer one definite and simplified characteristic—say, calories—which can be supplied only by one kind of good—say, food. Thus consumers' preferences for basic demands can be reduced to preferences for goods. In the case of selective demands, however, consumers possess, so to speak, prefer-ences for *nebulas* of characteristics. And each characteristic is only loosely linked with a nebula of goods. Selective demands are amor-phous. To overstate, selective demands may be satisfied by many com-binations of many characteristics which may be linked with many com-binations of physical or human means.

What is crucial in selective demands is, therefore, who is responsible for finding a satisfactory combination of characteristics and so of phys-ical and human means. Selective demands give rise to demands for programming under non-routine conditions. However, the services of programming, coordination, and implementation are difficult and costly in terms of human resources. In some cases, consumers them-selves carry out such services. In other cases, they try to find another person to take this job. For example, let us think of a consumer who is anxious to have a delicious dinner. One choice is his own cooking. In this first case, he has to learn recipes, collect materials, and coordinate cooking and seasoning. Another choice is, of course, a visit to an expensive restaurant. In this second case, he has to pay for services by manager, cook, sommelier, and waiter. Throughout his decision, he chooses a combination of characteristics and so of means, but the key choice is his selection of coordinating service. For another example, education is a "nebula" of characteristics such as technical learning, qualification for higher status, satisfaction of intellectual curiosity, communal atmosphere among students and teachers, and recreational activity. The key problem in consumers' educational demand is how to combine and coordinate these characteristics—which actually means what kind of educational coordination, or school, is to be chosen. Many selective demands in the era of affluence—the demands for ed-ucation, health, travel, hotels, restaurants, entertainments, sports, mass media, arts, parties, etc.—depend upon this choice of coordinat-ing services. To be sure, traditional tertiary industries—transportation, communication (in its narrow sense), public utilities, wholesale and retail trade, finance, insurance, real estate—will also expand. However, it is an expansion of demands for coordinating services under non-routine situations that makes us talk about the coming of the service economy.

However, marketability of services is, generally speaking, very poor, because they cannot be *identified* and *quantified*. Service cannot be standardized nor subjected to quality control. It cannot be quantified in terms of time unit, particularly when the service is a complicated and non-routine one such as coordinating, programming, and implementing.

To be sure, there are several kinds of effort to formalize or market services. In traditional tertiary industries, from transportation to real estate, the services are, in a fixed way, combined with respective flows of phsycial means. They are indeed marketable: the services are measured in terms of physical means.

Another similar example is an "embodied service," so to speak—an attempt to embody a fixed combination of services in a multipurpose consumer durable. A *deluxe* automobile is a classical example; today it is not only a travelling vehicle but also a racehorse, a smoking room, a telephone booth, and even a bedroom.

Another invention is pre-scheduling of services such as a commercialized scheduled tour, or, as one might call it, "packaged tour." However, consumers' demands are, generally speaking, too nebulous to be met by these packaged services. Therefore, a probable solution is, as the economist calls it, the "differentiation of products." In other words, each individual's selective demand is to be met by a particular service tailored to him. But it is well known that the principle of competition does not work among differentiated products. This suggests that the market fails to work efficiently.

The fashionable catchword "from quanitity to quality" symbolizes a gap between the non-routine demand for services and the standardized supply of services. As selective demand relatively increases, consumers' awareness of this gap is growing. However, a switch "from quantity to quality" implies that we are going to give up quantifying or even identifying demands, which is a severe loss in economic costs. For without standardization, there is no economy of scale. Hence, a change from quantity to quality will result in a steady rise in service prices. This will be one of the dominant reasons for inflationary trends in the advanced industrial societies.

All in all, an emergence of selective demands will give rise to a new kind of market failure, or, as we may call it, "marketability failure." This change may be expressed as "quantity to quality," "material to postmaterial," and so forth. However, it should be interpreted as a particular type of *income effect* rather than as value effect, though the two effects naturally interact.

Value Effect

A trend toward "the service economy" in the above sense is an unavoidable outcome of a rise in income. A value shift between instrumentalism and "consummatorism" will not affect this basis trend of demand change, but it will definitely affect a choice as to what kind of services are to be focused. Suppose, for example, that the value of instrumentalism is dominant as in the 1960s. In that decade, many authors including Daniel Bell, F. Machlup, V.R. Fuchs, and others agreed on a coming of the service economy, with a particular emphasis upon information industry or knowledge industry. In the case of Daniel Bell in the '60s, for example, a change from a goods-producing to a service economy was appreciated in an instrumental perspective—in the context of "the pre-eminence of the professional and technical class; the centrality of theoretical knowledge as the source of innovation and of policy formulation for the society; the control of technology and technological assessment; and the creation of a new 'intellectual technology'" (Bell, 1973, p. 14). "The service economy" in this sense is said to be instrumentalistic. On the other hand, we can also imagine a service economy of "consummatoristic" type, in which people's interests are esthetic rather than scientific, immediate rather than roundabout, and present-oriented rather than future-oriented.

Take an example of educational demand as one of the major service demands. In some societies, educational demands are instrumental; namely, education is viewed as a means or instrument to other higher ends. For one example, in premodern China, educational demand was strong among the people—at least those in the upper strata—as a means to enter the career of the famous Chinese mandarins. Its instrumental character was symbolized by the fact that education in the Chinese style was strictly standardized as learning and memorizing the great Chinese classics. Many present-day industrial societies present similar examples, in which people are eager to receive education because it opens chances for higher career status and income. Such "diploma disease" is prevalent in many countries. On the other hand, however, if people become more interested in "consummatory" aspects of education such as satisfaction of intellectual curiosity, communality among students as well as teachers, or even postponement of adulthood, the education will tend to aim at satisfaction in itself so as to become like entertainment rather than training.

Education is an example in which the two possibilities of instrumentalism and "consummatorism" are both still open. A growing demand for education is a basic fact due to the income effect of affluence, but what type of education will dominate depends on changes in values. The same is, more or less, true with other kinds of service demands. In most of them, however, a trend toward "consummatorization" seems already marked; in other words, a tendency toward immediate satisfaction is getting stronger. In many countries, large-scale gambling industries tend to prosper. Commercialized art, music, drama, literature, and mass media are becoming sensational, hedonistic, or even pornographic. Those "new service industries" try to explore demands for their products by remodelling them from one fashion to another. Thus, under the influence of privatized "consummatorism," the demands for new services are to diversify, differentiate, and alternate so that in the service industries there will not be such a demand explosion as we experienced for consumer durables like automobiles, TV, electric appliances, etc., and there will not be such well-defined productivity rises in the supplies of services as in the supplies of manufactured goods. By and large, "consummatorization" will be a factor in augumenting a failure to satisfy new selective demands through the market.

External Effect

Another important problem is that of external effects due to new selective demands. These effects may be classified into two classes: (1) old or cconomic external effects, and (ii) new or cultural external effects.

Like production activities, consumption activities give rise to external effects, positive or negative. Automobile discharges or household wastes are the negative external effects; they cause pollution just like industrial discharges from factories. Public goods, namely, those goods which exert positive external effects over the whole society—such as roads, bridges, water supply, sewage, and the like—are utilized not only by producers but also by consumers. Under affluence, those physical external effects may decline relative to the total scale of economic activities, but they may increase in terms of densities in certain localities.

However, more important in the present context is an effect due to the demand for communication in its widest sense as one of new selective demands. People are anxious to extend and intensify their communication with others. Education is a classic example: people want to receive education because they can belong to a kind of community where mutual communication is guaranteed. Hence, such demand for communication presupposes external effects from and to others.

Public education is justified for just this reason, because a diffusion of education is believed to profit all members of the society by improving mutual communication. Expressive activities such as art, music, drama, or literature are being performed, participated in, and appreciated on the basis of similar beliefs. In demanding these expressive activities, each person tries to find a reference group in which he can communicate. In particular, mass media provide a reference group for people and expand it. All these demands for communication aim at exerting external effects. Today we are more and more in a world of communicative externalities.

However, these communicative or cultural externalities are difficult to control. For one thing, their external effects are not always viewed as favorable to everyone. In the conventionally modern conception, education was regarded as always producing favorable external effect for everyone. However, as the hierarchy of values disintegrates, people are going to disagree about what kind of education is favorable for every-one. Such disagreement will be greater with art, drama, music, litera-ture, and so forth. To some people, those expressive activities may seem profane, pornographic, or criminal. These problems are as old as the problems of freedom of speech and expression. In the past (say, in the world of classical antiquity), such problems and activities were kept out of the economic sphere of the society; they were important public issues to be openly discussed among the citizens of the *polis*. Today, however, efforts are being made to market or commercialize these communicative activities. Such commercial efforts as in the mass media will reveal market failures due to communicative externality, and will engender political instability.

Considering all the foregoing arguments, the post-affluent market economy is likely to suffer from underconsumption, because new selective demands are difficult to meet via the market as they have less explosive momentum than demands for consumer durables during the postwar economic prosperity. In fact, family expenditure surveys in the U.K. as well as Japan (there are very few family expendi-ture surveys in other countries) show that the expenditure for marketed services did not expand relative to total family expenditure in the last twenty years—not only in real terms but even in nominal terms. There might be two prescriptions for this problem of underconsumption. One is unceasing differentiation and remodelling of the supply of services, which probably implies that service prices tend to rise. To be sure, the meaning of a deflator for services is ambiguous. If people accept price rises for services as improvements in quality, there will be no under-consumption in nominal terms. But it is also likely that people are going to be dissatisfied with such dazzling differentiation or remodelling and to shift their expenditure from services to other items, say, "household production." If this is the case, then underconsumption will ensue again.

Therefore, as the other possibility, the supply of services may be delegated to, or at least require intervention by, the government. Typical examples are education, health, transportation, and communication. If education, health, or transportation and communication were not supplied publicly, expenditure for these items would not show such spectacular increases as we now see. Indeed, increased public expenditures can compensate for private underconsumption. But the inefficiency of public enterprise is well known, and the danger of the free-rider problem is widely recognized. This explains the recent popularity of neo-liberalism or neo-conservatism. But it is an evident overstatement to say that the market mechanism can materialize post-affluent selective demands. Neo-liberalistic prescriptions are quite likely to lead to chronic recessions—a road to static *ordo*. As far as people in advanced industrial societies seek growth or development in some sense or other, the public sector will tend to increase in spite of all troubles and discontent with the performance of public enterprises and public intervention.

Political Demands and Alternative Scenarios

Our arguments may be summarized as follows:

(1) Affluence gives rise to a structural change in demand, that is, a change from basic to selective demands, or a transition to a service economy.

(2) New selective demands are difficult to satisfy through the market.

(3) Hence, some system other than an economic (market) system has to respond to these demands. There emerge new political demands.

In industrial societies, the political system has already been loaded with a number of tasks. The first category of task is classical governmental functions such as defense, justice, public works (like road, bridge, and port building), education, and, since the end of the nineteenth century, redistribution of income. Since World War II, Keynesian policies and welfare state policies have been recognized as the second cateogory. In addition to these first and second categories, the political system (as well as the government) has now to respond to emerging new selective demands. Thus the political system is going to be overloaded. The crucial issue at the present moment is whether the political system—in fact the parliamentary system—has enough capacity.

In answering this question, we may point to the following four trends:

(1) *Macro homogenization*: Affluence means high mass consumption, which results in unprecedented homogenization of life-style throughout the society. The new middle strata, or Giscard-d'Estaing's "*l'immense groupe centrale*," are forming. The old concept of class struggle does not hold and is becoming unacceptable because of this growing homogeneity. The two-party division between conservative and labor parties does not give a suitable grand partition.

(2) *Micro heterogenization*: New middle strata are, in a sense, conservative, because they possess vested interests obtained during the postwar economic prosperity. Numerous interest groups are formed. Those groups often overlap so that no grand partition is possible in a mutually exclusive and exhaustive way. Syncretic politics dominates. This also implies that strong minorities have vetos. Even premature ideology can come to the fore as a strong minority. Anti-activism and anti-individualism are over-represented under such conditions.

(3) *Demand for genuine growth*: New middle strata latently feel that they are not yet anti-activist. They know that economic growth in the conventional sense is no longer feasible nor satisfying to them. They will be increasingly aware of market failure around them. They will seek to find what kind of development is really genuine.

(4) *Need for technocrats*: The industrial society necessitates instrumental actions and values, and therefore their bearers. However, mass consumer-laborers tend to be "consummatory." Hence a potential need for bearers of instrumentality is growing. This actually means a need for able and impersonal bureaucrats, yet their full legitimation is difficult.

All these suggest that the conventional two-party parliamentary system will not work so efficiently as to respond to new political demands. Some restructuring of parliamentary systems is likely to be necessary. Scenarios for restructuring may be examined:

(1) *Quasi-classical formula*: New middle strata should become more and more like classical citizens. They are educated and their incomes are guaranteed. What is required of them is, therefore, that they be reasonable enough to balance instrumentalism and "consummatorism."

(2) *Quasi-syndicalist formula*: Each firm, factory, or workplace should be more like a community. Each member, blue-collar or white-collar, participates more actively, and the members' families are to be

incorporated in community-firms. The whole society is a republic of those community-firms.

(3) *Quasi-elitist formula*: New middle strata enjoy themselves in "consummatory" actions by delegating everything instrumental to techno-bureaucrats. The mass is nobility and the technocratic elites are slaves.

(4) *Totalitarian formula*.

An evaluation of feasibility of each formula is beyond the scope of this essay. Yet it may be suggested that the totalitarian formula will never be feasible in market-oriented affluent societies because of the prevalence of individualism, genuine or pseudo, until the economic system is totally upset and the other scenarios turn out to fail. Our choice at hand is among the first three alternatives. The second choice, the quasi-syndicalist formula, is unlikely to be harmonized with the rules and practices of existing parliamentary democracy based on the idea of individualism. More plausible scenarios are probably the "quasi-classical scenario," the "quasi-elitist scenario," or a combination of the two. What we now actually face is probably the problem of how to combine these two scenarios—another attempt at twentieth-century syncretism.

References

Arendt, Hannah. *The Human Conditon*. Chicago: University of Chicago Press, 1958.

Bell, Daniel. *The Coming of Post-Industrial Society*. New York: Basic Books, 1973.

Huizinga, Johann. *The Waning of the Middle Ages*, translated by F. Hopman. Harmondsworth: Penguin, 1955.

Inglehart, Ronald. *The Silent Revolution*. Princeton: Princeton University Press, 1977.

Lancaster, Kelvin. *Consumer Demand, A New Approach*. New York: Columbia University Press, 1971.

Maslow, Abraham H. *Motivation and Personality*. New York: Harper & Row, 1954.

Polanyi, Karl. *The Great Transformation*. Boston: Beacon Press, 1957.

LIST OF CONTRIBUTORS

YOSHIHIRO KOGANE was Deputy Director of the INTER-FUTURES team which was established within the Secretariat of OECD during 1976–79 to conduct an overall study of the future. He was Director of the Social Policy Bureau of the Economic Planning Agency of the Japanese Government from 1979 to 1982, and is now adviser to the Nikko Research Center, Ltd. He is the author of *Yuga Shakai no Kozu* ("Design of the Elegant Society"), *Nihonteki Sangyo Shakai no Kozo* ("The Structure of Japan's Industrial Society"), and *Nihon: Daini no Kaikoku* ("The Second Opening of Japan").

BERNARD CAZES heads the Division of Long-term Studies within the Commissariat General du Plan of the Government of France.

JONATHAN I. GERSHUNY is on the faculty of the Science Policy Research Unit at the University of Sussex, England.

YONEJI MASUDA, formerly Executive Director of the Japan Computer Usage Development Institute, is Professor at Aomori University and President of the Institute for Information Society, Tokyo.

YASUSUKE MURAKAMI is Professor of Social Sciences in the Faculty of General Education, University of Tokyo.

INDEX

achievement (value), 61
activism (value), 186, 193–96, 204, 211, 212; and industrialization, 196; and Judeo-Christian tradition, 186–87; limits to, 206–7
advanced industrial countries (AICs): competition with developing world, 47; contradictions within, 143–45; future of, 3; new demands in, 15; scenarios for, 33–36; structural changes in, 129
adventurousness (constellation of values), 60–61
affluence: and new demands, 220; and values, 208–9
altruism (value), 92
Arendt, Hannah, 185, 193, 194–95, 207
automation, development of, 156

Becker, Gary, 202
Bell, Daniel, 63, 139, 217
Bentham, Jeremy, 194
British Broadcasting Corporation (BBC), 111–12

capital goods, export of to developing countries, 46–47
Cathelat, Bernard, 58, 63, 68, 69, 70, 73, 74, 76, 77
centripetal values, 78, 79, 82
Childe, V. G., 198
Christianity, and industrialization, 191–92, 195–96
Club of Rome, 205
coexistentialism, 153, 154, 169
collectivism (value), 186, 187–88; and industrialization, 197; in preindustrial societies, 202–3
computer : and automation, 156; basis for information society, 173–75; development of, 169–70; and information production, 155–59; and technological development, 169
congruence (of economy and society)

hypothesis, 78–79
consummatorism (value), 143, 186, 188, 203, 210, 212
consumption : future trends in, 72, 73; structure of, 66–67
cooperation (value), 62
Crozier, Michel, 59

decentralization (in France), 71, 80, 82
de Gaulle, Charles, 60
demand-oriented products, 30
demands: changes in, 51–54, 185–86, 190, 213–20; dual nature of, 5–7; external effect on, 218–19. *See also* "new demands"
democracy, participatory, 159
determinism, in the social sciences, 86–87
Descartes, Rene, 193
developing countries: growth of formal sector in, 4; scenarios for future development of, 36–37. *See also* less developed countries; newly industrializing countries
development, economic vs. cultural, 4
differentiation of goods, 27, 28
discipline (value), 59

education: demand for, 215, 217–18; supply of by Welfare State, 26
egalitarianism, 52–53
employment, full. *See* unemployment
ethics, in future society, 180–82
European Community (EC), attitudes toward in France, 76
exports, 43, 46–47

family: in future society, 64, 70; in Japanese society, 98
feed-forward, law of, 162–63
firms, nature of, 201–2
forecasting, 163, 164
formal sector (market, Welfare State), 4, 7, 19, 24; development of, 34–35;

values: and affluence, 208-9; societal
  differences in, 87-88
Veblen, Thorstein, 138

Walras, Leon, 151
wants, vs. needs, 3-7, 9-10, 214
Weber, Max, 193
welfare: and allocation of time,
  141-43; changing perceptions of,
  132; demand for, 135-36; production
  of, 136-38; relation to income,
  132-33; supply and demand model
  for, 139-42

Welfare State: growth of, 28-29, 30,
  48, 49; and market function, 8-10; in
  myth and reality, 41-42; role of, 4,
  7, 9, 74; and services production, 26;
  weakness of, 131
well-being: measurement of, 10;
  self-production of, 19-21
White, W. H., 202
work, future attitudes toward, 71-72,
  81. See also leisure
women, employment in OECD
  countries, 13, 14, 53